BUILDINGS & LANDSCAPES

JOURNAL OF THE VERNACULAR ARCHITECTURE FORUM

VOLUME 23 | NUMBER 2 | FALL 2016

Buildings & Landscapes (ISSN 1936-0886) is published twice a year in the spring and fall by the University of Minnesota Press, 111 Third Avenue South, Suite 290, Minneapolis, MN 55401-2520. http://www.upress.umn.edu.

Published in cooperation with the Vernacular Architecture Forum (VAF). Members of the VAF receive the journal as one of the benefits of membership. For further information about membership, go to http://www.vernaculararchitectureforum.org/join.

Postmaster: Send address changes to *Buildings & Landscapes*, University of Minnesota Press, 111 Third Avenue South, Suite 290, Minneapolis, MN 55401-2520.

Manuscripts should be prepared to conform to the *Chicago Manual of Style*. Contributors agree that manuscripts submitted to *Buildings & Landscapes* will not be submitted for publication elsewhere while under review by the journal. Please feel free to direct any inquiries to either editor: Anna Vemer Andrzejewski, Professor, Department of Art History, University of Wisconsin–Madison, 800 University Avenue, Madison, WI 53711, avandrzejews@wisc.edu; Cynthia G. Falk, Professor of Material Culture, Cooperstown Graduate Program, SUNY Oneonta, P.O. Box 4, Cooperstown, NY 13326, cynthia.falk@oneonta.edu. Please send submissions to both editors, preferably in electronic form, illustrations included. Please see http://vafweb.org/submissions for author guidelines.

Address subscription orders, changes of address, and business correspondence (including requests for permission and advertising orders) to *Buildings & Landscapes*, University of Minnesota Press, 111 Third Avenue South, Suite 290, Minneapolis, MN 55401-2520.

Subscriptions: Regular rates, USA: individuals, 1 year, $60; libraries, 1 year, $125. Other countries add $5 for each year's subscription. Checks should be made payable to the University of Minnesota Press. For back issues, contact the Vernacular Architecture Forum. *Buildings & Landscapes* is a benefit of membership in the Vernacular Architecture Forum. Digital subscriptions to *Buildings & Landscapes* are available online through the JSTOR Current Scholarship Program at http://www.jstor.org/r/umnpress.

The Vernacular Architecture Forum is the premier organization in the United States studying ordinary buildings and landscapes. Established in 1979–80 to promote the appreciation of and scholarship on vernacular structures, it is an interdisciplinary organization composed of scholars from many fields, including history, architectural history, geography, anthropology, sociology, landscape history, preservation, and material-culture studies. Since its founding, the VAF has played a major role in the academic study and preservation of common buildings. The VAF holds an annual meeting, publishes an electronic newsletter and a journal, and maintains a website.

BUILDINGS & LANDSCAPES

JOURNAL OF THE VERNACULAR ARCHITECTURE FORUM
VOLUME 23 | NUMBER 2 | FALL 2016

A Reminder to Readers: Please remember to have a look at the digital supplement to *B&L*, which is hosted by JSTOR. A print and digital subscription to *B&L* is a courtesy of membership in the Vernacular Architecture Forum. If you've lost track of your username or password, select "Forgot Password" on the JSTOR.com login screen and enter your e-mail address.

CYNTHIA G. FALK AND ANNA VEMER ANDRZEJEWSKI

Preservation Forum

Peopling Preservation

A Forum in Honor of the Fiftieth Anniversary of the National Historic Preservation Act of 1966

The number fifty has special status in the historic preservation field. Cultural resources less than fifty years old are, in most cases, not eligible for listing on the National Register of Historic Places or for designation as National Historic Landmarks. There are, of course, exceptions—including sites associated with modern architecture and urban planning, the Cold War and the civil rights movement, and transformational individuals ranging from entertainer Elvis Presley to author and environmentalist Rachel Carson—that meet the test for "exceptional significance" even before the fiftieth anniversary of the events for which they are recognized.[1] But generally, the evaluation of historic significance requires a little more time. Although one could argue that the number fifty is arbitrary, the passage of five decades, or two generations, seems to provide a period long enough for a more objective analysis of importance. Time, as we know, provides perspective.[2]

To honor the fiftieth anniversary of the passage of the National Historic Preservation Act (NHPA), it seems only appropriate for the Vernacular Architecture Forum (VAF), through its journal *Buildings & Landscapes* (*B&L*), to reflect on what the act has meant to the study of vernacular architecture and landscapes and how trends in the field may inform future directions in historic preservation. This conversation started over a year ago when Davarian Baldwin of Trinity College provided a keynote lecture at the 2015 meeting of the VAF in Chicago on his research on Bronzeville and South Side Chicago, in which he explored the role of the University of Chicago in the transformation of surrounding neighborhoods. Baldwin's talk prompted a meaningful discussion among those in attendance, and the VAF opted to publish responses in the months following from Jennifer V. O. Baughn (Chief Architectural Historian, Mississippi Department of Archives and History), Jennifer Cousineau (Archeology and History Branch, Heritage Conservation and Commemoration Directorate, Parks Canada), and Louis P. Nelson (Professor of Architectural History and Associate Dean, School of Architecture, University of Virginia), as well as excerpts from Baldwin's keynote, online in the VAF's newsletter and *President's Blog*.[3] This *B&L* Preservation Forum builds on that discussion by going both back in time and across space to better understand the contours of historic preservation in the years leading up to the passage of the National Historic Preservation Act and in the context of the still contentious decisions made today, some fifty years later. At the center of this dialogue, we time and again find not just tangible physical resources but people—a powerful reminder for the historic preservation field today.

For many of the individuals and organizations affiliated with the VAF, the passage of the NHPA in 1966 was a transformative event in and of itself, even for those who were not yet alive to experience it. The National Historic Preservation Act created the National Register of Historic Places, the State Historic Preservation Offices, and the Section 106 review process for projects involving federal monies or federal permitting that might affect a property listed on or eligible for the National Register. In other words, it provided jobs in both the public and the private sector for those who wanted to study cultural resources, including historic buildings and landscapes. While everyday, vernacular resources still received less attention in many cases than bigger, better, more beautiful examples, the stage was set. A new generation of scholars undertook surveys, conducted research, reviewed projects, and began formal training programs in historic preservation. More than a decade later, the VAF itself emerged from the desires of folks working in the preservation and public history fields to document, foster appreciation for, and promote the protection of often overlooked aspects of the built environment. While in the United States an admiration for historic resources existed long before the passage of the National Historic Preservation Act, the new federal policies provided the mandates and structures—including the Advisory Council on Historic Preservation—to give preservation decisions consequence and garner greater support.

In the essays that follow, we come to understand the trends that have shaped the field and practice of preservation, perhaps most notably in urban areas, and led to calls for the preservation of historic resources in the years leading up to 1966. Erin Cunningham demonstrates how the University of Illinois's Chicago campus came to occupy an area that was already built up as the site of Jane Addams's well-known Hull House Settlement, which had served immigrants, combatted the effects of poverty, and provided a model for settlement houses across the United States (Figure 1). Caught up in a desire for imposing new, modern architecture and unwilling to see beyond the run-down, disorderly appearance of the settlement buildings, the university, notwithstanding significant community protest, saved only the Hull House mansion and the dining hall, which it relocated on the site.[4] In an era captivated by urban renewal and before any review of potentially negative impacts on Chicago's historic properties at the federal, state, or local level, the university removed much of the context for these two buildings, invented exterior appearances, and underfunded interior rehabilitation to create a shrine to Hull House founder Jane Addams. Cunningham's essay reminds us of the kinds of projects across the United States that prompted the passage of the NHPA while also offering a call for attention to the too often overlooked interiors of buildings, given the focus on more celebrated, public exterior features.

Fast-forward almost fifty years, and we find the University of Chicago making an equally contentious choice in deciding to "save" the Checkboard Lounge, the legendary blues club, by moving it—or at least the idea of it—to a new site closer to campus. Just as the decision makers who determined the fate of Hull House were steeped in the culture of their time, University of Chicago officials did not operate in a vacuum. As Davarian Baldwin explains in his essay, concerns about heritage tourism and the money it generates, along with contemporary planning goals emphasizing new mixed-use development including recognizable commercial chains and lodging in safe, accessible neighborhoods, informed a decision to move the building in the name of "preservation." Baldwin's analysis demonstrates that even after the passage of the National Historic Preservation Act, historic preservation, at least as defined in its purest sense, is only one consideration among many. The idea of preservation may also be enlisted in ways that ultimately work against the interests of some of the community's stakeholders. In Baldwin's example we find similar battles over who controls history and for what reasons to those in Cunningham's essay, in a setting not far removed in space but over a half century removed in time.

The cases of Hull House and the Checkboard Lounge as explored by Cunningham and Baldwin both emphasize the importance of the public in historic preservation, a field some see as fundamentally about infrastructure. From the people who populated the Hull House Settlement to those who patronized the Checkboard Lounge, it was members of the local community who advocated for the places they valued. In both cases the meanings of the buildings went far beyond bricks and mortar. A sense of place, marked by physical spaces, helped define groups who because of their race, immigrant status, or poverty were marked as different from those in power,

Figure 1. Jane Addams Hull-House Museum, Chicago, Illinois. During the Vernacular Architecture Forum's 2015 annual meeting, conference attendees visited the two remaining buildings from the Hull House Settlement and studied the museum's model of the settlement complex before redevelopment of the area by the University of Illinois at Chicago. Photograph by Cynthia G. Falk, June 2015.

including the educational institutions that ultimately prevailed.

In their observations about human agency, the authors in this forum critique any application of historic preservation principles that privileges a physical thing at the expense of the community of which it is part. Erin Cunningham reminds us of the importance of the lived experience, often more discernible on the interior, as opposed to the exterior, of a building. She could have just as pointedly asked the question of Hull House that Davarian Baldwin raises of Bronzeville: "Is historic integrity maintained when the descendants of the people we seek to commemorate can no longer afford to live near or are removed from the actual spaces where the buildings and landscapes exist?"

Bryan Orthel takes this argument still one step further. In what some will surely see as sacrilege, he argues that the demolition of a city block in Lexington, Kentucky, to make way for new development that never occurred was "good preservation." Orthel bases his argument on the fact that despite the loss of the buildings, some dating to the early nineteenth century, the community, or rather disparate groups within the community, came to better understand their pasts and their hopes for the future because they were forced to evaluate proposals, develop and promote their own views, and collectively address the loss. While Baldwin's analysis of the Checkboard Lounge suggests less-than-ideal, profit-oriented preservation scenarios, Orthel's evaluation of the creation of what is now a "pastured" block in the middle of downtown Lexington asks us to think differently about preservation. Orthel, like the other authors, puts people, rather than buildings, at the center of his narrative and in doing so forces us to look beyond the confines of the National Historic Preservation Act to think more broadly about historic places and what makes them meaningful. As one bystander poignantly explained of the demolition in Lexington, "When I see the puffs of dust rise up, it's like seeing the spirits of the people who used to inhabit those buildings."[5] There is clearly a sense of loss, but it is as much for the people, the community, and the lived experience as for the buildings themselves. Perhaps for this reason, the authors who write for this forum each mention the importance of music in the places they chronicle.

Cunningham notes in her study of Hull House that one of the failures of that project was that the community was shut out of the decision-making process. While today we are more aware of the importance of the local community to the success of preservation efforts, we are not always attuned to the multiplicity of voices that have a stake in historic preservation. The year 1966 saw not only the passage of the NHPA but demonstrations by the Southern Christian Leadership Conference in Chicago and by César Chávez in California, the founding of the Black Panthers and the American Indian Movement (AIM), and the Compton's Cafeteria Riot in San Francisco. The National Historic Preservation Act had its birth amid a revolution to recognize the rights of all human beings. Yet the history of historic preservation has often been dominated by a select group, sometimes to the exclusion of African American, Native American, Latino/a, LGBTQ, and other diverse communities. While this is slowly changing, we need to be cognizant of how past efforts have affected not only what is preserved but additionally who controls and composes the field. The essays in this forum remind us that we need to constantly scrutinize the roles of entrenched power, money, and knowledge in the preservation movement. And we need to find more and better ways to collaborate, incorporate diverse perspectives, and use preservation as a tool of local empowerment.

At *Buildings & Landscapes* we are committed to telling the stories of places and all the people who invest them with significance. We introduced the column Object Lessons in 2015 to allow for an in-depth study of buildings and landscapes that would offer us fresh ideas about how we might practice historic preservation and public history in more inclusive and publicly accessible ways. Our inaugural column by Jeff Klee traced the history of the reconstructed Anderson Blacksmith Shop at Colonial Williamsburg to remind us that a re-created building—even in the best of circumstances—can only approximate what came before it. In our most recent issue, Mauricio Castro explored Miami's Freedom Tower before, during, and after its time from 1962 to 1974 as the Cuban Assistance Center. Castro explores the significance of the building to the Cuban American community and the various proposals for its adaptive reuse, which eventually led to its stewardship by Miami Dade College and its use for art exhibitions and the Cuban American Museum. For those of us interested in everyday buildings and landscapes, the life of such places after their designated period of significance is yet another part of their evolving history. Preservation efforts—in this case by the Cuban American community—add another layer to the ongoing narrative.

Like the buildings we study, the National Historic Preservation Act was a product of its time. With that in mind, this issue includes not just this Preservation Forum but also a series of articles and research notes providing context for the passage of the NHPA. From rural electrification to interstate highways to urban renewal programs, much of the twentieth century was marked by a quest for the new and improved, with an emphasis on better, faster, and brighter. The NHPA arose as an antidote to those trends. Fifty years later, we can celebrate its accomplishments, criticize its shortcomings, and question how the future of historic preservation can better respond to the needs of an increasingly diverse American populace, interested in the past but still being propelled toward the future.

We hope that readers will want to be part of the continuing discussion. In June 2017 the Vernacular Architecture Forum will be meeting in Salt Lake City, Utah. There, participants will have the opportunity to respond to the issues raised in this forum, add their own observations and ideas, and engage in meaningful discussion about what the next fifty years can and should hold. We hope you can join us.

NOTES

1. Marcella Sherfy and W. Ray Luce, "Guidelines for Evaluating and Nominating Properties That Have Achieved Significance within the Past Fifty Years," *National Register Bulletin* 22 (Washington, D.C.: National Park Service, 1998), http://www.nps.gov/nr/publications/bulletins/nrb22/.

2. John H. Sprinkle, "'Of Exceptional Importance': The Origins of the 'Fifty-Year Rule' in Historic Preservation," *Public Historian* 29, no. 2 (Spring 2007): 81–103.

3. "Featured Dialogue: 50th Anniversary of the Historic Preservation Act," *Vernacular Architecture Newsletter* (Fall 2015), http://www.vafweb.org/VAN-Fall-2015; and Vernacular Architecture Forum website, *President's Blog,* September 30, 2015, http://www.vafweb.org/page-1821556/3554012.

4. Jane Addams' Hull-House, National Register of Historic Places Inventory—Nomination Form, http://focus.nps.gov/pdfhost/docs/NRHP/Text/66000315.pdf.

5. Beverly Fortune, "Reactions Mixed as First Buildings Leveled," *Lexington Herald-Leader,* July 3, 2008.

DAVARIAN L. BALDWIN

Preservation Forum

"It's Not the Location; It's the Institution"

The New Politics of Historic Preservation within the Heritage Tourism Economy

> *The local group used traditional preservation language and arguments to save their building, while the University of Chicago employed skewed marketing-speak to argue that they were saving an "institution" while knocking down that institution's building. That this kind of spin won the day proves nothing except that money and power and influence will usually win the day.*
>
> — Jennifer V. O. Baughn, Chief Architectural Historian, Mississippi Department of Archives and History[1]

A "Familiar" Story?

On the eve of the new millennium, South Side Chicago's infamous Douglas and Grand Boulevard neighborhoods were putting on their fancy clothes. Newly built condominium developments and renovated hundred-year-old greystones slowly overshadowed vacant lots and run-down storefronts. Under the larger heritage tourism banner of "Restoring Bronzeville," neighborhood boosters trumpeted the emergence of a cultural corridor along 47th Street housing a string of coffee shops, restaurants, public art, and monuments alongside restored historic buildings (Figure 1).[2] The name Bronzeville—once a statement of community self-definition and black pride—had become a municipally conferred historic landmark designation and marker of real estate value. At the center of urban revitalization stood the famed Checkerboard Lounge (Figure 2). Black residents hoped to renovate this historic blues venue as the signature showpiece of a "new Bronzeville," but owner neglect and municipal divestment made this desire a near impossibility.[3]

Figure 1. Ida B. Wells House, 3624 Dr. Martin Luther King Jr. Drive, Chicago, Illinois, 2008. Photograph by TonyTheTiger, Wikimedia Commons, CC BY-SA 3.0.

Then in November 2003, the University of Chicago (U of C) entered the picture. The university took notice of the Checkerboard dilemma and expressed a shared interest in the preservation of Bronzeville history and culture on the South Side. In a startling turn of events, U of C not only bought but also relocated the Checkerboard from 43rd Street to a new university-owned building inside the Hyde Park neighborhood's Harper Court shopping district (Figure 3). To be clear, U of C did not relocate the actual build-

Figure 2. The "Old" Checkerboard Lounge, 423 East 43rd Street, Chicago, Illinois, 2003. Photograph by discosour, Flickr Creative Commons.

ing but moved the "intellectual property" of the Checkerboard Lounge to Harper Court, while the actual building in Bronzeville was ultimately demolished along with its significance as a site of South Side blues history. Outraged, Restoring Bronzeville advocates immediately charged U of C with "cultural piracy." Bronzeville preservation advocate Bernard Lloyd led a protest to the campus where he argued, "You can't take the Checkerboard out of its physical and cultural context, or you create a different institution."[4] The university quickly responded that its acquisition and relocation was not only a simple economic transaction between owner and seller but also an act of black historic preservation, in the case of a venue neglected by its own community. U of C director of real estate operations Jo Reizner offered Lloyd a direct and simple response: "It's not the location; it's the institution."[5]

To many within the field of historic preservation, the Checkerboard controversy may hardly seem surprising. Jennifer V. O. Baughn, chief architectural historian at the Mississippi Department of Archives and History, described it as a very familiar story. For her, U of C's claim of "saving" the Checkerboard was not historic preservation but simply "skewed marketing-speak," a "spin" that "proves nothing except that money and power and influence will usually win the day."[6] Elsewhere, I have chronicled the rise of "UniverCities" and the growing power of higher education in shaping urban development, which confirms Baughn's suspicions about the for-profit real estate interests of institutions like U of C.[7] Yet the struggles here over the meaning of black historic preservation are less familiar than we may think. Restoring Bronzeville and U of C engaged in competing visions of black historic preservation—different urban plans based on a shared desire to generate capital by renovating a landscape that captures a piece of African American history. Ultimately, the Checkerboard controversy forces us to think about the present-day uses of historic preservation to serve both the needs of community stakeholders and the for-profit desires of capitalism. Preservationists

Figure 3. The "New" Checkerboard Lounge, 5201 South Harper Court, Chicago, Illinois, 2013. Photograph by Davarian L. Baldwin.

must also examine how language in the National Historic Preservation Act conflates *heritage* with *properties* in ways that open the door for the corporate interests of institutions like U of C to capitalize on marginal histories.[8] To dismiss U of C claims as "spin" misses an opportunity to reconsider the meaning of "traditional preservation language" just as we commemorate the fiftieth anniversary of the preservation act.[9]

Baughn's observations about the Checkerboard suggest a sharp distinction between the community interests of "modest and scrappy" preservationists, on the one hand, and the capitalist designs of "money, power, and influence," on the other. However, in the Checkerboard controversy we find local preservationists working *within* the boundaries of the National Historic Preservation Act's focus on properties—what architectural historian Louis P. Nelson has described as an almost single-minded celebration of the distinctive architectural design or material integrity of buildings.[10] Ultimately, both U of C and Restoring Bronzeville supporters advocated for a black historic preservation of property in order to acquire the economic benefits of "racial heritage tourism."[11] This new repackaging of Bronzeville's past is explicit about converting historic buildings and landmarks into capital that might draw new government aid and private consumers to a disenfranchised but culturally distinct community.

The case of the Checkerboard reveals that there is no pure divide between community heritage and capitalist hegemony within the world of historic preservation, especially for racially and economically disenfranchised groups. The Restoring Bronzeville group seized on the capitalist orientation toward properties already embedded within the National Historic Preservation Act in ways that both marginalized other visions of community development and commemoration and opened the door to U of C's equally property-based approach to black historic preservation. Bronzeville preservationists and university administrators converged in a common desire to build *neighborhood destinations,* with historic buildings and landmarks that could anchor rival urban growth machines. Ultimately, the Checkerboard controversy forces us to engage new and competing meanings of historic preservation within the heritage tourism economy of the twenty-first century.

Restoring Bronzeville

During the 1930s and 1940s, Bronzeville had been dubbed the Black Metropolis—a city-within-a-city. It was a neighborhood with a powerful collection of black churches, businesses, and cultural institutions that made this community the capital of black America. The story of Bronzeville, however, was not one of inevitable progress. Black Chicagoans waged battle with white residents and city leaders to turn a wide-ranging and municipally sponsored arsenal of segregation into a provisionally powerful space of congregation.[12] But by the late 1960s, Bronzeville had been left to die. Even the glowing name of Bronzeville itself fell out of vogue as the emerging black ghetto expanded to include the Oakland and Kenwood neighborhoods to the immediate southeast of Douglas and Grand Boulevard and directly north of Hyde Park (U of C's campus neighborhood).

The urban racial boundaries once fortified by racial violence, restrictive covenants, and redlining were subsequently reinforced with the concrete and steel of urban renewal projects. The high-rise public housing of Stateway Gardens (1955) and the Robert Taylor Homes (1961) alongside the highway construction of the Dan Ryan Expressway (1961) became the most infamous symbols of renewal and restriction. Once black residents were put in their place, federal housing laws and the decentralization of industrial production undercut the power of labor's increasingly interracial urban base. Federal resources also shifted from a social welfare agenda to one aimed at sponsoring finance capital speculation and profiteering. The informal economy of the drug trade and its violent gang-based struggles for market shares also took over where the flight of industry and commerce left off.[13]

One startling, if unexpected, consequence of municipal divestment and urban renewal was the sudden availability of cheap land in politically vulnerable communities and the subsequent real estate interest in the Douglas and Grand Boulevard neighborhoods.[14] Chicago was a factory town that faced unprecedented suffering from the flight of industry to the global south. Urban living and leisure spaces became key catalysts for economic growth as manufacturing gave way to the more service-oriented economy of information, culture, and education (ICE). A key aspect of the city's gradual rebirth in response was its focus on neighborhoods as attractive sites of creativity, livability, and innovation. Some saw this as a savvy way to repackage Chicago's notorious underwriting of spatial segregation into a celebration of distinct cultural enclaves. As early as the 1980s, municipal leaders began turning their gaze to the South Side, realizing that the northern border of what had been Bronzeville sat in close proximity to the city's central business district and the lakefront. At the same time, property values slowly rose when the nearby Illinois Institute of Technology (ITT) began to update and expand its facilities. Local black residents thought the looming specter of white residential gentrification was quickly coming around the corner. Many feared being displaced by big developers with deep pockets.[15]

At least partially generated by a fear of gentrification, black residents and activists seized on the opportunity to join the city, ITT, and community institutions to form the Mid South Planning Group in 1990. From this organization came the land use plan Restoring Bronzeville. Residents cogently understood that rising property values made it difficult to stay in a neighborhood dominated by absentee ownership. Stakeholders instigated an economic development strategy I call *cultural stewardship* by connecting historic land value to the neighborhood's present-day racial demographic. By the late twentieth century, preservation specialists advanced a concept of heritage that moved beyond built structures that were architecturally significant to include those that "provide context for the way people lived."[16] The new focus on context was quite advantageous for advocates of African American heritage tourism. Such an approach could benefit those who lived in neighborhoods where they did not own the buildings. Context also expanded understandings of historically relevant built environments to now include structures that may have failed to measure up to contemporary beliefs about meaningful architecture.

The Restoring Bronzeville land use and redevelopment plan embedded real estate value within racial heritage tourism. It called for the conversion of buildings remaining from Bronzeville's storied past into an attractive tourist and housing market that could draw consumers to an area that lacked a local economic base. At the same time, a racial heritage model of urban planning could, in the words of Greater Southwest Development director James Capraro, make it "hard to remove those people."[17] The racial trademarking of the area as a heritage tourism destination was a savvy attempt to claim ownership of the neighborhood through stewardship. Even if residents did not have actual deeds or development capital, they could argue that the value of a Bronzeville heritage tourism destination required black people actually live there.

The revived Black Chamber of Commerce used stories about historic Bronzeville's entrepreneurial luminaries such as banker Jesse Binga, *Chicago Defender* newspaper magnate Robert Abbott, and beauty culture entrepreneur Anthony Overton to enrich what amounted to an urban development plan of *economic aspiration*. Here, the possibility of a prosperous Bronzeville future was tied to the legacy of its vibrant black entrepreneurial past. Historic enterprises housed in grand structures were still extant, and such buildings became the rallying cry for local stakeholders to successfully lobby for federal and municipal preservation funding. Dollars were funneled into the neighborhood after eight individual buildings and one public monument, centered in the general vicinity of 35th and State Streets, were packaged together and awarded local landmark status as the Black Metropolis–Bronzeville Historic District (Figure 4).[18]

Six of the nine structures in the Black Metropolis–Bronzeville Historic District were previously listed individually on the National Register of Historic Places, and the local landmark district was created in 1998. This approach to urban development placed the area on the local and national heritage tourism landscape. Over the next two decades, such heritage-based placemaking also helped to ignite local history outreach programs, facilitated a Black Metropolis Research Consortium among area universities, and directed monies toward work-training programs and limited advocacy on behalf of residents displaced by public housing demolition.[19]

White residents were still slow to invest, live, or shop in Bronzeville, but longtime black residents and "returnees" began to capitalize on a Jim Crow past by converting racial heritage into economic development and ownership. A Bronzeville visitor's center moved into the former Supreme Life Insurance building, known for giving African Americans policies all over the country when mainstream institutions deemed them uninsurable. Cliff Rome reopened the famed Parkway Ballroom, where Nat King Cole and Billie Holiday performed, as a gallery, reception space, and headquarters for his catering business. Bronzeville advocates creatively utilized the 1913 Wabash Avenue YMCA building's history of black service and uplift to generate public and private support, including funds from the U.S. Department of Housing and Urban Development. This Renaissance Collaborative preservation project turned the old YMCA building into affordable single-occupancy housing with rehabilitative services for seniors on the ground floor, and it has won awards from the Landmarks Preservation Council of Illinois and the National Trust for Historic Preservation (Figure 5).[20]

Almost everyone celebrated the local landmark designation and development around the heritage of Bronzeville. Areas that were once called blighted were slowly becoming valuable assets on the real estate map. A growing black professional managerial class brought its tax base and expertise to the neighborhood in exchange for cheaper housing set in a market primed for growth. But more than a few voices grumbled that this top-down approach to urban development might confirm fears that, according to one of the last residents of the Robert Taylor Homes, Lisa Mayo, "they want to get us out of here."[21]

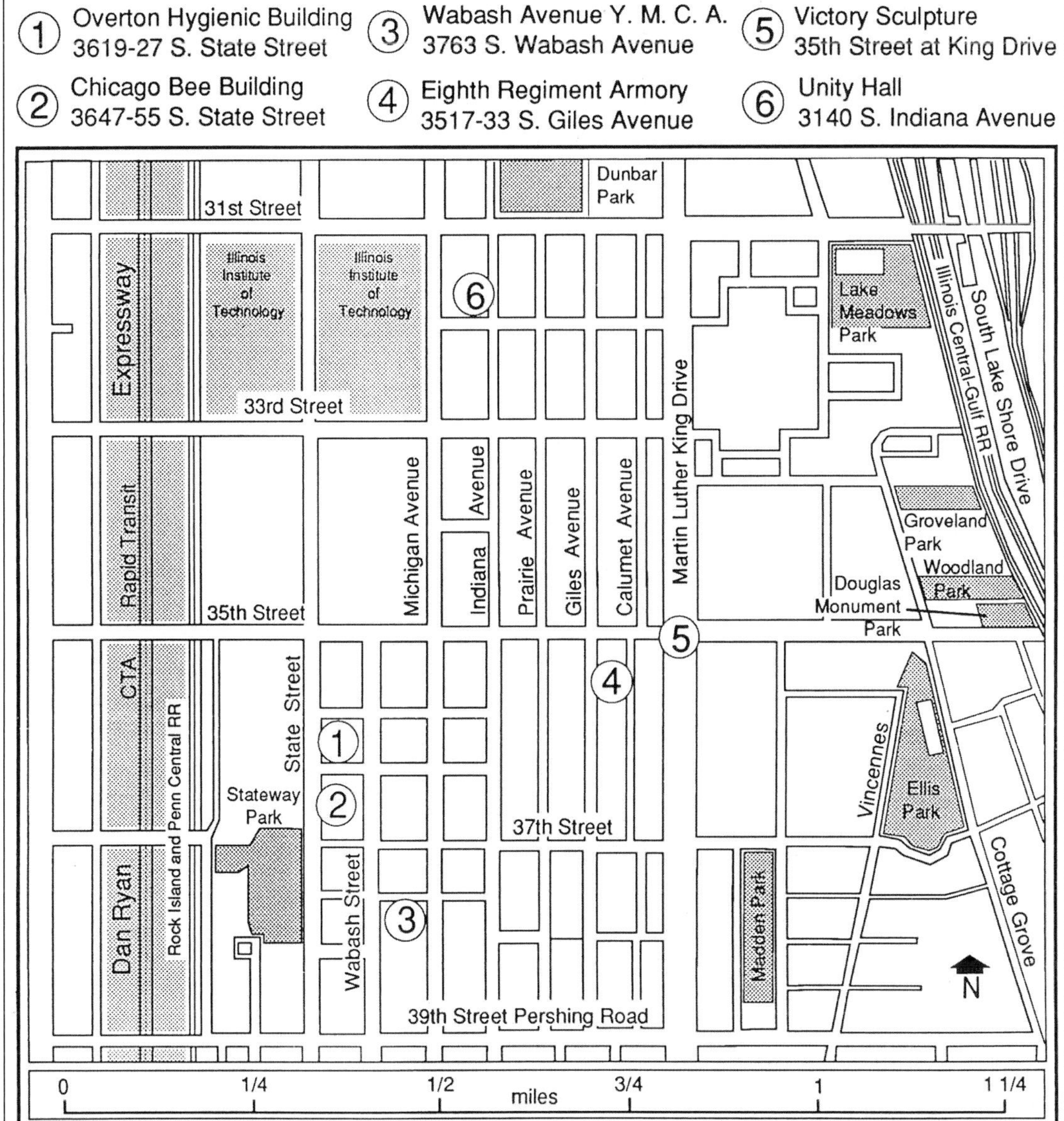

Figure 4. Map of the Black Metropolis–Bronzeville Historic District, Commission on Chicago Landmarks, March 1984.

There is no question that increased middle-class homeownership, a growth in small businesses to serve those "coming home," and the profits from an African American tourism market could generate an improved "quality of life," but the question remained: for whom?[22]

Celebratory proclamations about black residents reportedly coming back to Bronzeville belied the fact that black people had never left. Most housing and services marketed by Restoring Bronzeville were hardly directed within reach of those displaced by the demolition of the South Side's "vertical ghettos" of public housing starting in the mid-1990s. Here, gentrification had a black face and heritage brand, where apartments sold for six figures and replaced forty-dollar monthly rents. Community advocates presented black professionals and tourists with a redeveloped urban landscape wrapped in Bronzeville history (Figure 6).[23] Moreover, the cultural meaning of racial heritage tourism had specific constraints for how urban revitalization could be imagined.

The National Trust for Historic Preservation

Figure 5. Wabash Avenue YMCA, 3763 South Wabash Street, Chicago, Illinois, August 29, 2010. Photograph by Andrew Jameson, Wikimedia Commons, CC BY-SA 3.0.

defines heritage tourism as "traveling to experience the places, artifacts and activities that *authentically* represent the stories and people of the past."[24] Cultural critic Barbara Kirshenblatt-Gimblett reminds us, however, that while heritage is marketed as simply the recovery or preservation of something old and historically authentic, it is actually a new mode of cultural production.[25] Heritage tourism means that community space becomes legitimized as authentic based on the services it provides within the heritage tourism economy in the present. Experiencing black heritage in the safe confines of day spas, coffee shops, concert halls, and a blues corridor converts the Bronzeville community into the neighborhood destination of Bronzeville™.

The most popular narrative shaping Bronzeville™ justified the self-help renovation of designated black historic landmarks into black-owned half-a-million-dollar condominiums, small businesses, and cultural institutions. But black life as an urban museum hardly met the present-day needs of most Bronzeville residents. Listing single buildings on the National Register and creating the local historic district took place alongside the massive demolition of public housing, revealing the class pitfalls of the Restoring Bronzeville initiative and the limits of historic preservation. How did the preservationists' focus on buildings fail to capture the equally significant histories of public housing activism and community development that could have been leveraged to fight for the present-day needs of affordable housing? Could historic preservation work to maintain the integrity of public housing experiences as much as it intended to maintain the integrity of discrete properties? The racial heritage tourism model became a capital-generating venture brokered almost exclusively between municipal, neighborhood, and preservationist leaders. Bronzeville™ was constrained to serve the interests of consumers seeking to explore "foreign" locales and experience the past lives and staged excitement of cultural difference in the city. *Chicago Reader* journalist Jeff Huebner observed that after Hellenizing Greektown, Asianizing Chinatown, and Hispanicizing Pilsen through ethnic touches on monumental forms, landscape designs, and building rehabs, "the city ha[d] turned its sights on 47th Street" (Figure 7).[26]

Figure 6. Bronzeville Lofts, 50 East 26th Street, Chicago, Illinois, 2015. Photograph by Davarian L. Baldwin.

Urban developers sought to create a tourist landscape where travelers even step *out* of time, with directed routes through the neighborhood in clear evasion of the present-day lived community.[27] In fact, if there had not been overwhelming public protest, the Illinois Department of Transportation would have instituted its plan to close down approximately twelve Dan Ryan Expressway ramps that would have ultimately cordoned off the predominately black South Side from direct downtown access. Notable exceptions to the proposed closures included the 31st, 35th, and 55th Street exits, which brought consumers to the tourism developments in Bronzeville, the Illinois Institute of Technology, the White Sox ball park, and U of C.[28] A central question haunted

Figure 7. Alison Saar's Monument to the Great Northern Migration, built 1996, Dr. Martin Luther King Jr. Drive and 26th Street, Chicago, Illinois, 2015. Photograph by Davarian L. Baldwin.

Figure 8. Monument at once-proposed 47th Street Blues District, Dr. Martin Luther King Jr. Drive and 47th Street, Chicago, Illinois, 2015. Photograph by Davarian L. Baldwin.

the neighborhood space: would the proposed Bronzeville™ physically represent a community-wide revitalization for all to enjoy or an exclusive, suburban-style bedroom community valued for its proximity to downtown?

To be fair, within the larger ICE economy racial heritage tourism is offered as one of the few avenues for economic development in an impoverished black neighborhood. Yet in its current form, racial heritage tourism fails to address the needs and interests of the urban poor or even the working class. This approach to urban development has also proved largely ineffective for a black professional class of preservationists, returnees, and politicians who still struggle to bend the ear of public and private power in the city.[29] By 2009, Bronzeville residents hadn't generated enough private capital or political will to support large-scale "tourism-seeking efforts." Alderman Pat Dowell, who won the aldermanic seat from Dorothy Tillman, subsequently abandoned the 47th Street Blues District project, leaving monuments to Bronzeville music surrounded largely by vacant lots and decaying buildings (Figure 8). Pointedly, black professionals were perhaps best reminded of their limited social capital as early as 2003, when U of C came calling for the Checkerboard Lounge as the centerpiece of its new "university life" neighborhood destination plan.[30]

"Saving an Institution"?

The Checkerboard controversy most importantly revealed a potent struggle between the competing neighborhood-destination models of racial heritage tourism and university life. Bronzeville advocates sought to make the historic Checkerboard the centerpiece of their local development plan. At the same time, U of C also deployed the language of black historic preservation to explain its acquisition and relocation of the blues venue to the Hyde Park campus neighborhood. The National Historic Preservation Act of 1966 is important for the ways it has fostered the protection and rehabilitation of buildings and landscapes so central to historically disenfranchised communities, and preservationists and scholars continue to expand the notion of historical significance and refine applications of the act in practice. But at the same time, the act's continued focus on the property ownership of "buildings, structures, and objects" has the unintended consequence of potentially aligning with the for-profit logic of heritage tourism.[31]

Scholar Randall Mason has pointed out that the idea of "significance" within the practice of historic preservation makes the fixing of places and their meanings the primary emphasis. This approach to preservation encourages an undue focus on objects as repositories of memory and history. Mason calls for a "shift in the core purpose of the field from simply preserving material fabric to the more complicated tasks of preserving the significance of fabric and places." Ultimately, he suggests we must move from a fabric-centered bias that finds significance in fixing buildings. Instead, Mason proposes a values-centered theory of preservation, which prioritizes the ideas, memories, and motivations that give meaning to the built environment but may not be found in a physical architectural landmark at all. In this context, heritage values are not presumed to be fixed to a particular building but are created by the people who occupy buildings, and thus preservation takes on a more social as well as architectural focus.[32]

The criteria for the National Register have always been expansive enough to include built structures that are not considered architecturally significant but are significant under Criterion A, meaning they are "associated with events that have made a significant contribution to the broad patterns of our history."[33] For example, Camp Atwater of North Brookfield, Massachusetts, offers an extremely well-manicured but rather conventional set of buildings and grounds mirrored in many similar campsites across the country. But Atwater, founded in 1921, is listed on the National Register because it is considered the oldest black-owned-and-operated camp in the nation.[34]

At this moment of the National Historic Preservation Act's fiftieth anniversary, we have the opportunity to consider a revised notion of preservation that would better recognize marginal communities that leave a less definitive footprint in the built environment as well as buildings and sites with a lower level of integrity, including the villages of the enslaved, back-alley communities, and other "shadow landscapes."[35] Because the National Register focuses on preserving historic properties, the historically significant experiences of marginal communities with more clandestine, itinerant, and unstable relationships to physical places may be at times difficult to capture within the dominant logic of preservation as defined in the National Register guidelines. And so building on Mason's call, we should move toward a more values-centered approach to historical significance that does not undermine the preservation of buildings and landscapes but adds a focus on preserving the social experiences that may or may not be fixed to discrete properties.

Preservation law and practice must also encourage a more robust discussion about how to preserve the actual people (and their descendants) who produce the historical significance captured in these buildings and landscapes, whether they maintain or rebuild an easily legible marker in the built environment or not. Is historic integrity maintained when the descendants of the people we seek to commemorate can no longer afford to live near or are removed from the actual spaces where the buildings and landscapes exist? The National Historic Preservation Act is a powerful weapon that has been effectively wielded by preservationists, but the law, even with strict criteria, does not exist in a vacuum. Instead of parsing out competing notions of preservation as true or false, as community based or money motivated, we must contend with the capitalist consequences already embedded within the National Register through its focus on discrete private properties or districts as the primary manifestation of heritage.

The Checkerboard controversy demonstrates that even with the best intentions, historic preservation's focus on distinct properties, without also considering the experience of the people who make properties distinct, dovetails directly with the even more explicitly for-profit motivations of the heritage tourism economy. Let's be clear: U of C was not concerned with National Register criteria or local landmark district status when it moved the Checkerboard. In preservation practice, moving, much less demolishing, a building is rarely considered a legitimate solution. But rather than simply dismissing these manipulations of preservation language, we need to directly contend with how preservation is embedded within a shifting economic and political landscape. Because true to the focus on property at the center of the 1966 act, when Bronzeville preservationists charged "theft," a Hyde Park resident countered that relocation of the Checkerboard was in fact "saving an institution" that was in danger of being lost forever.[36]

Both U of C administrators and Hyde Park stakeholders offered creative claims on black heritage preservation that appealed to private contracts, economic growth, and even community development. Jim Wagner, chair of the Committee to Restore Jazz to Hyde Park, added that owner L. C. Thurman's decision to sell the Checkerboard Lounge was ultimately a basic contractual agreement between owner and lessee. A Hyde Park booster smugly scoffed that because "Harper Court is just 15 blocks from the old location," protests worked against the interests of the "whole near south community." But when talking to university audiences, Wagner argued the Checkerboard relocation would "spawn an entertainment district" in the commercially deficient Hyde Park, so U of C "students won't have to travel north" for blues.[37] In the end the Checkerboard debate revealed U of C's distinctive use of historic preservation language to serve the urban planning interests of "university life," to the detriment of Bronzeville's racial heritage tourism ambitions.

U of C remains Hyde Park's biggest landowner, but the racial and class composition of the neighborhood has diversified. Questions about safety, both real and perceived, continue to challenge the attractiveness of the campus community for students and tourists alike. Moreover, the university's urban renewal schemes from the 1950s and 1960s both limited the economic possibilities for neighboring communities like Bronzeville and left the Hyde Park area with little of the commercial development so central to the new ICE economy. The importance of turning campus communities into neighborhood destinations was clear when Wagner made the case for a university acquisition of the Checkerboard by pointing out the "steady U of C crowd" at the lounge in Bronzeville.[38] U of C contained research laboratories, conference rooms, and computer stations to draw young professionals and empty nesters, but it failed to possess the university lifestyle of wide sidewalks teeming with cafes, bookstores, galleries, nightclubs, and museums that would compel them to stay.

As chair of the Committee to Restore Jazz in Hyde Park, Wagner also recounted how urban renewal destroyed what he described as a thriving jazz scene in Hyde Park. In its acquisition of the Checkerboard, U of C deployed the language of historic preservation, but Wagner made such an appeal based on interests in preserving Hyde Park's musical past and stimulating a present-day interest in live music for the consumer base of students and faculty.[39] It is a telling piece of development history that the Checkerboard Lounge was relocated to Hyde Park's Harper Court commercial district.

Harper Court was originally created as a refuge for artists and small shopkeepers displaced by the university's urban renewal initiative (Figure 9). Founded in August 1965, Harper Court was opened with literal fireworks as one of the four designated shopping centers meant to compensate for the university's demolition of

Figure 9. The "Old" Harper Court, Chicago, Illinois, 2008. Photograph by Eric Allix Rogers, Flickr Creative Commons.

area businesses under the Hyde Park–Kenwood Urban Renewal Plan. Flash forward forty-five years, and U of C would own Harper Court, which served as the clearest manifestation of a university desire to reorganize the neighborhood as an extension of the campus. The plans for a redesigned Harper Court captured larger efforts to "reimagine" 53rd Street as a Hyde Park commercial corridor or, as community news officer for the university Kadesha Thomas tellingly paraphrased, to "make sure we will be able to shop, eat out and have fun, without leaving our neighborhoods."[40]

The new Checkerboard Lounge in Hyde Park would be situated within a redesigned $200 million Harper Court mixed-use complex. The Danville-based Vermillion Group won the design contract because it had a "a portfolio of projects in university towns." Vermillion confirmed, "What we are really trying to do is create a sense of destination."[41] The older bungalow-style buildings on the site were demolished to make way for a new design that included two new streets and a performance space where the streets could be closed off to create private festival grounds. The proposal also included retail space on the lower levels of office buildings, a two-hundred-room boutique hotel, two midrise apartment buildings, and a condominium tower on top of parking. According to Susan Campbell, associate vice president of civic engagement at the university, the primary goal was to create an environment where the office space and hotel ensure a captive consumer base "during both daytime and evening hours."[42]

Figure 10. Vacant lot where the Checkerboard Lounge once stood, 423 East 43rd Street, Chicago, Illinois, 2015. Photograph by Davarian L. Baldwin.

As already mentioned, Hyde Park had become a much more economically and racially diverse neighborhood since the mid-twentieth century. Therefore, some feared that boutique hotels and high-priced condominiums would reproduce what one resident described as an economic and lifestyle "moat around the university area." Moreover, the Harper Court redesign destroyed critical pieces of Hyde Park's own black history. Most shops became "casualt[ies] of the growing pains of a neighborhood on the move." Gone is the Dixie Kitchen & Bait Shop restaurant, a onetime favorite of Barack Obama. The Hyde Park Hair Salon that once trimmed the locks of Muhammad Ali, Obama, and Harold Washington also did not make the cut of revitalization and was relocated. Many appreciated the previous configuration of stores because they were affordable. Bronzeville native Katrina Everett concluded that the university "wants an environment of stores and restaurants its rich students are used to going to."[43]

On November 18, 2005, the New Checkerboard Lounge for Blues 'n' Jazz opened to great fanfare. Less than two years later, however, the Checkerboard became a casualty of the university life vision. The lounge faced low customer turnout and profit loss; the Hyde Park Jazz Society even moved its jazz night to (of all places) Bronzeville's 43rd Street. Coming full circle, 43rd Street was now home to a vacant lot where the original Checkerboard Lounge once stood (Figure 10). But plans for an even larger Harper Court shopping and entrainment complex forged ahead. The New Harper Court celebrated its opening in November 2013 with Mayor Rahm Emanuel, U of C president Robert Zimmer, Grammy Award–winning R & B vocalist Estelle, and the Kenwood Academy Choir all in attendance.[44]

U of C may have saved the *idea* of a dying black institution, but the new lounge and its location within a redesigned Harper Court seemed to confirm the fears of black residents in Bronzeville and Hyde Park. The new Checkerboard served as the centerpiece of a manicured Harper Court streetscape of simulated urbanity, designed to serve the largely suburban interests of students, young urban pioneers, and potential tourists (Figure 11). Framed by two perpendicular private streets (almost alleyways), the architectural layout suggests that all actions within the space are regulated by the dictates of commercial exchange, allowing for mixed but regulated uses without the messiness of mixed social classes.

Benches and sidewalk commerce exist in the absence of public restrooms or public streets. Gone are the walls and ceilings of the suburban mall. They have been supplanted by what I call the *open air enclosure,* a privatized public experience of socializing under the shadows of office and retail towers made of glass and steel. The Hyde Park Hair Salon, Dixie Kitchen, and Calypso restaurant were replaced with some student-friendly local retailers, but these black businesses were primarily displaced by national retail chains, including Starbucks, Chipotle, L.A. Fitness, and the Hyatt Place Hotel. Harper Court recalls what Michael Sorkin once called "Variations on a Theme Park," looking more like City Walk at Disney World or any suburban office park island instead of a city street on the South Side.[45]

Figure 11. The "New" Harper Court, Chicago, Illinois, 2013. Photograph by Leslie Schwartz Photography.

The Checkerboard's move to Hyde Park was not simply a result of black disinterest and university salvation. Bronzeville had lost to U of C in a new phase of urban planning, preservation, and economic development in creating what both saw as neighborhood destinations.

The National Historic Preservation Act at Fifty

It is precisely at the fiftieth anniversary of the National Historic Preservation Act that we should celebrate the amazing successes this legislation has afforded practitioners and academics. Whole swaths of U.S. history, both architecturally significant and socially marginal, would have been lost without the labors and advocacy of preservationists. At the same time, fifty years is also a perfect time to revisit the original stipulations of the act and consider how they speak to the present moment. The social and cultural landscape of 1966 was structured by a relatively rigid Jim Crow spatial order that still intimately tied race and culture to place. In many ways a group's identity could be framed and understood through geography. However, such an association may no longer exist, if it ever did, suggesting problems with understanding heritage strictly through its association with physical properties.

Preservationists are correct to require that the legislation maintain a strong system of criteria and evaluation in order to ensure legitimacy and authority when appealing to politicians and the wider public. However, the Checkerboard controversy reveals how a focus on rigid criteria and physical properties can work against the noble endeavors of preservationists and academics. By moving the Checkerboard Lounge, U of C violated what is accepted preservation practice, which is preserving a context for a building by keeping it in situ. But a focus on property integrity disconnected from a discussion of *community integrity* fails to fully engage the realities of forced neighborhood turnover, whereby a "Bronzeville" historic district could have few black residents or become an exclusively middle-class black enclave. Both U of C and the Restoring Bronzeville group are nonprofit institutions that make claims to serve the public good. And they both used traditional preservation language to serve their capitalist needs within the for-profit heritage tourism economy. What appeared to be a titanic struggle between the preservationist David fighting for the public good and a profiteering university Goliath was in fact both sides working within the capitalist notion of properties as defined by the act.

Practitioners and academics must engage the degree to which the ICE economy of heritage tourism shapes not only the ambitions of the moneyed and powerful but also the hopes of the disenfranchised. At the same time, reconsidering preservation practice may also expose the potential class inequalities embedded within our approach and the specific challenges faced by marginal stakeholders who reject or are not able to embed their history within built structures. With waves of gentrification separating well-established communities from their historic landscapes, is there a way that preservationists can argue for the integrity of the people who produce historically significant neighborhoods as much as we advocate for the buildings as a marker of their presence? Finally, U of C's relocation of the Checkerboard brand, without a relocation of the actual building, begs for a greater interface between historic preservation and the exploding field of intellectual property rights whereby cultures can become simply a series of material artifacts and objects (buildings?) and authenticity is manifest through contractual ownership. I take this as an exciting time in which the advocacy and practice of historic preservation must be as nimble and adaptive as the challenges we face.

AUTHOR BIOGRAPHY

Davarian L. Baldwin is the Paul E. Raether Distinguished Professor of American Studies at Trinity College. Alongside numerous essays and scholarly articles, he is author of *Chicago's New Negroes: Modernity, the Great Migration, and Black Urban Life* and coeditor (with Minkah Makalani) of the essay collection *Escape from New York: The New Negro Renaissance beyond Harlem* (Minnesota, 2013). He is currently working on *Land of*

Darkness: Chicago and the Making of Race in Modern America and *UniverCities: How Higher Education Is Transforming Urban America.*

NOTES

I thank Virginia Price and D. Bradford Hunt for their original invitation to present my ideas before the Vernacular Architecture Forum at the 2015 meeting in Chicago as well as the audience for its insightful feedback. I thank Gretchen Buggeln for organizing a forum in the *Vernacular Architecture Newsletter* around my lecture commemorating the fiftieth anniversary of the National Historic Preservation Act of 1966 and Cynthia Falk for editorial discussions about this essay.

Portions of this essay were previously published in Davarian L. Baldwin, "Chess Moves on a Checkerboard: Heritage Tourism, University Life, and the New Face(s) of Urban Development," in *Race and Real Estate*, ed. Adrienne Brown and Valerie Smith (New York: Oxford University Press, 2015).

1. Jennifer V. O. Baughn, "Responses to Davarian Baldwin's Keynote," part of "Featured Dialogue: 50th Anniversary of the Historic Preservation Act," Vernacular Architecture Forum website, *President's Blog*, September 30, 2015, http://www.vafweb.org/page-1821556/3554012.

2. The name Bronzeville has become less an expression of community integrity and now functions to claim municipal resources while beckoning commercial investors, private home buyers, and cultural tourists to the area. See Kari Lydersen, "Chicago's Bronzeville Is Ready for Reprise," *Washington Post*, November 6, 2004, AO3; Terry Armour,"Bronzeville: South Rises Again," *Chicago Tribune*, August 26, 2005, 1; Sandra Guy, "Cottage Grove Area Poised for Takeoff," *Chicago Sun-Times*, February 14, 2005, 75; "Kenny Johnson, "Commentary," *Chicago Defender*, November 19–21, 2004, 21; "Front Row: An Up-Close View of Chicagoland's Entertainment," *Chicago Tribune*, August 26, 2005, 5. Racial heritage tourism in Bronzeville is the subject of Michelle R. Boyd, *Jim Crow Nostalgia: Reconstructing Race in Bronzeville* (Minneapolis: University of Minnesota Press, 2008). See also Southside Partnership, "Rebuilding Bronzeville through Collaborative Action: A Position Paper" (February 1999, in the author's possession).

3. Blues great Buddy Guy and small business owner L. C. Thurman opened the Checkerboard in 1972; sitting on 43rd Street amid a collage of shacks, joints, and jukes, most agree that Chicago's amplified "urban blues" sound was born here. Known as the Home of the Blues, the Checkerboard hosted legendary jam sessions that included Muddy Waters, the Rolling Stones, Eric Clapton, Junior Walker, and KoKo Taylor. See James Porter, "The Last Juke Joint," *Time Out Chicago*, June 9–16, 2005; Celeste Garrett, "Legendary Blues Club Runs Out of Encores," *Chicago Tribune*, May 26, 2003, 1.1; Jim Sonnenberg, "Last Call at the Checkerboard Lounge," *Crain's Chicago Business*, February 15, 2003; "The Thrill Is Going," *Crain's Chicago Business*, February 17, 2003, 1; and Jeff Huebner, "Whose Blues Will They Choose," *Chicago Reader*, December 1, 2000, http://www.chicagoreader.com/chicago/whose-blues-will-they-choose/Content?oid=904036. See also David Grazian, *Blue Chicago: The Search for Authenticity in Urban Blues Clubs* (Chicago: University of Chicago Press, 2005).

4. See Deanna Isaacs, "The 800-Pound Gargoyle: The University of Chicago May Not Be the Only Force That Shaped Hyde Park and Kenwood but It's the Biggest," *Chicago Reader*, March 4, 2010; and "Friends of the Checkerboard Lounge, U of C Committing Act of Cultural Piracy: Open Letter to University of Chicago President Don Randel," *Hyde Park Herald*, November 19, 2003.

5. Todd Spivak, "Competing Plans for the Checkerboard," *Hyde Park Herald*, October 15, 2003, 1.

6. This essay came out of my plenary lecture to the Vernacular Architecture Forum at its annual 2015 conference in Chicago. VAF president Gretchen Buggeln followed by sponsoring a series of solicited responses from University of Virginia architectural historian Louis Nelson, Mississippi Department of Archives and History architectural historian Jennifer Baughn, and Canadian architectural historian Jennifer Cousineau. See "Featured Dialogue: 50th Anniversary of the Historic Preservation Act," *Vernacular Architecture Newsletter* (Fall 2015), *http://www.vafweb.org/VAN-Fall-2015; and* Vernacular Architecture Forum website, *President's Blog*, September 30, 2015, *http://www.vafweb.org/page-1821556/3554012*. This essay serves as my response to the dialogue.

7. The work examining the interface between higher education and urban development comes out of my work in progress "UniverCities: How Higher Education Is Shaping Urban America" and my essays "Chess Moves on a Checkerboard: Heritage Tourism, University Life, and the New Face(s) of Urban Development," in *Race and Real Estate*, ed. Adrienne Brown and Valerie Smith (New York: Oxford University Press, 2015), 237–59, and "'The 800-Pound Gargoyle': The Long History of Higher Education and Urban Development on Chicago's South Side," *American Quarterly* 67, no. 1 (March 2015): 81–103.

8. See the language on properties in "National Historic Preservation Act of 1966, as amended through 1992" (Public Law 102-575).

9. Baughn uses the terms "spin" and "traditional preservation language" in Baughn, "Responses to Davarian Baldwin's Keynote."

10. For comments from Baughn and Nelson, see "Featured Dialogue: 50th Anniversary of the Historic Preservation Act"; "National Historic Preservation Act of 1966."

11. Michelle Boyd defines racial heritage tourism as the development of sites that "celebrate the history and culture of racial and ethnic groups through the preservation and restoration of historic structures, districts, and cultural practices" in order to draw minority tourists to a growing travel market. See "Reconstructing Bronzeville: Racial Nostalgia and Neighborhood Development," *Journal of Urban Affairs* 22, no. 2 (2000): 107; see also Anastasia Loukaitou-Sideris and Konstantina Soureli, "Cultural Tourism as an Economic Development Strategy for Ethnic Neighborhoods," *Economic Development Quarterly* 26, no. 1 (2012): 50–72; Hal K. Rothman, *The Culture of Tourism, the Tourism of Culture: Selling the Past in the American Southwest* (Albuquerque: University of New Mexico Press, 2003); Carol Mansfield and Elizabeth Smolcic, *Black Heritage Tourism: Exploitation or Education?* (Washington, D.C.: Partners for Livable Places, n.d.).

12. Earl Lewis, *In Their Own Interests: Race, Class, and Power in Twentieth-Century Norfolk, Virginia* (Berkeley: University of California Press, 1993), 90. On black Chicago, see Jeffrey Helgeson, *Crucibles of Black Empowerment: Chicago's Neighborhood Politics from the New Deal to Harold Washington* (Chicago: University of Chicago Press, 2014); Adam Green, *Selling the Race: Culture, Community, and Black Chicago, 1940–1955* (Chicago: University of Chicago Press, 2007); Davarian Baldwin, *Chicago's New Negroes: Modernity, the Great Migration, and Black Urban Life* (Chapel Hill: University of North Carolina Press, 2007); and St. Clair Drake and Horace R. Cayton, *Black Metropolis: A Study of Negro Life in a Northern City* (New York: Harcourt and Brace, 1945).

13. Natalie Y. Moore and Lance Williams, *The Almighty Black P Stone Nation: The Rise, Fall, and Resurgence of an American Gang* (New York: Lawrence Hill Books, 2011); Andrew J. Diamond, *Mean Streets: Chicago Youths and the Everyday Struggles for Empowerment in the Multiracial City, 1908–1969* (Berkeley: University of California Press, 2009); Mary Pattillo, *Black on the Block: The Politics of Race and Class in the City* (Chicago: University of Chicago Press, 2007); and Sudhir Venkatesh, *American Project: The Rise and Fall of a Modern Ghetto* (Cambridge, Mass.: Harvard University Press, 2000); Arnold R. Hirsch, "Containment on the Home Front: Race and Federal Housing Policy from the New Deal to the Cold War," *Journal of Urban History* 26 (January 2000): 158–89; Thomas J. Sugrue, *Origins of the Urban Crisis: Race and Inequality in Postwar Detroit* (Princeton, N.J.: Princeton University Press, 1996); Douglas S. Massey and Nancy A. Denton, *American Apartheid: Segregation and the Making of the Underclass* (Cambridge, Mass.: Harvard University Press, 1993); Raymond A. Mohl, "Race and Space in the Modern City: Interstate-95 and the Black Community in Miami," in *Urban Policy in Twentieth-Century America*, ed. Arnold R. Hirsch and Raymond A. Mohl (New Brunswick, N.J.: Rutgers University Press, 1993), 100–158; and John M. Hagedorn with Perry Macon, *People and Folks: Gangs, Crime, and the Underclass in a Rustbelt City* (Chicago: Lake View Press, 1989).

14. See Pattillo, *Black on the Block;* and Boyd, "Reconstructing Bronzeville."

15. On the ICE economy, see Andrew Ross, "Universities and the Urban Growth Machine," *Dissent Magazine: A Quarterly of Politics and Culture*, October 4, 2012. On the "new Chicago," see Larry Bennett, *The Third City: Chicago and American Urbanism* (Chicago: University of Chicago Press, 2012); Dominic A. Pacyga, *Chicago: A Biography* (Chicago: University of Chicago Press, 2009); John Koval, Larry Bennett, Michael Bennett, Fassil Demissie, Roberta Garner, and Kiljoong Kim, eds., *The New Chicago: A Social and Cultural Analysis* (Philadelphia: Temple Univer-

sity Press, 2006); and Janet L. Abu-Lughod, *New York, Chicago, Los Angeles: America's Global Cities* (Minneapolis: University of Minnesota Press, 1999).

16. Huebner, "Whose Blues Will They Choose?"; and Boyd, "Reconstructing Bronzeville." On racial heritage tourism in Bronzeville, see Boyd, "Reconstructing Bronzeville"; Southside Partnership, "Rebuilding Bronzeville"; Ray Quintanilla, "Alderman Keep Firm 'Hold' on Bronzeville," *Chicago Reporter*, January 1994; Sandra Guy, "Cottage Grove Area Poised for Takeoff."

17. Quote comes from Quintanilla, "Alderman Keep Firm 'Hold' on Bronzeville." See also Mid-South Planning and Development Commission, *Mid-South Strategic Development Plan: Restoring Bronzeville* (Chicago: City of Chicago Department of Planning and Development, 1993).

18. Huebner, "Whose Blues Will They Choose"; and Timothy Samuelson, *Black Metropolis Historic District* (Chicago: Department of Planning and Development, 1994).

19. See Bronzeville Organizing Strategy Sessions, *The Bronzeville Community Manifesto and Covenant* (Chicago: A. E. Rowe Press, 1998).

20. See Ari Sims, "Historic Bronzeville Visitor Center Set to Open Soon," *Chicago Defender*, July 17–18, 2006, 15; *Issues and Initiatives: Housing, Wabash YMCA: The Renaissance Apartments* (National Historic Trust for Historic Preservation, October 25, 2009), *http://www.nationaltrust.org/issues/housing/Wabash_YMCA_IL.html*; Lydersen, "Chicago's Bronzeville is Ready for Reprise."

21. Brian Rogal, "Inside Story: Uncertain Prospects," *Chicago Reporter*, September 26, 2007.

22. Pattillo, *Black on the Block*; and Boyd, *Jim Crow Nostalgia*.

23. Lydersen, "Chicago's Bronzeville Ready for Reprise"; Rogal, "Inside Story"; Ferman Beckless, "Bronzeville's New Look," *Chicago Defender*, April 17, 2004, and "Bronzeville Just Won't Be the Same," *Chicago Defender*, April 10, 2004. See also Derek S. Hyra, *The New Urban Renewal: The Economic Transformation of Harlem and Bronzeville* (Chicago: University of Chicago Press, 2008).

24. National Trust for Historic Preservation, "Heritage Tourism," *http://www.preservationnation.org/information-center/economics-of-revitalization/heritage-tourism/#.Uz7tU1flvqE* (emphasis added).

25. See Barbara Kirshenblatt-Gimblett, *Destination Culture: Tourism, Museums, and Heritage* (Berkeley: University of California Press, 1998). See also Nezar Al Sayyad, ed., *Consuming Tradition, Manufacturing Heritage: Global Norms and Urban Forms in the Age of Tourism* (London: Taylor and Francis, 2000); Greg Ringer, ed., *Destinations: Cultural Landscapes of Tourism* (New York: Routledge, 1998); John Urry, *The Tourist Gaze: Leisure and Travel in Contemporary Societies* (Thousand Oaks, Calif.: Sage Publications, 1990).

26. See Huebner, "Whose Blues Will They Choose?" On the process of "Hispanicizing" the Pilsen neighborhood, see Oscar Avila, "Hispanic Condo Buyers Seen as Pilsen Threat," *Chicago Tribune*, April 22, 2005, 1. Notably, while the official "Blues District" was placed on 47th Street, most know the legacy of the blues was located on 43rd. It has been argued that 47th was chosen as the "home of the blues" not for historical authenticity but because of the properties held there by influential community officials.

27. See Boyd, *Jim Crow Nostalgia*, 138–43; and John Hannigan, *Fantasy City: Pleasure and Profit in the Postmodern Metropolis* (New York: Routledge, 1998).

28. On the Dan Ryan, see Virginia Groark, "Proposal for Dan Ryan Set to Shift: Ramp Closings Upset Neighbors," *Chicago Tribune*, December 21, 2003, 4; Chinta Strausberg, "Blacks Enraged over Ramp Closings: Asks Justice Department to Halt Ryan Reconstruction," *Chicago Defender*, December 16, 2003, 1; and Stephanie Zimmerman, "IDOT Ends Panel on Ryan Expy. Work: Task Force Had Offered Criticism—'Outreach Campaign' Replaces It," *Chicago Sun-Times*, April 12, 2004, 4.

29. On heritage tourism and urban development in Bronzeville, see Matthew B. Anderson and Carolina Sternberg, "'Non-white' Gentrification in Chicago's Bronzeville and Pilsen: Racial Economy and the Intraurban Contingency of Urban Development," *Urban Affairs Review* 49, no. 3 (December 2012): 435–67; and Yue Zhang, "Boundaries of Power: Politics of Urban Preservation in Two Chicago Neighborhoods," *Urban Affairs Review* 47, no. 4 (March 2011): 511–40.

30. See Antonio Olivo, "No Encore for the Blues: Grand Plan to Revive Bronzeville's Past as a Musical Hot Spot Quietly Fizzles Out," *Chicago Tribune*, February 27, 2009, 1. See also Arlene Dávila, "Empowered Culture? New York City's Empowerment Zone and the

Selling of El Barrio," *Annals of the American Academy of Political and Social Science* 594, no. 1 (July 2004): 49–64.

31. National Historic Preservation Act of 1966.

32. See Randall Mason, "Fixing Historic Preservation: A Constructive Critique of 'Significance,'" *Places* 16, no. 1 (Fall 2003): 64, 68.

33. "How to Apply the National Register Criteria of Evaluation," *National Register Bulletin* 15 (Washington, D.C.: U.S. Department of the Interior National Park Service Cultural Resources, 1990), i, 2, *www.nps.gov/nr/publications/bulletins/pdfs/nrb15.pdf.*

34. Henry Thomas (president, Camp Atwater Committee), interview with author, June 26, 2015.

35. "Featured Dialogue: 50th Anniversary of the Historic Preservation Act"; and "How to Apply the National Register Criteria of Evaluation," i.

36. "How to Apply the National Register Criteria of Evaluation," 2; and Sam Ackerman, "Checkerboard Tradition Will Continue on 53rd," *Hyde Park Herald,* December 17, 2003, 4.

37. Jim Wagner, "Checkerboard Owner Asked for U of C's Help," *Hyde Park Herald,* December 17, 2003; Sam Ackerman, "Checkerboard Tradition Will Continue on 53rd," *Hyde Park Herald,* December 17, 2003, 4; and Jeff Johnson, "Famed Checkerboard Lounge to Reopen in Hyde Park," *Chicago Sun-Times,* November 3, 2005.

38. Wagner, "Checkerboard Owner asked for U of C's Help." On the consequences of Hyde Park urban renewal, see Stevens, "Learning from the 'Terrible Mistakes' of Urban Renewal."

39. Johnson, "Famed Checkerboard Lounge to Reopen in Hyde Park"; and Wagner, "Checkerboard Owner Asked for U of C's Help."

40. "University of Chicago Purchases Harper Court, Partners with City to Revitalize 53rd Street," University of Chicago News Office, *http://news.uchicago.edu/news.php?asset_id=1363;* and Kadesha Thomas, "What's Up with Harper Theater," *53rd Street Blog, http://fiftythird.uchicago.edu/2009/07/27/whats-harper-theater.*

41. Kate Hawley, "Harper Court Developer Selected," *Hyde Park Herald,* January 20, 2010, 1; Steve Kloehn, "Community Hears the Latest Ideas for Harper Court," *53rd Street Blog, http://fiftythird.uchicago.edu/2010/02/17/community-hears-latest-ideas-harper-court.*

42. Kadesha Thomas, "Harper Court Moving Forward—Three Contenders Remain," *53rd Street Blog, http://fiftythird.uchicago.edu/%202009/09/17/harper-court-moving-forward-three-contenders-remain.*

43. John Slania, "Hyde Park's Big Test," *Time Out: Chicago,* February 17, 2010; Kate Hawley, "Big Plans Dominate Hyde Park Real Estate in 2008," *Hyde Park Herald,* December 31, 2008, 2; Lisa Grant, "U of C Needs to Work in Partnership with Community," *Hyde Park Herald,* August 27, 2008. On closings and controversy, see Deva Woodley, "Growing Pains: Dixie Kitchen Closing June 7th," *53rd Street Blog, http://fiftythird.uchicago.edu/2009/06/02/growing-pains-dixie-kitchen-closing-june-7th;* Slania, "Hyde Park's Big Test"; Wendell Hutson, "Black Restaurants to Be Displaced by Redevelopment Project"; and Johnathon Briggs, "Hyde Park Haircut Hub in the Move: U of C Redevelopment Plan Forces Out Neighborhood Institution," *Chicago Tribune,* December 27, 2006; and Jeremy Adragna, "Bagel Store Closes after Lease Spat with U of C," *Hyde Park Herald,* February 11, 2004. See also Christopher Mele, *Selling the Lower East Side: Culture, Real Estate, and Resistance in New York City* (Minneapolis: University of Minnesota Press, 2002); "Black Restaurants to Be Displaced by Redevelopment Project," *Chicago Defender,* May 27, 2008.

44. See Anthony Bishop, "Checkerboard Seeks New Ways to Attract Business," *Hyde Park Herald,* May 10, 2006, 3; and Lindsay Welbers, "Harper Court Celebrated," *Hyde Park Herald,* November 13, 2013, 6.

45. See Celia Bever, "O-Issue: Harper Court and 53rd Street Development," *Chicago Maroon,* September 22, 2013, and "ULI Case Studies: Harper Court," Urban Land Institute, October 2013, http://uli.org/case-study/uli-case-studies-harper-court. See also Michael Sorkin, ed., *Variations on a Theme Park: The New American City and the End of Public Space* (New York: Hill and Wang, 1992).

BRYAN D. ORTHEL

Preservation Forum

Preservation and Negotiation of History and Identity in Lexington, Kentucky

> *I want modernism to emerge as a distinctive patterning of mental and technical possibilities. . . . "Modernity" means contingency. It points to a social order which has turned* from the worship of ancestors and past authorities to the pursuit of a projected future—*of goods, pleasures, freedoms, forms of control over nature, or infinities of information. This process goes along with a great emptying and sanitizing of the imagination. Without ancestor-worship, meaning is in short supply—"meaning" here meaning agreed-on and instituted forms of value and understanding, implicit orders, stories and images in which a culture crystallizes its sense of the struggle with the realm of necessity and the reality of pain and death. . . .*
>
> *We know we are living a new form of life, in which all previous notions of belief and sociability have been scrambled. And the true terror of this new order has to do with its being ruled—and obscurely felt to be ruled—by sheer concatenation . . . that is, by a system without any focusing purpose to it, or any compelling image or ritualization of that purpose.*
>
> — T. J. Clark, *Farewell to an Idea*[1]

In the fall of 2010, visitors to downtown Lexington, Kentucky, saw an unusual urban contradiction. An entire city block in the figural and physical heart of the city was empty.[2] Instead of buildings, the block was covered with grass and fenced like a horse paddock on one of the farms surrounding the city (Figures 1 and 2). Dynamically painted, full-size, fiberglass horses—a public art project—stood on sidewalks and outside prominent buildings throughout downtown. The public art project coincided with the World Equestrian Games hosted by Lexington that year.[3] Several of the fiberglass horses appeared to stroll the sidewalks adjacent to the empty block. The block was opened for concerts and other gatherings during public celebrations. A passerby on Main Street could have seen a herd of people enjoying themselves within the fence, while horses outside the fence wandered the streets. Not only were roles reversed, but the city had been turned inside out. A block of the city developed almost since the town's founding had been cleared and transparently, if paradoxically, transformed into a version of the agricultural landscape threatened by the city's continued, sprawling growth. This "pastured" block—both as re-created pasture and sanitized history—represented a continuous, ongoing fight over the city's identity. Buildings had been demolished; history destroyed; the relationship of powerful subsets of the community questioned; and the city's status quo interrupted. The events surrounding the pastured block reveal deep questions about how Lexington residents interact with each other and understand who they are as modern individuals. These events exist in a context of other community struggles that address race, economics, and the politics of space. The pastured block demonstrates the residents' twenty-first-century fight for identity through understanding of the past and what they imagine the future will be.

Initial reaction to the pastured block's narrative may focus on destruction and loss. Few preservationists would initially describe the outcome as good. Fifteen buildings dating from the 1820s to the 1940s were torn down in preparation for something new. Yet this essay argues the story of the pastured block was in effect good

Figure 1. The pastured block, downtown Lexington, Kentucky. Adjacent to the block, nineteenth- and twentieth-century commercial buildings front the street. In this view a pedestrian can see the old county courthouse and the mixture of buildings in various states of repair. The grass and paddock fencing in the foreground cover the block that once held fifteen buildings, including a Woolworth's store and a row of 1820s-era buildings. Photograph by Bryan D. Orthel, 2010.

preservation. Lived experiences and human interactions surrounding the demolition of the buildings were (and continue to be) active preservation. Put another way, preservation operates as social outcomes separate from the survival (or change) of physical landscape or material culture. Preservation exists as knowledge, information, and understanding about ideas of self-identity. The preservation of Lexington as a community—and the preservation of individuals living as a social community—was advanced by changes brought on by the block's demolition. The debate about the block extended beyond a typical part of the community concerned with old buildings. People actively engaged with their own understandings of history. Preservation happened in how these individuals thought about the past and the future as both related to them. They pushed their ideas into public fora (e.g., neighborly discussions, social media, public meetings). In turn, they also used these understandings of Lexington's past and future to advocate for how the community should exist in the sociocultural and physical present. This social product is sometimes tangentially referenced in preservationists' discussions of gentrification or educational outcomes but rarely recognized as the vital result of individuals' choices about preservation.

Stories about the pastured block reveal the social meanings of spaces. Understanding the stories requires exploring the discrete perceptions of individuals and groups.[4] Lexington's pastured block is reminiscent of other redevelopment projects that altered physical, social, and cultural places. Block 37 in downtown Chicago spent over a decade in limbo between public and private uses after redevelopment plans were delayed and ultimately changed.[5] The cultural history of the site of Crown Hall at the Illinois Institute of Technology demonstrates the complicated layers associated with place and memory.[6] Renegotiations of social and public spaces can also involve extant buildings (e.g., Portland's Pioneer Courthouse Square, Louisville's Galleria mall, or Detroit's Michigan Central Station). The conceptual reunderstanding of private–public, individual–communal relationships happens every day (e.g., Ground Zero in New York City or the digital framing of online communities). Lexington's pastured block is not unique in this way. This essay focuses on the contemporary, ongoing, ordinary discussion about the pastured block to frame a point about the fluidity of preservation and history in modern society: *we actively use history to define how we (as individuals and social groups) continue.*

In the case of Lexington's pastured block, fifteen buildings were demolished beginning in 2004 in anticipation of a proposed high-rise redevelopment project. Over seven years, the proposed redevelopment changed from a single, forty-story, monolithic building covering the entire block to a mixture of smaller-scale, mixed-use buildings.[7] At the time of this writing, the form and uses for the buildings to be constructed on the site continue to be negotiated.[8] The demolished buildings included a Woolworth's store and a row of 1820s-era buildings that were some of the oldest remaining in the city (Figures 3 and 4). Residents, business owners, and civic organizations fought to prevent the demolition of the historic buildings and the loss of the businesses that occupied them. A few of the businesses successfully relocated within the downtown core, but most closed. Different subsections of the community saw distinct meanings and opportunities:

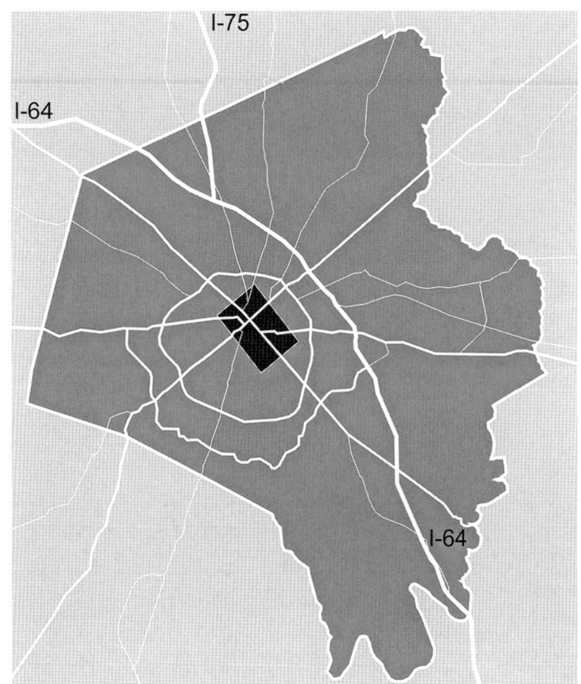

Lexington-Fayette Urban County Government area

Figure 2. Map of downtown Lexington, Kentucky, with inset (*above*) of the surrounding region. Downtown is wrapped by residential areas (*medium gray*) and dotted with small parks (*stippled*). The pastured block (*star*) is in the heart of the downtown. Main Street runs diagonally from northwest to southeast. Neighborhoods sit around the core. Drawings by Bryan D. Orthel.

WESTERN SUBURB
GRATZ PARK
ARENA
ARENA PARKING
MAIN STREET
SOUTH HILL
UPPER
LIMESTONE
VINE
EAST END
MAXWELL

Downtown Lexington environs

- The developer questioned the historic value of the demolished buildings: "It's not like Lincoln ever shopped there."[9]
- A citizen noted that the same proposed hotel, residential, office, and retail space built in the suburbs would require eighty acres.[10] The downtown loss saved part of the pastoral setting that surrounded the city.
- The then mayor championed the project, while his detractors questioned it.[11]

While the debate went on, the block was transformed through demolition and the eventual planting of grass. Construction was repeatedly delayed. In mid-2014, construction on an underground parking garage started even as revisions to the proposed building plans continued.[12] Construction halted in 2015 as the project was again reconsidered.[13] While construction on the garage subsequently resumed, the ultimate form and use of the site remain unknown.

The site held different values for the developer, the elected officials who sought economic development, and the community residents who wanted a different future. Views about whether the project is progress or destruction remain strong and distinct between subsections of the community. Questions around the block's demolition and redevelopment challenged residents to consider their past, their imagined future, and how their *immediate now* fit between. In 1999 T. J. Clark described modernity as a shared idea about the future, an agreement that the future was to be controlled by potential, not how we had lived before (see this essay's epigraph). He concluded, though, that Western society's present situation is no longer modern. We no longer agree on the future. Instead, we act, frame, connect, balance, re-create, abuse, and otherwise use our understanding of the past to assert our individually desired futures. We forcefully string together a way forward that requires continual improvement and negotiation because we do not agree. Our collective diversity of historical understanding (or consciousness) requires that we make society anew using parts of the past that we do not understand or describe in the same way.

We do not control time. Yet we strive to shape what it looks like. The way people live and the ways they express themselves in their environments inherently preserve identity, the status quo, and the *self*. Most individuals do not intend to destroy themselves or their way of life; for their self-interest, their actions are preservative. Human awareness of the passage from past to present—and the implication of a continu-

Figure 3. Historic photography of buildings on the pastured block, circa 1920. The image shows part of the western face of the buildings along Main Street from South Upper Street (*at right*) toward Limestone Street. The three northernmost buildings were extant until demolition in 2008. Courtesy of the Asa C. Chinn Downtown Lexington, Kentucky Photographic Collection, University of Kentucky Libraries.

ing future—prompts our consideration of how we exist in that passage.[14] The modern heart of downtown Lexington exists as such a re-creation of time and physical space. Lexington's heart is understood as both an evolving landscape and an experienced and remembered space that is intimately linked with individual memory and perceptions. The linked immediacy of this re-created *now* and *then* demonstrates preservation's role in the continuation of identity and history.

Figure 4. F. W. Woolworth Building on the pastured block. The Woolworth building (1947–48) was occupied until 1990. Despite multiple efforts to identify an adaptive use for the building after the store closed, the owners demolished the building in 2004 to expand the adjacent parking lot. Courtesy of Cynthia Johnson, circa 2000.

Stories as Narratives

This essay relies on a sequence of ideas drawn from Clark's discussion of the breakdown of a modern sense of continuity and Anthony Giddens's and Jane Grenville's separate descriptions of history's existential role in an individual's continuity of self. These ideas frame a critical understanding of identity. However, they require a way to access meanings that are not obviously visible in the daily, everyday ways that we interact through the exchange of ideas. Hayden White's description of marking meaning through historical storytelling provides a key way to examine individuals' understanding and use of history. The inclusion of four interdisciplinary theoretical reference points is intentional (i.e., Clark, art history; Giddens, sociology; Grenville, archaeology; White, history). Their conclusions are largely parallel and reinforce this essay's overall argument in a way that would not emerge from a single, disciplinary vantage point.

We often tell stories—shared out loud or marked into the physical world around us—to state what we believe. Without our understanding of these stories, we are left exposed and unsupported. How and what we say matters.[15] Stories may be physical remnants (e.g., the "old church" or a brass plaque) or events and memes that are canonized into statements of solidified cultural knowledge.[16] All of this is history. But as Clark suggested, these stories (or markers) are challenged by our individual experience.[17] We intend for stories to help us better explain and understand time and our situation. Giddens argued that the modern, existential self creates and maintains its coherent storyline of identity through such ongoing efforts. Grenville reasoned further that "understanding [our] ontological (in)securities" frames our existential sense of where we are: now versus then, here versus there.[18] The destruction of an individual's coherent storyline or understanding would mean the end of self.[19] Security in one's sense of self, time, and experience provides "the confidence that most human beings have in the continuity of their self-identity and the constancy of the surrounding social and material environments of action."[20] But to return to Clark, this continuity is challenged by changes in what we understand and competing stories told by others.

White argued that telling stories of history requires turning facts into meanings.[21] Stories allow each individual to restate and structure her or his understanding of time and experience. What we understand and believe may change. The stories we tell change. Stories, like the landscape, are edited. Further, isolated stories may hold meaning but are not narratives. Any single story may or may not contribute to an individual's overall narrative of self-identity. An individual may not be conscious of how a story supports or contradicts his or her broader narrative. Understanding the uses of stories requires seeing what is allowed to remain and listening (or reading) what people say.[22] Examining many stories shared by different individuals reveals a clearer narrative about both individual and communal understanding. In Lexington, like other places, no single story line controls the identity of all residents. Yet the continuous roll of time links the contested (and, to some, disagreeable) past with the present in negotiating individual and social understanding.

Stories about Lexington's history were gathered through interviews with ten residents of downtown Lexington and from media reports about the city's downtown neighborhoods and the pastured block. The media reports contextualized the stories with many details left out of oral retellings. The stories were further framed with observation of the landscape to visualize the physical clues and experiential characteristics of the stories' settings. Landscape observation also revealed unspoken conditions that influence individual understandings. Interviewees were selected for geographic distribution in the downtown neighborhoods and their willingness to participate. The interviewees varied in age, duration of residence in the downtown area, community involvement, and gender, economic, and racial background. As part of the research protocol, interviewees were promised anonymity that precludes individual description.[23] The interviews were analyzed using a narrative protocol to understand the meanings inherent in stories rather than just the words used.[24] The narrative analysis process maintains the complexity of an interviewee's story, which often reveals the shifting character of human identity that may be "assembled and dissembled, accepted and contested" by the interviewee across different aspects of the story.[25]

Interviews were transcribed, returned for participant confirmation, and coded for narrative structure, types of preservation actions, and characterizations of historical consciousness.[26] Coding was cross-compared to identify patterns of meaning and distinctions in how individuals described and used history. The interviews with downtown residents focused on their perception and use of history in their daily lives, not redevelopment projects within the downtown area. Nevertheless, each interviewee spontaneously discussed the pastured block and described his or her perceptions of history in relation to the public debates about the project. Archival research, observations of cultural landscapes, and examination of open, public social media discussions (e.g., message boards, newspaper discussion areas) supported the analysis and enriched subsequent discussion of the findings. The quotations and stories recounted in this essay represent contextualized conclusions from those residents' stories. The stories the residents told reflect the private process by which we artificially connect together our understanding of history so that we can maintain our current sense of self and claim who we want to be in the future. As the stories reveal, this process relates to the physical environment but depends more on individual perception and abstract conceptions (e.g., memories) of the way things are.

Telling, Acting, and Framing Lexington's History

Lexington's founding residents named their settlement in honor of the first battle of the American Revolution at Lexington and Concord, Massachusetts (1775).[27] By 1820 the town was recognized as among the largest and wealthiest communities west of the Allegheny Mountains. Its reputation as the "Athens of the West" was supported by a series of firsts: the first newspaper in the west (*Kentucke Gazette,* 1787), the first institute of higher learning west of the Alleghenies (Transylvania University, 1789), the first library in Kentucky (1795), and the first Episcopal congregation in the west (1796). Lexington also identified itself as the home of John Wesley Hunt, reportedly the west's first millionaire, and of a list of nationally influential individuals central to the Civil War.[28]

During the Civil War, Lexington remained predominately under Union control, except for one month in 1862. Yet Confederate raids on the town led by General John Hunt Morgan repeatedly threatened the residents' sense of security. General Morgan's family home was located in the prominent Gratz Park area of the downtown. The Union headquarters were located less than three hundred feet across the park from the Morgan family home. Today, the Hunt-Morgan House is a house museum operated by the Blue Grass Trust for Historic Preservation. Although the city's role in the Civil War was limited, parts of the community maintained divided cultural, economic, and political systems throughout the nineteenth century and into the twentieth century.

Lexington built a manufacturing and research base in the twentieth century. In the 1950s, IBM moved its typewriter division to Lexington. The electronic Selectric typewriter and the Courier font, which became synonymous with progressive business across the nation, formed the foundation for Lexington's new research and manufacturing base.[29] Tobacco trading and banking also continued to be part of the city's economy. At the same time, African American residents lived in segregated neighborhoods or hamlets in the community, developed their own parallel cultural and economic centers, and attended separate Rosenwald schools.[30] In February 1960, residents held a sit-in at the Woolworth's lunch counter in downtown Lexington in support of a similar protest in Greensboro, North Carolina. The East End neighborhood's Charles Young Center not only provided the cultural center for the city's African American community but also served as the organizational grounds for civil rights marches and boycotts in the adjacent downtown area.[31]

For many Lexington residents, the city's history derives from the list of firsts and superlatives that are part of its past. Lexington is not a representation of the American idea; these residents understand themselves and their city as a *quintessential* part of the story about the nation's birth, struggles, and prosperity. While the historical pedigree of Lexington remains the dominant spirit of the place, local residents do complicate their historical understanding with many other simultaneous perspectives. Some understand Lexington as the primary city of eastern Kentucky. Others recall the past role of tobacco, coal, and other agricultural products in the city's growth. Another set of residents view Lexington's past and present through the framework of unresolved racial and social issues. A small but vocal group sees the city's potential as an innovation center. And of course, many people celebrate the city's links to its horse racing heritage.

The contested past is (at least conceptually) known in the dominant narratives of place. The separate ways that the city remembers white and African American owners, trainers, and jockeys involved in the horse racing industry demonstrate these contrasts within the community. Thoroughbred Park, a downtown green space, contains sculptures and plaques identifying individuals from the region's horse racing past (Figure 5). The park "captures and reenforces through its physical presentation a very sharp, longstanding (140 years-old) race/class divide in the city."[32] While Thoroughbred Park sits next to the East End neighborhood and the site of the city's original racing track, it does not reference the many prominent African American trainers and jockeys who lived within sight of the park.[33] Instead, members of the neighborhood are developing their own memorial space to recognize that past as their own.[34]

Figure 5. Thoroughbred Park, Lexington, Kentucky, looking to northeast. The topography of Thoroughbred Park visually separates the East End neighborhood from the primary roads leading into downtown Lexington. The landscape of the park is dotted with sculptures and plaques identifying individuals associated with the horseracing industry. Photograph by Bryan D. Orthel, 2013.

Conflicts around space and place have been a part of Lexington's identity since at least the mid-nineteenth century.[35] In the twentieth century, this conflict reshaped Lexington's downtown and structured part of the community's social order. For example, the Blue Grass Trust for Historic Preservation, a nonprofit preservation education and advocacy organization, was founded in 1955 in response to the threatened demolition of several buildings in the Gratz Park neighborhood of downtown. A small group of Lexington residents could not believe that part of the town's history could be removed for parking. The group's efforts were not universally accepted, but the organization became a prominent voice in the community. As the organization grew, it advocated for preserving specific places that connected the city to the past, developed a revolving loan fund to preemptively purchase threatened historic buildings, and founded a house museum at the John Wesley Hunt house in Gratz Park (now known as the Hunt-Morgan House).

As in many communities, the change brought by redevelopment and growth prompted concern and promise. Lexington's residents were proactive in protecting and advancing their values. In response to growth after World War II, Lexington created the nation's first urban growth boundary in 1958. The urban growth boundary limited the outward sprawl of developed area and protected the horse racing–related landscape that surrounded the city.[36] Beginning in the 1990s, nonprofit organizations and the municipal government started programs to purchase development rights or secure use easements to further protect the racing landscape from suburban development. In the East End, residents actively campaigned for redevelopment to strengthen the neighborhood's declining retail and cultural core.[37] Development, growth, and change repeatedly prompted residents of the city to create new ways to protect what they valued.

Preservation of history and buildings was a specific issue in downtown Lexington across the twentieth century. The city's downtown was reshaped in form and use. Augustus, a longtime Lexington resident and downtown businessman, described how the downtown adjusted to the development of car-based culture. In the 1950s and 1960s, Lexington saw "a pattern of demolition of historic structures . . . the fabric of the commercial district, to create room to park cars."[38] Downtown property owners tried to "mask [their] historic architectural buildings to look like something you'd find in a mall or the suburbs," and "the face of Main Street" was dramatically altered.[39] Prominent projects that introduced new, more suburban building types into the center of the city reshaped the downtown commercial core. The removal of the railroad lines bisecting downtown opened up new land and prompted further redevelopment projects in the 1970s and 1980s.[40]

In the mid-1970s, residents fought to protect sixteen acres of the Historic South Hill neighborhood from demolition.[41] Part of the neighborhood was cleared. The site is now the parking lot for the city's convention center and arena complex.[42] In the early 1980s, a local businessman purchased the Phoenix Hotel in downtown, demolished the building, and proposed a multistory office and residential complex to be known as the World Coal Center.[43] The promised building never materialized. To improve the aesthetics of the vacant site prior to the regional NCAA basketball tournament hosted by Lexington in 1985, the empty lot was transformed into a temporary park.[44] Eventually, the city's main library, a residential tower, and a permanent park were built on the site (Figures 6 and 7). The permanent park was named Phoenix Park after the demolished hotel. Also in the 1980s, private developers demolished the Ben Ali Theater across Main Street from the Phoenix Hotel site to build a high-rise apartment building.[45] The site sat empty for more than a decade. The Phoenix Hotel and Ben Ali Theater sites are immediately south and southeast of the pastured block. Ultimately, a new county courthouse complex was built on the Ben Ali site (2001–2).

In 1984 the redevelopment of sixteen buildings in one Main Street block created a retail, art, and entertainment complex (originally known as Victorian Square) that emphasized the buildings' Italianate and Victorian features. An adjacent three-quarter block was demolished to become a shopping mall (and parking garage) inspired by festival markets (e.g., Faneuil Hall Marketplace and Quincy Market in Boston or Harborplace in Baltimore) that mix shopping, entertainment, history, and spectacle. Other building projects replaced large pieces of downtown urban blocks with modern office buildings, hotels, and retail space.[46] During the 1990s the *Lexington Herald-Leader* reported on the steady decline and bankruptcy of the festival market and other once-promising downtown projects.[47] The city's growth continued to shift toward the suburban rings and away from downtown, while downtown mimicked suburban-style building patterns. Parking garages and high-rise buildings were built where blocks of mixed-use, lowrise buildings had been. Since 2000, new lowrise, mixed-use construction and renovation of existing buildings have provided additional opportunities for living in the downtown core and revitalized its commercial activity. The downtown of 2016 is significantly different in physical structure and social makeup than its 1970s self.

Individuals who lived or worked in the downtown neighborhoods repeatedly came together to respond to these specific changes and the ongoing growth of Lexington. Residents protested against some of the proposals (e.g., the 1970s arena parking lot plan) but embraced others (e.g., the 1980s Victorian Square and festival market). And the reaction to proposals differed depending on the subsection of the community. While residents and neighbors of the area to be cleared for the arena parking lot fought the demolition, other residents embraced the change brought about by the new venue. Community organizations and residents struggled with the proposed loss, the progress promised by the new arena, and whether Lexington would embrace a "community preservation movement" that included protecting diverse areas and histories.[48] In the end, part of the neighborhood was demolished to become the parking lot.

Albert, a longtime resident of Lexington, described the neighborhood loss as a watershed in how the community viewed itself: "I think the case had a major impact on empowering downtown neighborhoods. Since that time, people don't make plans (like the plans demolishing that neighborhood) without consulting the existing neighborhoods."[49] Still, less than a decade later, residents felt powerless to stand against some proposals for continuing downtown redevelopment (e.g., World Coal Center).[50] Residents fought first to take care of their immediate neighborhoods and their individual senses of self. As recently as 2004, residents of the Martin Luther King neighborhood rejected the city's efforts to designate their neighborhood as a historic district.[51] They resented the imposition of someone else's reading of "history" on their neighborhood. They also feared gentrification would force them to move. Individuals and groups dealt with the issues in their own backyards and neighborhoods before joining together to address broader community concerns.

Figure 6. The pastured block in the context of 1970s- and 1980s-era commercial development. The removal of the railroad tracks that had transected downtown Lexington opened up new land for development. The railroad tracks ran parallel with the southwestern edge of the pastured block. The three commercial towers (*starting from the right*) were developed after the tracks were removed. A few historic structures along the track route remain (see two-story structure, *center right*). The residential tower (*at the left*) was built on the site of the Phoenix Hotel. Photograph by Bryan D. Orthel, 2013.

Although the Blue Grass Trust remains the dominant preservation organization in the city, its own history as a traditional, socially oriented, and small-*c* conservative organization prompted some residents to challenge its role as the city's primary preservation group. In October 2006, Preserve Lexington was founded to advocate against the demolition of the buildings on the now pastured block.[52] Preserve Lexington aimed "to preserv[e] downtown Lexington's historic fabric, voic[e] the interests of diverse groups and cultures, and promot[e] quality infill and design."[53] Preserve Lexington's and the Blue Grass Trust's advocacy represented different subsets of the community and different views of preservation. Preserve Lexington aimed to speak for young professionals who wanted to aggressively fight demolition.[54] The Blue Grass Trust and its socially prominent membership roster approached preservation and interactions with the city's power structures more cautiously. They were more likely to lobby in private, through social settings, or official channels than in headline-grabbing press releases or social media. The Blue

Figure 7. Demolition of the Phoenix Hotel, Lexington, Kentucky. The Phoenix Hotel (constructed circa 1914 and 1954) was demolished in 1981–82 in anticipation of a high-rise development. The proposed building was not built. Courtesy of the University of Kentucky General Photographic Prints, University of Kentucky Libraries.

Grass Trust preferred to work quietly to influence decisions affecting the city's past.[55]

These two groups were not alone in advocating for the protection of the community's resources. Other community organizations supported specific approaches for preserving the city and the surrounding region. These groups included Bluegrass Tomorrow (regional planning), the Bluegrass Conservancy (land trust), Bluegrass PRIDE (local sustainability), the Fayette Alliance (farmland preservation and community development), the Lexington-Fayette County Urban County Government's program to purchase development rights (agricultural open space), and the Dry Stone Conservancy (stone fence preservation). A group of interested citizens associated with multiple viewpoints created a digital forum, ProgressLex, in 2010 to supplement discussions surrounding the pastured block and build social capital for protecting the community.[56] Whether through the Blue Grass Trust, Preserve Lexington, or ProgressLex, small groups of residents coalesced into more formal organizations representing distinct approaches to understanding and protecting the city's history. This history of Lexington's physical and social landscape is, in itself, not unique. Many other American communities were transformed by similar processes and reacted with similar community organization and social responses.

The effort to prevent the demolition of the buildings on the pastured block crossed racial, economic, and geographic lines. The block's historic value related to the broad community, not just one subset. Opposition to the demolition drew support from residents who lived in the downtown neighborhoods but also motivated individuals who lived in the suburbs to become involved.[57] More recently, a proposal to save and restore the First African Baptist Church was also framed as the responsibility of Lexington to know its whole self. The church was not just for the African American community.[58] With time, residents and organizations have recognized issues that affect the wider community beyond their immediate, individual concerns. Redevelopment, change, and preservation have moved the community forward while individuals alternatively resist and embrace the past and future as part of their identity. Augustus explained that the residents increasingly valued and understood histories in the neighborhoods and were working to make them what they had been: "It's almost like the neighborhood['s] coming back to life."[59] This repeated and retold history suggests that the community is as it always has been, if also different. As the story continues, multiple parts of Lexington's identity—and the identities of its residents—assert themselves. Individualized understandings of history that are linked with communal ideals of the past are used by the individuals to make connections between their past and their present.

Linking Community and History

The stories individuals in Lexington tell about their histories and identities follow three lines. First, the stories reveal how meanings and historical narratives are developed. Second, the diversity of stories requires that individuals reconcile the conflicts separately and as groups. Third, reconciling differing stories incorporates histories and identities together. The result is the preservation of identities, meanings, and histories that, while now changed, address the confusion between the past and the future.

The story of the pastured block weaves together the twentieth-century history of Lexington with how individuals and communities view themselves and choose to act. In fighting to protect buildings on the now pastured block, individuals were fighting to protect their status quo—their view of the past and future. History was frequently invoked, but the bigger concern was holding onto that muddled, time-spanning *immediate now* experienced by each individual. Individuals were actively telling personalized historical stories (à la White) to make sense of their existence (e.g., Clark, Giddens, and Grenville). When the first demolition on the pastured block was proposed in 2002, the executive director of the city's Downtown Development Authority described his concern about repeated losses undermining the wholeness of the place: "It bothers me that the smile along Main Street is going to have a few more missing teeth."[60] Change prompted individual reflection and concern about a perceived threat. At the same time, redevelopment of the block fit within a larger sense that Lexington's downtown should revitalize and become more integral to the city.[61] Some individuals sought change to create a new, desired future. Many online comments noted that there was "nothing downtown":

> Besides a few people that work in the offices and bball every now and then at Rupp [Arena] . . . what else is there to do? . . . a few bars and restaurants. . . . There aren't many shops. . . . If this project is going to work, Lexington needs to up the "bustle meter" and get more people downtown.[62]

Several redevelopment projects that also started between 2002 and 2008 produced mixed-use residential and commercial buildings along Main Street and its cross streets. These individual buildings have drawn visitors to new shops and offices and increased the downtown population living in lofts and live-work units. Longtime downtown business owners positively received many of the redevelopment ideas and recognized that "things will never go back to being exactly the way they were in the 'good old days.'"[63] But perception challenges remained. Amanda, a lifelong resident, described Lexington's culture this way: "Lexington really has a hard time using the word *new*."[64] *The sense of continuity between the past and present required simultaneously recognizing the place as unaltered—and wholly different* (for example, Figure 8). For many residents the redevelopment on the pastured block was difficult to fit within this coexisting dichotomy.

Protecting History, Identity, and the Status Quo

The first part of the story about the pastured block reveals many ways that meanings and identities are tied into historical understanding through the stories we tell. In 2000 the pastured block contained fifteen two- and three-story commercial buildings. Although not the first demolition on the block, the loss of the art deco–inspired Woolworth building raised community interest about the block (see Figure 4). The Woolworth store had operated from the mid-1940s through 1990.[65] A fifteen-year attempt to find a suitable reuse failed, and the building was demolished in 2004. After that point the developer's efforts to demolish the rest of the buildings progressed steadily. The other fourteen buildings on the block were demolished in July 2008. Lexington residents enlisted a substantial group of state and national experts to make the case that the buildings should not be demolished. Although arguments were made for the historic value of several buildings, the signature buildings of the preservation campaign were Morton's Row (Figures 9 and 10). The three buildings of Morton's Row dated to 1826 and were described as the "most important early buildings in downtown

Figure 8. Collage of historical markers reflecting emphasis on the "good old days." The community's sense of continuity required seeing Lexington as unaltered from its past and wholly different. Clockwise from the top left are a plaque identifying the oldest house in town, a Blue Grass Trust plaque, a privately dated building, a plaque indicating a building listed on the National Register of Historic Places, a municipal sign, and a tongue-in-check plaque. Photographs by Bryan D. Orthel, 2011.

Lexington, both historically and architecturally."[66] Commercial uses had occupied Morton's Row since the buildings' construction over 180 years before. The developer repeatedly argued: "None of [the to-be-demolished] structures was on the National Registry [*sic*] of Historic Places."[67] Further, the developer questioned the historic value of the buildings because Lincoln had not shopped in them.[68] The buildings did not match the developer's understanding of history. To the developer and property owners, the question of historic value was a false argument being used to prevent the development.[69] Residents of Lexington expressed particularly strong concerns about the public process that led to the demolitions, the value of the lost buildings, and what their loss meant for the city. Conflicting understandings of what could be historic and should be valued created the precise conditions that Clark described as scrambled and "without any focusing purpose."[70] Because different parts of the community valued the buildings and downtown for different reasons, it was initially difficult to establish a consistent narrative among the stories individuals wanted to tell.

Social Reaction

Public comments on blog and newspaper discussion boards convey the strength of opinion on both sides of the controversy. The comments—and the cumulative narratives that emerged from them—reveal individuals negotiating a scrambled world. Some people praised the redevelopment proposal. One online post shared optimism about the proposed new building as "just the right kind of development that can spur other quality projects to happen nearby."[71] Others were skeptical. A former resident discussed how he had hoped that Lexington could be both the place he loved growing up and the place that he dreamed it would be. The demolition of these buildings demonstrated to him that Lexington did not yet "deeply value" what it was:

> Regardless of intent, what comes across in [the decision to allow demolition of the block] is a heavy-

Figure 9. Morton's Row, Lexington, Kentucky, circa 1920. At the time of the photograph, the buildings of Morton's Row housed business offices, a barber shop, a laundry, a restaurant, and retail space. Courtesy of the Asa C. Chinn Downtown Lexington, Kentucky Photographic Collection, University of Kentucky Libraries.

> handed demolition of centuries of history with no true effort or desire to celebrate all the different elements present in this block. What also comes across is that Lexington is not a place for dialogue and incorporation, for creativity and compromise.[72]

For the individuals engaged in the debate, the redevelopment proposal and buildings' demolition required framing the city's heart, identity, past, and future in a new and different way.

As with many stories, the conflict took several forms. Patrons of music venues, the farmers' market, and artist spaces on the block organized a public funeral for the demolished buildings. The funeral included a procession around the block and a 1980s-themed party.[73] The 1980s theme was a reference to the city moving backward three decades to when the same developer had previously demolished several city blocks for new buildings. Procession signs read: "I mourn the greed," "I mourn the loss of civic input," and "I mourn the loss of music."[74] One sign said: "I mourn the lack of imagination."[75] Other responses channeled discontent through more formal formats. An editorial in the university newspaper noted that students "lost not only their favorite weekend hangouts, but also their faith in the local government when the city ignored the pleas of many to halt the destruction of our downtown."[76] Parts of the community expressed frustration with the developer, the government, the proposal, and the process.[77] The mayor, vice mayor, and city council members supported opposing sides of the proposal and openly debated the issues at public meetings and in the media. The city's zoning processes were attacked for providing layers of protection for some buildings and none for others. Significantly, individuals expressed disbelief that other people did not recognize the truth as they understood it. For example, a letter to the editor asked: "Only in Lexington would groups like Preserve Lexington and the Blue Grass Trust try to preserve a pawn shop and a honky-tonk establishment. . . . What loss will they be?"[78] The debate highlighted the complexity of maintaining a self-coherent sense of history.

The value and meaning of history itself was challenged by the stories individuals shared. Proponents of the redevelopment argued that the Morton's Row buildings were not historic enough to warrant preservation. One individual asked, "How can a building dating back to 1826 not be historical?"[79] A proponent of the redevelopment responded by comparing the buildings to the droppings of a Civil War–era horse:

> If someone had a stool sample from John Hunt Morgan's prize horse it could also be considered as "historic" but does that mean that it's something worth preserving? Just because something is old,

Figure 10. Morton's Row, circa 2006. The buildings of Morton's Row housed a restaurant and a pawn shop. Courtesy of Janie-Rice Brother, 2006.

> it doesn't mean we have a sacred interest in preserving it. The same thing applies for this block of "structures." I am not a fan of modern architecture. I was a history major at the University of Kentucky and I own two log homes dating back to 1792 so obviously I do love history and believe in preservation. The simple fact is however that there is nothing in this block worth preserving.[80]

The two competing understandings of history are conflicting paradigms. Neither individual was open to hearing the other's story.

Some members of the community felt the buildings' loss was the destruction of part of their own history. One resident watching the demolition said, "When I see the puffs of dust rise up, it's like seeing the spirits of the people who used to inhabit those buildings. It's sad."[81] Another resident expressed her grief even before the demolition had begun in a letter to the editor:

> As a Lexingtonian, I have quietly watched the beauty of downtown wrecked, razed and bulldozed over the years.
>
> I still remember shopping at Stewart's, Lowenthal's, Embry's, Wenniker's, Wolf Wile, Hymson's and Town and Country. I remember lunching in the Phoenix Hotel dining room or sitting at the counter of Woolworth's with my grandmother on Saturday afternoons. There were people on the streets visiting and shopping. . . .[82]
>
> I strongly encourage the city to slow down and think about the block known as Morton's Row. . . . I would like to see the . . . project scale back and incorporate the historically significant buildings there.[83]

Even though only one of the stores mentioned in her letter remained in downtown and only one other was still in business, her memories of these experiences were strong. She understood that the downtown was wholly different, but it was also somehow part of an unaltered status quo—*her* modern present. For her—like others—history, identity, and the present mixed and needed to be protected. Three years after the demolition at the pastured block, Amanda described the demolition with strong personal emotion. Her voice broke as she said, "It's going to be hard for me to get past that one—but I'm going to."[84] Meaning and understandings of history framed different identities for Lexington's residents.

Balancing Value, History, and Community

The second part of the pastured block's narrative shows the complexity of reconciling diverse views of history and its individualized meanings. The value of Lexington's history remains contested and differently recognized among parts of the community. The building that one person values as personal history represents economic opportunity through new development to another or burden to a third (Figure 11). Tom Eblen, a columnist for the local newspaper, expressed this contradiction:

> As I watch The Dame [a music venue] on Main Street being demolished, I see a neglected, century-old building that could have been reused to give the proposed . . . development more character and class. But many others—people the age of my daughters—see something different: They see the loss of an important piece of their culture. To them, it's almost as if somebody took a wrecking ball to the Lexington Opera House or the grandstand at Keeneland.[85]

Eblen's comparison is appropriate on several levels. The buildings on the pastured block arguably had deeper history in the community than the Opera House or Keeneland grandstand, but they did not fit the cultural impression of real—or "Lincoln-like"—history. *Further, for part of the community, the demolished buildings were not formal history but regularly lived experience.* A columnist in a university newspaper wrote:

> This spot was the heart of the city—a spot where both people from [the University of Kentucky] and people from Lexington at large got together to listen to good music, hang out with good people and to have fun. All that is gone now, in favor of a large dirt pit which may in the future hold an opulent, 35-story hotel. . . . Welcome to Lexington. Sorry to say it's a little lamer than it used to be.[86]

The ways that individuals and subcommunities balance their understanding of the past and its

Figure 11. Different perspectives on redevelopment. During 2014 the pastured block was excavated in preparation for construction of an underground parking garage that was part of the proposed redevelopment (*foreground*). The photograph shows the row of historic nineteenth- and twentieth-century buildings along the northeastern edge of the block along Main Street. Many of these buildings are being renovated for adaptive uses. Photograph by Bryan D. Orthel, 2014.

value define the larger community's identity. In Clark's words, agreed-upon "meaning [was] in short supply."[87] Residents strung together individual experiences in places and their immediate social relationships as personal *presents*—individualized, *immediate nows* that defined their identity in the modern world. The demolished buildings on the pastured block had provided opportunities for such presents through social gathering and business or simply as markers reminding an individual about the past. The shared experiences in those places were understood and retold in stories that overlapped but had different meanings.

Diverse Perspectives

The debate over the demolition of the fifteen buildings eventually brought together a diverse group of people in an uneasy, if united, front. Allen, a longtime Lexington resident, explained that no one part of the community dominated the drive to protect the buildings:

> [The] concern came out of a lot of corners and that's why I say communities. It was a loose coalition that was, sort of—managed to hold together. It could easily have fragmented, because we had people who didn't give a damn about the buildings per se, but they really cared about the businesses that were inside those buildings. . . . Then you'd obviously have people . . . who came out of a preservation community . . . so their interests were slightly different, but they were able to work together. . . . You had people who were concerned purely because of the height of the building. . . . There were people who worked for downtown design guidelines. . . . But they managed to work together.[88]

The reasons for saving the buildings varied, but individuals shared a collective goal. They agreed that demolition would have a negative impact. The group became a tentative, temporary community.[89] At the same time, some parts of the coalition were "visibly uncomfortable dealing" with individuals who approached the issues from different perspectives.[90] The "young, college-aged hipsters" and people representing establishment perspectives were an uneasy fit at the same table.[91] Support and opposition to the proposed development required individuals to reconcile their own stories with others' view of the Lexington they wanted for the future.

Public and Private Expectations

The public process surrounding the redevelopment of the privately owned block complicated the communal negotiation of value, history, and identity. Although the block was privately owned, many distinct parts of the community claimed the space as part of their self-representation.[92] The redevelopment proposal was mostly privately financed and to be built on land privately acquired for this specific project. The proposal was required to comply with public regulation and policies. Competing perceptions of history blurred the lines between community obligation, public expectation, and private rights.

Several parts of the community desired a voice in the project. Even as they opposed the demolition of the block, residents and organizations sought a compromise that would incorporate the façades of the historic buildings into a version of the proposed development.[93] Prominent community members proposed alternative development ideas.[94] The then vice mayor called for an international design competition to think more innovatively about how to redevelop the block.[95] The University of Kentucky invited architects from Los Angeles and Chicago to a public design workshop focused on exploring alternatives for the site.[96] A group of middle school students put together proposals for redeveloping the block.[97] The developer responded with "a few changes" to the plans but argued that the company had the right to demolish the buildings and that it was "too late to consider alternative suggestions from architects, preservationists or citizens."[98] Again, different views of the desired future were in conflict. Individuals continued to navigate the stories they used to define who they were in the present. A communal narrative had not yet emerged from the many stories.

To many people the proposed redevelopment did not fit with how they saw Lexington. A downtown businessperson was quoted as saying, "The architect hadn't spent enough time in Lexington to get the design right."[99] Many residents of Lexington felt that the proposed development did not represent the community and that they had little control over the change that was being imposed. Although history was frequently invoked, the bigger, largely unspoken concern was maintaining a clear vision of whom the individuals and community would become. Residents not only were worried about how the city would be defined but expanded that concern to considering how their individual identities would be affected.

Community Values Moving Forward

After the buildings were demolished and construction postponed, the community discussion focused on the process that surrounded the redevelopment plan. People recognized that the process was not as open or inclusive as they desired. The process was called "frustrating" and "backwards."[100] Only a month after the last building came down, the newspaper asked: "What can Lexington learn from the . . . fiasco?"[101] In 2010, almost two years after the demolitions, the question of how the community should grow and develop remained unresolved. ProgressLex argued that continuing to discuss the unresolved issues was not beating a dead horse:

> The nag is dead all right, dead and buried in the giant paddock in the middle of downtown. But if we don't ask why, if we don't demand an accounting of all that went wrong, not just with [the redevelopment] plans, but with the behavior of the [city boards and mayor], if we don't perform a "post-mortem" on [this] corpse, then, mark my words, this won't be the last dead horse we bury in the heart of our city.[102]

Three years later, in January 2013, residents proposed using the pasture for a living room—literally organizing sofas in its center—to have a discussion about how the city should move forward.[103] Ultimately, a diverse group of citizens worked together to rewrite the zoning and design guidelines for development and building in downtown. The newspaper's editorial board summed up the popular sentiment: "Developers need to accept that others have [a] stake in downtown project[s], too."[104] Although this issue is more complex, in this case a heartfelt vision about growth from one part of the community was trumped by a different perspective of growth from another section of the community.[105] That rift was difficult to bridge. The process of individuals reconciling these different views brought out myriad understandings of history, challenged individuals, and socially reshaped the community's process for creating the future of downtown. Bringing those understandings of histories into view primed the social and intellectual environment to protect important meanings and reinforce shared values.

Using History as Ideals and Daily Action

The third part of the pastured block's narrative demonstrates the change and continuity that emerges from incorporating others' stories into individual and community histories. Once it became evident that construction on the demolished, vacant block would not begin soon, citizens of Lexington expressed regret and exchanged volleys of "I told you so." The newspaper's editorial board noted that Lexington had extended good faith to the developer who promised to reinvigorate downtown:

> Humiliation abounds on the block bounded by Main, Upper, Vine and Limestone. That's where Lexington's earliest commercial history was destroyed last summer to make way for a $250 million development that a compliant mayor and an easy-talking developer assured us would transform and invigorate our downtown. . . . The result is not a shining tower rising in our midst but a muddy, empty lot surrounded by construction fencing. . . . Faith rewarded with humiliation.[106]

Problems accessing the developer's primary financing delayed construction. Eventually, that financing was withdrawn. While some people voiced incriminations, others sought a temporary solution to the vacant, muddy block in the middle of the city.[107] The vice mayor demanded the developer fill the block with top soil, plant grass, and reopen the closed sidewalks.[108] The police removed people who used the empty block for unsanctioned purposes, like pick-up sports.[109] A year after proposing the project and nine months after the demolitions, the developer agreed to seed the block to grass and replace the construction fence with plank fencing similar to fencing on the region's horse farms.[110] The developer put a positive spin on the compromise: "We wanted to dress it up, make it look nice."[111] But planting grass on the block was greeted with relief and derision.[112] A critic wrote:

> These may be heartfelt gestures, but they are no substitute for the profound respect and visionary stewardship deserved by this unique region. The . . . absurdity degrades both farm and city, and should wake us up to the fact that we can no longer afford to surrender the character of our city and country to decisions driven by expediency. Power brokers must be held accountable to standards that recognize the good sense and integrity inherent in preservation and inspired design.[113]

A newspaper columnist wondered if Lexington was doomed to repeat its own history following the troubled 1980s-era downtown redevelopment projects. Members of the community moved forward by recrafting the story of the block into a future more compatible with their own, now changed, stories.

With time the redevelopment proposal evolved to relate more closely to the history and physical context of the prepastured block. In March 2011 the developer hired a new architectural team to explore alternatives for the redevelopment. At the suggestion of the mayor, the developer selected Studio Gang, an internationally known Chicago firm.[114] Once reports of the new architectural team were made public, Lexington's residents quickly started to suggest their own new ideas for reusing the pastured block. Tom Eblen stated that Lexington would not accept a generic solution in one of his newspaper columns. Instead, he asked, "What if, for example, the design could find ways to reference Lexington's rich 19th century architectural heritage with a unique, contemporary twist?" (Figure 12).[115]

The original redevelopment proposals featured a centralized tower of condominiums and hotel rooms sitting on a four-story plinth of commercial space. The tower filled the block with a single building. The design was symmetrical and solid and criticized for being placeless, overbearing, and too large for the context. Studio Gang's proposal divided the site into a series of smaller buildings that mimicked the scale of the still extant nineteenth- and twentieth-century buildings on nearby blocks. A series of narrower, independent buildings would cover the site. The new proposal incorporated public outdoor space. Studio Gang specifically sought to divide the design work for the project between multiple architecture firms to allow the buildings to develop distinct characteristics that could complement the diversity of Main Street's historic buildings. Some preservation advocates saw the design as vindication of their efforts. As one online comment put it:

> I kinda like the way the [developer] paid Gang to tell them what was on that block was better than what the [developer] wanted to build there. What a kick in the head![116]

Gang's new proposal emerged from research about the existing urban structure and Lexington's history, rather than imposing a new order on the scale and systems of the city.[117] Public comment on the design proposals was invited at two community meetings. Individuals and groups were asked how they viewed the new designs and how the designs could be improved.[118] The same people who had argued against the demolition of the block softened their opposition. The developer was hailed for a new community spirit.[119] The newspaper's editorial board praised the architecture team: "Jeanne Gang and her team studied the surrounding buildings, the history of the block, the Central Kentucky landscape and created something that honors each of them."[120] Less than a year later, another team of architecture firms was selected to revise the Studio Gang proposal, but their work followed the multiple building approach. The Studio Gang proposal shifted the topic and tone of the debate about the redevelopment of the block.[121] Construction on an underground parking garage started in 2014 but halted after the block had been excavated while the project's focus was reevaluated. Construction on the parking garage restarted in 2016.

The stories Lexington residents began to tell about the pastured block took on a different character. In the context of Clark, Giddens, Grenville,

Figure 12. Pastured block with skyline. The view across the pastured block toward the northwest shows the openness of the block, several three-story nineteenth-century buildings (similar to the fifteen demolished buildings), and twentieth-century office buildings along the Vine Street corridor. The buildings to the left were constructed along the path of the removed railroad tracks. The glass tower (*center*) replaced most of another downtown block during the 1980s. Note the fiberglass horse in the left foreground. Photograph by Bryan D. Orthel, 2011.

and White, these new stories actively explained new meanings to support the recrafted modern identities that emerged from the pastured block situation. The public discussion about the proposed design by Studio Gang moved beyond a debate about the relative historic value of the lost buildings. With the buildings gone, people focused on the other attributes of the block, the redevelopment, and the downtown that they valued and wanted to see continued. Individuals began to agree about the meanings necessary for a communal understanding of history in downtown Lexington. Redevelopment on surrounding blocks demonstrated different ways individuals and the community could move forward. For some individuals the pastured block had already become an integral part of the downtown experience and was now the desired status quo to be protected (Figure 13). Newspaper articles about the new redevelopment designs prompted comments urging protection of the pastured block as green space:

> I like that block the way it is now. Plant some trees, plop down some picnic tables and create a parking area for taco trucks and call it a day.[122]

and

> There is NO DESIGN that would be an improvement over leaving the space open as a small park. "Heart of The Bluegrass" and we have NO park downtown—disgraceful. Every great city in the world has a park near downtown.[123]

In May 2015 a Twitter thread explored alternative uses for the block after the construction on the proposed underground parking garage was delayed. On Twitter residents suggested new uses that varied from a giant swimming pool to a public transportation hub.[124]

While shared meanings increased, many social media commentators questioned the economic viability of the project and expressed their worries that the block would remain empty or worse, become home to a building without users.[125] A few people continued to focus on the way the site was but did so with more insight than they had expressed two years earlier. A conversation thread from an online discussion board shows this shift:

> It doesn't matter what they build on this spot, it won't replace what this city lost: It's [*sic*] character.[126]

> > Oh boloney. If Lexington's character was defined by the collection of derelict, tumble downs that occupied that block then the town is the municipal equivalent of a bum. What Jeanne Gang is proposing is inspired. And it's especially cool that local architects have been invited to the table. The previous structures are now long-gone (and themselves had replaced previous structures.) We need to move on.[127]

> > > What [the first comment] means is when they tore down the old buildings, what was taken away was a community marketplace of ideas. The Dame, Buster's, Underlying Themes and Mia's were the main places downtown that local artists and musicians would congregate to perform, rub elbows, exchange skills and plan projects. It was part of the real cultural backbone of the city.[128]

The story was no longer about the destruction of historic buildings but was now recognized as a point of disagreement about the future. The many stories that residents had told were no longer understood as threats to the future (e.g., reminiscences that focused toward the past) but increasingly seen as part of new social structures and community vitality. The evolution of the discussion framed a broader view of preservation that focused on the goals of individuals working together rather than the relative merit of physical structures.

Overall, the pastured block demolitions were part of a renewed interest in downtown.[129] Over several years people and groups assimilated the immediate history of the block's demolition into their individual understanding of the city, its identity, their identities, and the present. Having lost the buildings, many individuals and community groups turned to protecting the social community and building the type of commercial activity that supported their shared visions for the downtown area. The demolition and pastured block displaced the downtown farmers' market, which had used parking areas and sidewalk on the block. A market pavilion was built on Cheapside, the public space adjacent to the old county courthouse (Figure 14).[130] A new regular Thursday Night Live event drew people into downtown for entertainment, food, and social activity. Downtown grocery stores opened to support more urban living. Augustus described the new energy in downtown:

> I think that most of what's happened downtown with the revitalization of not only historic architecture, but also the creation of additional attractive, fun, inviting kinds of uses and things to do and see and be available to you downtown, has been received by the community in a really positive way. . . . And now I walk out [of work] at 5:30 on Thursday and I see 3,500 people gathered in the public square enjoying themselves, enjoying the city.[131]

New and old businesses continue to relocate and prosper in the downtown.[132] The city's subsequent discussions about the revitalization of the convention center and arena complex (two blocks northwest of the pastured block) included questions about ideas that would link the two sites.

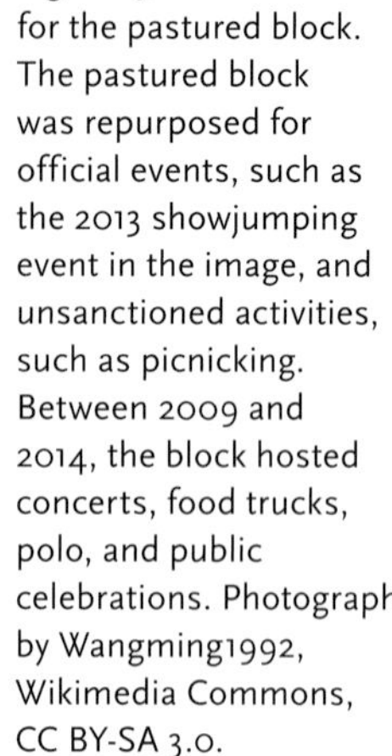
Figure 13. New uses for the pastured block. The pastured block was repurposed for official events, such as the 2013 showjumping event in the image, and unsanctioned activities, such as picnicking. Between 2009 and 2014, the block hosted concerts, food trucks, polo, and public celebrations. Photograph by Wangming1992, Wikimedia Commons, CC BY-SA 3.0.

Designs to renovate the arena complex and restore a waterway through downtown relied on connections to both the pastured block and the city's sense of history.[133]

The end of the pastured block's story remains unwritten, but histories and identities have been preserved while change continues.

Maintaining and Re-creating Understanding

As Lexington's downtown revitalized and changed, individuals and groups involved in the debate about the pastured block did not abandon their understanding of history or its value. Their actions ultimately deployed that history in different ways that looked forward rather than resting on the past or the status quo. History increasingly was a practical and symbolic representation to be used—part of the stringing together of the city's present and future as a shift from physical-and-concept to concept-and-action. The individual and group understandings of history grew to encompass a larger perspective. People began to understand the places, buildings, and sense of community they valued in more abstract ways that could be translated or imitated in the present.

The demolition of the pastured block in downtown Lexington can be read as loss, progress, commonplace event, and sarcastic tragedy. Many passersby (and readers) may conclude that the situation is a poor example of preservation. The buildings on the site were lost, something new will be built, a pattern repeats, and irony abounds. But demolition of the buildings prompted the preservation of something that is not physical. In response to the destruction, individual members of the community re-created their identity and history in more vibrant ways. These individuals were forced to reconcile their own perceptions of the status quo with other viewpoints. Their sense of "what was" clashed with others' views. Ultimately, this meant the individuals had to restructure their understanding of the past and actively recraft their presupposed future. Preservation in this case occurred at the individual scale—in assertions of historical knowledge, in changes in living to reinforce a different perspective, and in considering what was happening in the immediate now as real past and future.

Figure 14. Cheapside Pavilion with statue of John C. Breckinridge, Lexington, Kentucky. Cheapside, the public square next to the old courthouse, has been transformed into a farmers' market and entertainment pavilion as part of the revitalization of the downtown. In the nineteenth century, Cheapside was a site for slave auctions. Photograph by Bryan D. Orthel, 2014.

The story of Lexington's pastured block is not an argument to destroy buildings. Demolishing the buildings did not preserve them. A photograph, drawing, or digital model remains unequal to the experiential landscape. The Lexington example also does not provide an ideal approach for structuring individual and public debate about identity and community form. The residents who lived through the debate, demolition, and delayed construction experienced very real dread, loss, and concern. The demolition was part of the complicated challenge of living in the present. Our knowledge and understanding of the past frames what we expect will happen next. I have argued elsewhere that each individual is entitled to her or his understanding of history.[134] As Grenville and Giddens argued, denying individuals their understanding of history also denies them their sense of self.[135] Others reason that heritage must be a universal human right.[136] That position does not require that everything be saved—nor that historical chaos reign. Instead, the Lexington example demonstrates how preservation is significantly more complex than most policy or professional efforts suggest. The ways that people use and protect history extend far beyond physical resources. Individuals understand their past, present, and future as strings of ideas, events, and moments. Clark supposes that in the current world the individual must craft his or her understanding of time and self from disparate pieces.[137] As White described, this understanding must be converted into meanings and symbols: whether physical things or retold as stories.[138] The stories that residents of Lexington tell about their pastured block show that process of making meanings and understanding the immediate present.

The residents' stories and comments comprise a different way to frame preservation: as individually lived understanding rather than protection of physical artifact or cultural practice. Preservationists and historians should explore the historical consciousness and preservation-based actions of individuals to develop a more complete understanding of history's value for the contemporary and future world. The first step to recognizing and dealing with this preservation frame requires documenting and accepting individual meanings of place and discrete understandings of lived experience. Ultimately, addressing preservation from this perspective forces preservation professionals to acknowledge that preservation designs history through the choices that are made. Preservation is neither naïve nor neutral. Preservation is a wicked, systematic problem. Preservation immediately alters an individual's understanding of history, self-identity, and conception of position in time.

The connection of the present and future *into* the past requires social and communal structure. The individual's understanding of the past, present, and future is simultaneous and changing rather than sequential. The case of the pastured block is based on the stories, actions, and memories of individuals working in relationship to each other. Individually, people understand their own history, but the communal understanding of history requires exchanging information and building relationships of knowledge. The known past, whether individual or communal, becomes the status quo of the present because people understand who they are based on who they recognize they have been. An individual can (mostly) be protected from the unknown future by refusing to challenge the status quo. But historical meaning relies on social exchange. History's value differs between individuals. Social interaction and negotiation of value is necessary for determining not only what is important but how the individual fits within communal representations of history. In the example of Lexington's pastured block, this process is ongoing. Individual decisions to preserve a piece of history (e.g., an idea, a building, a tradition) relate to the larger scale of communal understanding of history; equally, the communal group must endeavor to understand the meanings of individuals' stories and actions. In this way the authority of the past is exerted into the present and future.

AUTHOR BIOGRAPHY

Bryan D. Orthel is assistant professor at Kansas State University. With a background in architecture and historic preservation, his research focuses on the ways that individuals understand and use history, also known as historical consciousness.

NOTES

The author is indebted to the many residents of Lexington who agreed to interviews and offered their insight into the city. In addition, the many residents who expressed their viewpoints about the project through social media and newspaper discussion boards are thanked for providing a rich, living data source. The editors and reviewers for this journal shared insightful and engaging criticism that strengthened the essay. The author is thankful for their comments and guidance. Finally, the author is profoundly grateful for invaluable advice and direction provided by Phil Gruen (Washington State University) during the research and writing phases of this project.

1. T. J. Clark, *Farewell to an Idea: Episodes from a History of Modernism* (New Haven, Conn.: Yale University Press, 1999), 7–8 (emphasis added). All references to Clark within the essay refer to this excerpt.

2. Adrian, a lifelong resident, described the redevelopment of the pastured block as "the big hole in the heart of the city." Adrian, interview by author, transcript K10.100.

3. The World Equestrian Games are the world championship competitions in dressage, driving, endurance, eventing, jumping, para-dressage, reining,

and vaulting. The games occur on a four-year cycle spaced between the Olympic games. Lexington, Kentucky, was the first host city outside Europe.

4. Dennis Domer, "Old but Not Good Old History: Prospects and Problems of Freezing Time in Old Buildings," *Journal of Architectural and Planning Research* 26, no. 2 (2009): 95–110.

5. Peter Bacon Hales, "Public Arts in Public Places: Contests and Spectacles in Block 37" (paper, American Studies Association, Washington, D.C., 1997).

6. Daniel Bluestone, "Chicago's Mecca Flat Blues," *Journal of the Society of Architectural Historians* 57, no. 4 (December 1998): 382–403.

7. Beverly Fortune, "$250 Million Tower Would Reshape Downtown," *Lexington Herald-Leader*, March 4, 2008; Steve Lannen and Michelle Ku, "Webbs Tweak CentrePointe Design," *Lexington Herald-Leader*, May 30, 2008; Beverly Fortune and Cheryl Truman, "Dudley Webb Submits Scaled-Down Version of CentrePointe," *Lexington Herald-Leader*, July 9, 2010.

8. Dan Dickson, "City Brokers Meeting with New CentrePointe Developers, Consultants Weighing City Hall Plans," *Business Lexington*, December 15, 2015.

9. Tom Eblen, "We Need to Balance Past, Future in Historic Preservation Debates," *Lexington Herald-Leader*, March 3, 2012.

10. Jeff Jefferson, letter to the editor, *Lexington Herald-Leader*, April 6, 2008.

11. Beverly Fortune, "Merge Old Buildings, New Plan, They Say," *Lexington Herald-Leader*, June 25, 2008; Jim Gray, "What Will City Get for CentrePointe Subsidy?," *Lexington Herald-Leader*, June 6, 2008.

12. Jim Warren, "Boom Goes the CentrePointe: Blasting Begins Monday at Downtown Block," *Lexington Herald-Leader*, March 15, 2014; Beth Musgrave, "Design Panel Approves CentrePointe Changes, Including Adding Five Floors on One Building," *Lexington Herald-Leader*, May 14, 2014.

13. Beth Musgrave, "Lexington Officials Send Webb Companies Letter Demanding CentrePointe Site Be Filled In," *Lexington Herald-Leader*, May 28, 2015; Beth Musgrave, "New Investors Plan to Take Over CentrePointe, Want City Hall to Be Part of Project," *Lexington Herald-Leader*, August 11, 2015.

14. Frederick Nietzsche stated: "Then man says 'I remember' and envies the animal which immediately forgets and sees each moment really die, sink back into dark night extinguished for ever. . . . *The unhistorical and the historical are equally necessary for the health of an individual, a people and a culture*." Friedrich Nietzsche, *On the Advantage and Disadvantage of History for Life*, trans. Peter Preuss (Indianapolis, Ind.: Hackett Publishing, 1980), 9–10 (emphasis in original).

15. Eugene McCann, using another example from Lexington's cultural landscape, framed this as the layered reality of "conceived, perceived, and lived" experience within Lefebvre's political space. Eugene J. McCann, "Race, Protest, and Public Space: Contextualizing Lefebvre in the U.S. City," *Antipode* 31, no. 2 (April 1999): 167.

16. John Bodnar, *Remaking America: Public Memory, Commemoration, and Patriotism in the Twentieth Century* (Princeton, N.J.: Princeton University Press, 1992).

17. Clark, *Farewell to an Idea*; McCann, "Race, Protest, and Public Space."

18. Jane Grenville, "Conservation as Psychology: Ontological Security and the Built Environment," *International Journal of Heritage Studies* 13, no. 6 (2007): 458.

19. David Lowenthal expanded on this by noting that memory is often falsified (intentionally or subconsciously) to preserve an existing sense of self-identity. Anthony Giddens, *Modernity and Self-Identity* (Stanford, Calif.: Stanford University Press, 1991); David Lowenthal, "History and Memory," *Public Historian* 19, no. 2 (Spring 1997): 30–39; Grenville, "Conservation as Psychology."

20. Quoted in Grenville, "Conservation as Psychology," 448. Original quotation from Anthony Giddens, *The Consequences of Modernity* (Cambridge, U.K.: Polity Press, 1990), 92.

21. Hayden White wrote: "One cannot represent the meaning of historical events without symbolizing them. . . . What can be explained about historical events is precisely what constitutes their non- or a-historical aspects. What remains after events have been explained is both 'historical' and 'meaningful' insofar as it can be understood. And this remainder is understandable insofar as it can be 'grasped' in a symbolization, that is, shown to have the kind of meaning with which plots endow stories." Hayden White, "The Question of Narrative in Contemporary Historical Theory," *History and Theory* 23, no. 1 (February 1984): 30.

22. Stories and landscape combine intentionality (e.g., editing, structuring, and intentional inclusion)

with the unintended. As Peirce Lewis states, the landscape is also our "unwitting autobiography, reflecting our tastes, our values, our aspirations, and even our fears, in tangible, visible form." In living, we reveal more than we may believe about who we are and what we value. Peirce F. Lewis, "Axioms for Reading the Landscape: Some Guides to the American Scene" in *The Interpretation of Ordinary Landscapes: Geographical Essays,* ed. Donald W. Meinig (New York: Oxford University Press, 1979), 12.

23. The human subject portion of this research was conducted following a protocol review by the Washington State University Institutional Review Board and approved per federal regulation 45 CFR 46.110 (b)(1). Interview participants consented to recording of the interviews, understood the potential implications for participation, and released the recordings and transcripts of the interviews for use in academic research and publication. The names of research participants have been altered to shield their identities.

24. Catherine Kohler Riessman, *Narrative Analysis* (Newbury Park, Calif.: Sage Publications, 1993); Catherine Kohler Riessman and Lee Quinney, "Narrative in Social Work: A Critical Review," *Qualitative Social Work* 4, no. 4 (December 2005): 391–412.

25. Riessman and Quinney, "Narrative in Social Work," 394.

26. Preservation actions included choices or actions to preserve based on the following: negative reasons (e.g., to not would destroy self or meaning), paradigmatic reasons, metaphorical reasons, and utilitarian reasons. These reasons included preservation actions that were populist, essential, entrepreneurial, and private. Coding for historical consciousness included empirical knowledge, passive knowledge (including nostalgia), transferred consciousness, semantic knowledge, moral consciousness, and theoretical consciousness. Dag Myklebust, "Preservation Philosophy: The Basis for Legitimating the Preservation of Remains of Old Cultures in a Modern World with New Value Systems," in *Proceedings from International Council on Monuments and Sites 8th General Assembly: Old Cultures in New Worlds,* vol. 2 (Washington, D.C.: ICOMOS, 1987); Christopher Koziol, "Historic Preservation Ideology: A Critical Mapping of Contemporary Heritage Policy Discourse," *Preservation Education & Research* 1 (2008): 41–50; Bryan D. Orthel, "The Story of Shoes in Trees: Understanding History as an Existential and Social (but Not Temporal) Narrative," *Preservation Education & Research* 6 (2013): 59–71.

27. "Lexington, Kentucky: The Athens of the West: A National Register of Historic Places Travel Itinerary," National Park Service website, undated, http://www.nps.gov/nr/travel/lexington/athens.htm.

28. Mary Todd Lincoln, wife of Abraham Lincoln, grew up in Lexington. Henry Clay, the Great Compromiser and Speaker of the House of Representatives, based his estate in Lexington. John C. Breckinridge served as Vice President of the United States (1857–1861) and Confederate Secretary of War. Jefferson Davis, President of the Confederate States of America, attended Transylvania University. "Lexington, Kentucky: The Athens of the West"; George W. Ranck, *History of Lexington Kentucky: Its Early Annals and Recent Progress* (Cincinnati, Ohio: Robert Clark & Co., 1872), 124–27; "John C. Breckinridge," *Wikipedia,* accessed 2012, http://en.wikipedia.org/wiki/John_C._Breckinridge.

29. Scott Sloan, "Lexington's Famed Selectric Typewriter Turns 50," *Lexington Herald-Leader,* July 30, 2011; "Courier (typeface)," *Wikipedia,* accessed 2012, http://en.wikipedia.org/wiki/Courier_(typeface).

30. Krista L. Schneider, "Negotiating the Image of the Inner Bluegrass," *Landscape Journal* 26, no. 1 (January 2007): 134–50; "Cadentown Rosenwald School, Caden Lane, Lexington, Fayette County, KY," Prints and Photographs Online Catalog, Library of Congress, http://www.loc.gov/pictures/item/ky0414/.

31. Adrian, transcript K10.289.

32. Richard H. Schein, "Belonging through Land/scape," *Environment and Planning A* 41, no. 4 (April 2009): 821.

33. An early horse racing track and grandstand adjacent to downtown Lexington hosted the first running of several important race series and built the careers of the African American jockeys and trainers who lived in the nearby East End neighborhood. Isaac Murphy, who raced in the 1880s and 1890s, still has the highest percentage of wins of any jockey. The East End neighborhood is experiencing a revival through self-investment, changing demographics, and the return of people who grew up there. "Kentucky Association," *Wikipedia,* accessed 2011, http://en.wikipedia

.org/wiki/Kentucky_Association; "Isaac Burns Murphy," *Wikipedia,* accessed 2012, http://en.wikipedia.org/wiki/Isaac_Burns_Murphy. See also Schein, "Belonging through Land/scape"; Merlene Davis, "Comments Sought on Proposals for Signature Piece at Isaac Murphy Memorial Art Garden," *Lexington Herald-Leader,* January 30, 2012.

34. See for example Angela, interview by author, transcript K05.67+; Davis, "Comments Sought on Proposals for Signature Piece at Isaac Murphy Memorial Art Garden"; Merlene Davis, "Isaac Murphy Garden Delayed, but Organizers Hope for Completion in 2013," *Lexington Herald-Leader,* November 5, 2012; Merlene Davis, "Discover the History of Lexington's East End in a Walking Tour," *Lexington Herald-Leader,* April 29, 2013. In May 2015 a new linear park was proposed for the downtown core. The park would begin at the Isaac Murphy Memorial Art Garden before connecting to Thoroughbred Park and a series of other existing downtown public spaces. Beth Musgrave, "Town Branch Commons, a Park through Downtown Lexington, Could Cost $75 Million," *Lexington Herald-Leader,* May 19, 2015.

35. In 1855 an heir to Henry Clay demolished the federal-style house that had been Clay's Ashland estate to replace it with a new dwelling. (To capitalize on Clay's fame, the heir sold walking sticks made out of wood salvaged from the house.) The editor of the *Louisville Journal* was incensed by the senseless destruction of a landmark associated with Henry Clay, his national reputation, and Lexington's influence in the nation. The editor called the destruction "barbarism unparalleled in the annals of fathers and sons." In response the heir challenged the editor to a duel. Although the editor refused, the ideas of history and continuity were significantly intertwined as Lexington negotiated its modernity. James D. Birchfield, *Preservation in the Bluegrass: Remarks on the 50th Anniversary of the Blue Grass Trust, April 17, 2005* (Lexington, Ky.: Colophon, 2009), 9.

36. *Lexington, Kentucky College Town Study* (public report, Lexington-Fayette Urban County Government, Lexington, Ky., December 2002).

37. The promised restoration of the Lyric Theatre, a local African American landmark in the East End neighborhood, waited more than twelve years for funding while other projects (e.g., a basketball museum) were completed quickly. The theater project funding was finally approved by the city in 2009 under threat of legal action to enforce the earlier agreement. The divide in Lexington also separates economic classes. The 2007 extension of Newtown Pike deeper into the downtown area cut through a small neighborhood of very low-income residents. The new road was named Oliver Lewis Way in honor of the jockey who won the first Kentucky Derby in 1875. (The name was selected through a public voting process. The second-place name was Mary Todd Lincoln Boulevard.) The project raised contentious social issues surrounding the relocation of residents to temporary and affordable housing within the immediate area. The downtown area is heterogeneous. Some areas retain desirable status while adjacent areas are considered socially out of bounds. The sense of a divided city has changed, but remains. Beverly Fortune, "Council Gets Details of Plans for Lyric," *Lexington Herald-Leader,* July 1, 2009; Ed Lane, "Why I Voted against Funding Renovation of the Lyric Theatre," *Business Lexington,* April 2, 2009; Karla Ward, "Newtown Pike Extension to Be Renamed Oliver Lewis Way," *Lexington Herald-Leader,* August 31, 2010; Jennifer Hewlett, "Davis Bottom Residents Displaced by Newtown Extension," *Lexington Herald-Leader,* January 1, 2011; Abe, interview by author, transcript K03; Angela, transcript K04; Andrew, interview by author, transcript K05; Amanda, interview by author, transcript K07; Albert, interview by author, transcript K09.

38. Augustus, interview by author, transcript K06.108.

39. Augustus, transcript K06.114.

40. The redevelopment of the Vine Street corridor continues in the present day. Parking structures from the 1970s and 1980s were designed to hold upper-level development. In the past decade several proposals have explored building on top of these parking structures to maximize the land use. Surface-level parking on Vine Street also remains underdeveloped.

41. Albert, transcript K09.76.

42. The city-sponsored Rupp Arena, Arts, and Entertainment District Task Force examined strategies for renovating and improving the convention center and arena and suggested that the sixteen-acre, empty parking lot be redeveloped to provide denser parking, pedestrian-friendly open space, and buildings to promote year-round use of the space. The task force

specifically noted the positive development value of having historic neighborhoods on three sides of the parking lot. Rupp Arena is named for Adolf Rupp, forty-year coach of the University of Kentucky men's basketball team. *The Rupp Arena, Arts, and Entertainment District Executive Summary and Recommendations* (public report, Lexington-Fayette Urban County Government, Lexington, Ky., January 2012).

43. "World Coal Center," *Wikipedia*, accessed 2011, http://en.wikipedia.org/wiki/World_Coal_Center.

44. Jacqueline Duke, "Plans Call for 'Lake Wilkinson' to Be Replaced by Temporary Park," *Lexington Herald-Leader*, May 11, 1984.

45. Jacqueline Duke, "Apartments for Elderly Are Planned for Downtown," *Lexington Herald-Leader*, May 14, 1985.

46. The Vine Center (now World Trade Center Kentucky) and a hotel replaced an entire city block. The Fifth Third Bank tower covers half a block adjacent to the old county courthouse. Several parking garages also replaced historic buildings. Other buildings were built on land cleared when the Town Branch streambed was enclosed and the railroad line through town was removed in the 1970s.

47. In particular, the failure of a downtown mall modeled on the festival market concept drew significant attention. The project and its adjacent parking garage had been partially financed with publicly supported bonds. Regular reports in the newspaper on the openings, closings, and eventual bankruptcy read like a sports report of trades, game analyses, and the what-ifs of postgame thinking. The city government was entangled in the bankruptcy through the publicly supported bonds. The developer for the failed festival market is the same developer who proposed the redevelopment of the pastured block. The festival market building has been repurposed as commercial office space. "From the Ground Up," *Lexington Herald-Leader*, July 6, 1985; "Webb Says He Can't Pay Festival Market Loan, Baesler Says City Won't Defer Payments," *Lexington Herald-Leader*, December 15, 1991; "Lexington Receives $1.7 Million Payment," *Lexington Herald-Leader*, February 27, 2007.

48. Ambrose, interview by author, transcript K08.365.

49. Albert, transcript K09.85.

50. Albert, transcript K09.301.

51. "Vote to Create Historic District Is Canceled, MLK Area Residents Had Protest Planned," *Lexington Herald-Leader*, April 23, 2004.

52. Eric Thomason, mass e-mail message, October 23, 2006.

53. Preserve Lexington, mass e-mail message, March 20, 2007.

54. Preserve Lexington is no longer active. Many of the individuals behind the organization continue to participate in the community in different ways.

55. While the Executive Committee, board, and membership of the Blue Grass Trust might not agree with this assessment, I base it on first-person experience with the organization. Between 2002 and 2006, I served in various volunteer and leadership roles with the trust, including as chair of the Community Preservation Committee and, briefly, as a member of the Executive Committee. My involvement with the trust did not include any of the organization's responses to the situation leading to demolitions on the pastured block. I was involved in approving applications for the plaques illustrated elsewhere in the paper.

56. Dan Rowland, "Welcome to ProgressLex," *ProgressLex* (blog), February 28, 2010, http://www.progresslex.org/2010/02/28/welcome-to-progresslex/.

57. Allen, interview by author, transcript K01.176.

58. Brent Leggs, "Can You Imagine a Future Lexington without an African American Past?," *ProgressLex* (blog), May 27, 2010, http://www.progresslex.org/2010/05/27/can-you-imagine-a-future-lexington-without-an-african-american-past/; Tom Eblen, "Lexington Must Learn from Preservation Mistakes," *Lexington Herald-Leader*, May 30, 2010.

59. Augustus, transcript K06.299.

60. Five other downtown buildings on different blocks were demolished in the same month as the Woolworth building. Michelle Ku, "Historic Woolworth Building in Lexington, Ky., to Become a Parking Lot," *Knight Ridder/Tribune Business News*, September 21, 2002; Margaret Foster, "Downtown Lexington's Next Loss: Woolworth's," *Preservation Magazine*, August 17, 2004, online only (site discontinued).

61. Esther Marr, "Standing Pat and Poised," *Chevy Chaser*, September 21, 2007.

62. madtony8k, comment in response to "Lexington | CentrePointe | 550 FT | 35 FL | U/C," SkyscraperCity discussion forum, March 21, 2008, 5:52 p.m., http://www.skyscrapercity.com/archive/index.php/t-590639.html.

63. Marr, "Standing Pat and Poised."

64. Amanda, transcript K07.297.

65. Cynthia Johnson, *F. W. Woolworth Building* (Kentucky Heritage Council, National Register of Historic Places Registration Form, 2002), 7.1.

66. Walter Langsam quoted by Tom Eblen, "There's a Lot of History on CentrePointe Block," *Bluegrass and Beyond* (blog), June 22, 2008, http://tomeblen.bloginky.com/2008/06/22/theres-a-lot-of-history-on-centrepointe-block/; Bill Johnston, "Centrepointe Counterpoint," *Lexington Herald-Leader,* June 16, 2008.

67. R. Dudley Webb, *A Prepared Statement by R. Dudley Webb Relative to the Status of "CentrePointe"* (prepared statement to the LFUCG Urban County Council, May 5, 2009).

68. Tom Eblen, "We Need to Balance Past, Future in Historic Preservation Debates," *Lexington Herald-Leader,* March 3, 2012.

69. The former executive director of the Lexington Downtown Development Authority, a municipally sponsored nonprofit organization, was quoted as questioning the very definition of historic: "The historic fabric is important to downtown, but right now I don't think anybody can say what the historic fabric is." Ryan Hrvatin, letter to the editor, *Lexington Herald-Leader,* April 6, 2008.

70. Clark, *Farewell to an Idea,* 7–8.

71. starbuc jupiter, comment in response to "Lexington | CentrePointe | 550 FT | 35 FL | U/C," SkyscraperCity discussion forum, March 18, 2008, 11:47 p.m., online only (site discontinued).

72. Grits, comment in response to "There's a Lot of History on CentrePointe Block," *Bluegrass and Beyond* (blog), June 26, 2008, 2:55 p.m., http://tomeblen.bloginky.com/2008/06/22/theres-a-lot-of-history-on-centrepointe-block/.

73. Laura Clark, "Dame May Relocate Soon," *Kentucky Kernel,* September 11, 2008.

74. Beverly Fortune, "Funeral Procession Circles Lost Block," *Lexington Herald-Leader,* September 14, 2008.

75. Danielle Pritchett, "Patrons Grieve Loss of City Block," *Kentucky Kernel,* September 14, 2008.

76. Taylor Shelton, "Thomason Will Best Serve University, Commonwealth in 3rd District Seat," *Kentucky Kernel,* October 28, 2008.

77. Longtime preservation advocates supported the proposed demolition and redevelopment. Residents who supported the redevelopment of downtown and were generally prodevelopment rallied against the demolitions. The developer expressed the opinion that the local newspaper and other organizations unfairly targeted the project for criticism. Editorials, columns, and articles in the local daily paper, a university student newspaper, and the local business journal expressed strong concerns about the demolition and specific redevelopment plans even while supporting the general idea of redevelopment. Foster Ockerman Jr., "Downtown Block Lacks Historic Context for Preservation," *Business Lexington,* June 13, 2008; Dudley Webb, "Point-by-Point on CentrePointe," *Lexington Herald-Leader,* November 9, 2009; Webb, *A Prepared Statement by R. Dudley Webb Relative to the Status of "CentrePointe"*; "New Building Is Still Excessive," *Kentucky Kernel,* November 12, 2008; David Mohney, "Progrowth vs. No Growth: CentrePointe Revives Age-Old Fight," *Chevy Chaser,* April 5, 2008; Tom Eblen, "When Will CentrePointe Construction Begin? We'll See," *Lexington Herald-Leader,* January 9, 2009; Tom Martin, "Straightforward on CentrePointe: Questions and Answers," *Business Lexington,* July 5, 2011.

78. Gilbert Jones, letter to the editor, *Lexington Herald-Leader,* May 24, 2008.

79. Mari Adkins, comment in response to "There's a Lot of History on CentrePointe Block," *Bluegrass and Beyond* (blog), June 23, 2008, 1:02 p.m., http://tomeblen.bloginky.com/2008/06/22/theres-a-lot-of-history-on-centrepointe-block/; Beverly Fortune, "Reactions Mixed as First Buildings Leveled," *Lexington Herald-Leader,* July 3, 2008.

80. David Feather, comment in response to "There's a Lot of History on CentrePointe Block," *Bluegrass and Beyond* (blog), June 24, 2008, 8:22 p.m., http://tomeblen.bloginky.com/2008/06/22/theres-a-lot-of-history-on-centrepointe-block/. The reference to John Hunt Morgan's horse connects to well-known local mythology about the statue of General Morgan on the old courthouse lawn.

81. Fortune, "Reactions Mixed as First Buildings Leveled."

82. Leslie Beatty, letter to the editor, *Lexington Herald-Leader,* May 19, 2008.

83. Beatty, letter to the editor.

84. Amanda, transcript K07.259.

85. Tom Eblen, "Passing of 'The Dame' a Blow to Young People," *Bluegrass and Beyond* (blog), July

30, 2008, http://tomeblen.bloginky.com/category/austincommerce-lex/. The Lexington Opera House is a restored late nineteenth-century building in the downtown core. The Keeneland grandstand, a mostly modern hodgepodge of construction, represents the iconic status of the horse racing industry in the Lexington region.

86. Robert Kahne, "New High-Rise Hotel Creates Eyesore for Downtown Lexington," *Kentucky Kernel,* August 26, 2008.

87. Clark, *Farewell to an Idea,* 7–8.

88. Allen, transcript K01.333 and K01.348. The discomfort between generations and parts of the community apparently included the developer. In a letter to the editor, a local citizen wrote: "[The developer] has demonstrated his disdain for places like The Dame, Buster's and Mia's. During his initial appearance before the Urban County Council, when asked if he would consider allowing those establishments to be a part of [the development], he became visibly uncomfortable and indicated that while he thought those establishments had their place in Lexington, that place could not be within two blocks of his upscale hotel." Some community members expressed concern that the developer would seek to prevent homeless residents from using the sidewalks near the proposed building or nearby park spaces like Phoenix Park. Charles Baldwin, "Evidence Needed," *Lexington Herald-Leader,* May 24, 2008; cartomanlex, comment in response to "Lexington | CentrePointe | 550 FT | 35 FL | U/C," SkyscraperCity discussion forum, August 27, 2008, 4:38 a.m., http://www.skyscrapercity.com/archive/index.php/t-590639-p-3.html.

89. See Adam Przeworski, "Deliberation and Ideological Domination," in *Deliberative Democracy,* ed. Jon Elster, 140–60 (New York: Cambridge University Press, 1998).

90. Allen, transcript K01.343.

91. Allen, transcript K01.342.

92. See for example McCann, "Race, Protest, and Public Space." McCann's discussion of Lefebvre's *Politics of Space* as applied to Lexington's racialized landscapes aligns with T. J. Clark's framing of modern identity. The representation of identity in contrast to (or in confluence with) power asserts position within the future. Significantly, the multilayered complexity of this lived experience reduces the past to a flexible, alterable, and re-created palette to use in drawing the distinct, modern-ruled path forward.

93. Fortune, "Merge Old Buildings, New Plan, They Say."

94. Joe Graves and Graham Pohl, "Go Back to Drawing Board," *Lexington Herald-Leader,* July 7, 2008.

95. Richard S. Levine, "City Deserves First-Class Building on Old Woolworth Block," *Lexington Herald-Leader,* July 6, 2008.

96. These designs were ridiculed as "bizarre" and "unrealistic." In an online poll, Lexington residents favored the then-current developer's proposal over the university ideas by a margin of two to one. Beverly Fortune, "UK College of Design Takes Crack at Its Own Downtown Project," *Lexington Herald-Leader,* July 17, 2008; Beverly Fortune, "CentrePointe Alternatives Unveiled," *Lexington Herald-Leader,* July 22, 2008; Tom Eblen, "Sound Thinking behind Strange-Looking Designs," *Lexington Herald-Leader,* July 1, 2008.

97. Mary Meehan, "Winburn Students Create Alternative Uses for CentrePointe," *Lexington Herald-Leader,* July 6, 2010.

98. Tom Eblen, "Two Developers' Approach to Projects Radically Different," *Lexington Herald-Leader,* July 9, 2008.

99. David Mohney, "Lexington's Not London," *Chevy Chaser,* July 25, 2008.

100. Fortune, "CentrePointe Alternatives Unveiled."

101. Tom Eblen, "What Can We Do Next Time?," *Lexington Herald-Leader,* August 10, 2008.

102. Hayward Wilkirson, "CentrePointe: A Much-Needed Autopsy," *ProgressLex* (blog), April 2, 2010, http://www.progresslex.org/2010/04/02/centrepointe-a-much-needed-autopsy/.

103. Nathan Dickerson, "The Public Living Room," *ProgressLex* (blog), January 25, 2013, http://www.progresslex.org/2013/01/25/the-public-living-room/.

104. "Webbs Miss Center Point," *Lexington Herald-Leader,* April 7, 2008.

105. The conflict over how the downtown core will continue to grow and change remains an active issue. In 2010, ProgressLex led an effort to change the design of a proposed CVS store at the southwestern edge of the downtown area. The controversy drew considerable media attention and support from across the city. Some downtown residents questioned how far the city

should go in imposing development standards. One blogger asked why the design of the CVS was "vulgar" in downtown but acceptable in the suburban reaches of the city. New standards proposed in response to the situation remained incomplete in 2015. Andrew Battista, "The Downtown Brand Wars," *North of Center* (blog), May 20, 2010, http://noclexington.com/?p=699; Albert, transcript K09.138; Beverly Fortune, "Lexington Council Delays Action on Proposed Design Standards for New Downtown Buildings," *Lexington Herald-Leader,* September 8, 2015.

106. "Dead Man Balking," *Lexington Herald-Leader,* April 11, 2009.

107. See for example Beverly Fortune, "Firm Suggests a Farm in Town," *Lexington Herald-Leader,* May 14, 2009.

108. Beverly Fortune, "Vice Mayor Demands Action on CentrePointe," *Lexington Herald-Leader,* April 29, 2009. A letter to the editor sarcastically suggested the introduction of goats to the grassed site to provide milk, cheese, and meat, ritual slaughters to the development gods, and entertainment for the city's residents. Joseph Binford, letter to the editor, *Lexington Herald-Leader,* August 4, 2009.

109. Fortune, "Vice Mayor Demands Action on CentrePointe."

110. Beverly Fortune, "Webbs to Bring Soil, Grass to Empty Site," *Lexington Herald-Leader,* April 29, 2009; Beverly Fortune, "Horse Farm Fence Being Built around CentrePointe Site Downtown," *Lexington Herald-Leader,* October 2, 2009.

111. Fortune, "Horse Farm Fence Being Built around CentrePointe Site Downtown."

112. A local blogger commented: "f$&king @#$^. Centrepointe is all but dead, and now he states he can get fill dirt in to plant grass to 'shut these people up.' Thanks Webb for demolishing numerous historic properties—including the oldest commercial structure in Lexington, and replacing it with a block of dirt." Sherman Cahal, comment at "Re: Lexington, KY: Centrepointe | 550 ft. | 35 fl. | U/C, reply #101," *Urban Ohio.com* (blog), June 4, 2009, 4:42 p.m., http://www.urbanohio.com/forum2/index.php/topic,11809.140.html?PHPSESSID=ogduvdgm3uba8d62rvnqve8kp4.

113. Graham Pohl, letter to the editor, *Lexington Herald-Leader,* October 18, 2009.

114. Beverly Fortune, "Chicago Architect to Offer Ideas for CentrePointe Design," *Lexington Herald-Leader,* April 7, 2011.

115. Tom Eblen, "From Bad Times to Opportunities," *Lexington Herald-Leader,* April 30, 2009.

116. Beever, comment in response to "Downtown Brainstorms: Welcome Ideas for Park, Empty Block," *Lexington Herald-Leader,* April 20, 2011, posted April 20, 2011, 2:24 p.m., http://www.kentucky.com/2011/04/20/1713839/downtown-brainstorms-welcome-ideas.html#comment-188344158.

117. Albert, transcript K09.253. Informally, several Lexington residents have expressed to the author their admiration for the research and thought behind Studio Gang's work. One noted with approval that the cell-like structure of the proposed thirty-story tower derived from the molecular structure of the limestone bedrock common to Lexington.

118. Tom Eblen, "New Architect Impresses CentrePointe Skeptics," *Bluegrass and Beyond* (blog), June 2, 2011, http://tomeblen.bloginky.com/2011/06/02/new-architect-impresses-centrepointe-skeptics/.

119. Albert, transcript K09.244.

120. "CentrePointe Design: Smaller Projects Most Exciting Aspect," *Lexington Herald-Leader,* July 28, 2011.

121. In October 2011 the developer selected a third architectural team to carry forward the basic master plan proposed by Studio Gang. The third team, led by a Lexington architecture firm, released revised building proposals in mid-February 2012 and at the end of February. While the proposed buildings differed stylistically and programmatically from the Gang proposal, the scale and multipart structure of the block remained similar. Different local architecture firms were selected to design the separate buildings. After seeing the latest version, a downtown resident commented, "I'm trying to convince myself this is a positive result, and in many ways it is." Beverly Fortune, "Architect Jeanne Gang No Longer Involved with CentrePointe, Developer Says," *Lexington Herald-Leader,* October 28, 2011; Eblen, "Latest Version of CentrePointe Shows Progress in Lexington's Design Process"; Fortune, "Latest Incarnation of Redesigned CentrePointe Block Gets Positive Reception"; Beth Musgrave, "Unnamed Development Group Expresses Interest in Lexington's CentrePointe Development," *Lexington Herald-Leader,* May 7, 2015.

122. DevilAnse, comment in response to "CentrePointe Redesign Process Points Way for Lexington Center Redevelopment," *Lexington Herald-Leader,* July 17, 2011, posted July 16, 2011, 10:16 p.m., www.kentucky.com/2011/07/17/1813690/tom-eblen-centrepointe-turnabout.html#comment-254298085.

123. mysticheadlice, comment in response to "New CentrePointe Design Includes 30-Story Tower of Tubes," *Lexington Herald-Leader,* July 14, 2011, posted July 13, 2011, 11:20 p.m., http://www.kentucky.com/2011/07/14/1810725/new-centrepointe-design-includes.html#comment-252105094.

124. #FillCentrePit, Twitter, https://twitter.com/search?q=%23FillCentrePit.

125. In April 2012 another developer announced plans to renovate four buildings on an adjacent block into a boutique hotel and restaurant complex by 2014. In May 2013 a restaurateur suggested he would open a restaurant on part of the pastured block in mid-2015. The restaurateur withdrew from the project in May 2015. Beverly Fortune, "Lexington's 21C Hotel to Include Three Parcels Next to First National Building," *Lexington Herald-Leader,* April 10, 2012; Charles Bertram, "Restaurateur Jeff Ruby Tweets He's Opening in Lexington, Says No More," *Lexington Herald-Leader,* May 17, 2013; Beth Musgrave, "CentrePointe Developers Threaten Legal Action If City Does Not Rescind Notice to Fill in the Site," *Lexington Herald-Leader,* May 1, 2015.

126. Kevin Martinez, comment in response to "New CentrePointe Design Includes 30-Story Tower of Tubes," *Lexington Herald-Leader,* July 14, 2011, posted July 14, 2011, 11:54 a.m., http://www.kentucky.com/2011/07/14/1810725/new-centrepointe-design-includes.html#comment-252116877.

127. SWDN, comment in response to "New CentrePointe Design Includes 30-Story Tower of Tubes," *Lexington Herald-Leader,* July 14, 2011, posted July 14, 2011, 2:58 p.m., http://www.kentucky.com/2011/07/14/1810725/new-centrepointe-design-includes.html#comment-252116877.

128. jo_somebody, comment in response to "New CentrePointe Design Includes 30-Story Tower of Tubes," *Lexington Herald-Leader,* July 14, 2011, posted July 14, 2011, 3:40 p.m., http://www.kentucky.com/2011/07/14/1810725/new-centrepointe-design-includes.html#comment-252116877.

129. Augustus, transcript K06.204.

130. Beverly Fortune, "Cheapside Taking on New Life as Downtown Destination," *Lexington Herald-Leader,* April 3, 2010.

131. Augustus, transcript K06.204.

132. Fortune, "Cheapside Taking on New Life as Downtown Destination."

133. Tom Eblen, "Rupp Arena Task Force's Work about to Become More Public," *Lexington Herald-Leader,* July 31, 2011; Beverly Fortune, "Final Report of Rupp Taskforce Envisions $300 Million Project with Many Sources of Financing," *Lexington Herald-Leader,* February 1, 2012; "Arena Plan: Great Vision of Downtown's Future," *Lexington Herald-Leader,* February 5, 2012; Beverly Fortune, "New York Firm Chosen to Design Town Branch Project through Lexington," *Lexington Herald-Leader,* February 4, 2013.

134. Orthel, "The Story of Shoes in Trees"; Bryan D. Orthel, "Ordinary Wallpaper: Identity and Use of History," *Interiors: Design, Architecture, Culture* 5, no. 3 (2014): 361–88.

135. Grenville, "Conservation as Psychology"; Giddens, *Modernity and Self-Identity.*

136. See for example Melissa F. Baird, "Heritage, Human Rights, and Social Justice," *Heritage & Society* 7, no. 2 (2014): 139–55.

137. Clark, *Farewell to an Idea,* 7–8.

138. White, "The Question of Narrative."

ERIN CUNNINGHAM

Preservation Forum

Interiors, Histories, and the Preservation of Chicago's Hull House Settlement

In June 1967 the Jane Addams Hull-House Museum opened on the new University of Illinois campus in Chicago (Figure 1). Designed to commemorate Hull House founder Jane Addams, the museum was constructed from the remnants of the nationally renowned Hull House Settlement, which only six years earlier, in 1961, had spanned an entire city block on Chicago's West Side.[1] In contrast to the sprawling settlement, the museum included only two of the original thirteen structures: a mansion built in 1856 for Chicago real estate broker Charles Hull and a brick dining hall Jane Addams had built in 1906. Completely refaced with new brick, the exterior of the mansion was restored to approximate its 1856 appearance—that of an Italianate Victorian mansion with Corinthian columns, a large portico, and a hipped roof, which had stood on the outskirts of Chicago. The mansion's restored exterior did not hint at its storied life. Before Addams and her cofounder, Ellen Gates Starr, rented the mansion in 1889, it was successively a hospital, a saloon, a tenement, a home for the elderly run by the Little Sisters of the Poor, and a desk factory. By the end of the century, the mansion was "almost submerged" with additions that architectural firm Pond & Pond had built, reflecting the influences of the English Tudor, arts and crafts, and prairie styles.[2]

On the interior the restored mansion's orderly center-hall plan also did not reveal the full extent of its remarkable transformation from a two-story suburban home to a sprawling interconnected complex that Eleanor Roosevelt once likened to a "rabbit warren" and social activist Beatrice Webb described as a "continuous passage leading nowhere in particular" (Figure 2).[3] The double parlors were staged as mid-nineteenth-century interiors furnished with newly polished wood floors, replica "oriental" rugs, and custom-made electric chandeliers—a direct reference to the house's original gas lighting. The reception room showcased photographs of Addams and images and maps of the Hull House Settlement. And the octagon room housed a simple memorial to its founder; at its center stood a bronze bust of Addams on a pedestal. The Hull-House Museum's careful reconstruction and tidy presentation concealed not only the evolution of its interiors but a divisive restoration, at once celebrated as "immaculate" and condemned as "bastardized."[4]

Figure 1. Photocopy of restored Jane Addams's Hull House mansion and Chicago Circle Center behind, Chicago, Illinois, 1968. 057-00-01 Chicago Circle Center (1968), UIC ARCHIVES, University of Illinois at Chicago Library.

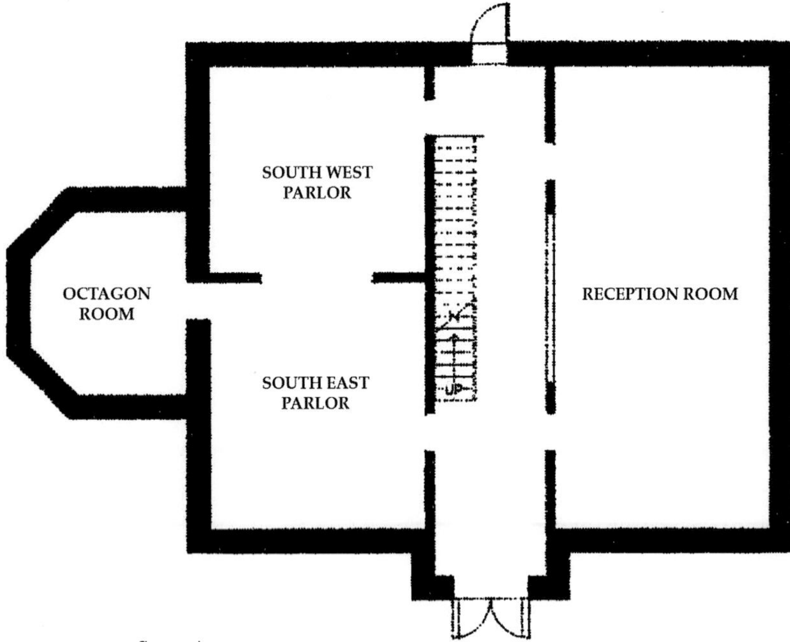

Figure 2. First-floor plan of the restored Hull House. Drawn by Erin Cunningham, 2016.

The Hull House project invigorated officials, residents, and preservationists in 1961, almost two years before New York's infamous demolition of Penn Station and five years before the passage of the National Historic Preservation Act. This story of the preservation of Hull House's interiors highlights the voices of multiple, and sometimes conflicting, stakeholders. These stakeholders include Hull House's community—residents, neighbors, and associates—as well as the University of Illinois and its bureaucracy, which handled the restoration of Hull House between 1962 and 1967. In interpreting Hull House's current incarnation, these voices are critical. The decisions of the Subcommittee on Memorabilia, which was appointed by the university in 1963 and ultimately oversaw the interior restoration of the mansion, contribute yet another layer. Building on Hull House's histories, the testimonies of people associated with Hull House, and archival evidence, this investigation turns our attention to the inside, to the places we inhabit, and draws on stakeholder voices to put people at the center of the preservation of interior spaces.[5]

The Community

When the city council approved the Harrison-Halsted site for the new University of Illinois at Chicago campus in 1961, it ignited disbelief from Hull House residents and neighbors, from the Chicago community, and from the larger, national social work community. Letters flooded the offices of Chicago mayor Richard Daley, University of Illinois president David Dodds Henry, and Chicago-area newspapers. These letters describe instances of individual, personal connections to Hull House, emphasizing its architecture and its mission and stressing its enormous national significance. They are colorful, impassioned reminders of relationships forged at Hull House; they label the settlement as a shrine and an "object of pilgrimage" and describe its proposed demolition as "callousness," "wanton destruction," a "black eye to America throughout the world," a "national catastrophe," and an "act of vandalism."[6] Social worker Louis Cirrincione was not alone when he likened tearing down Hull House to "sinking the 'Constitution,' plowing up Gettysburg, or doing away with Mt. Vernon."[7] Earl Planty, a University of Illinois professor, expressed his surprise that "an educational institution would think of such a desecration," while Chicagoan John A. Leiser wrote, "We have barbarians in our own country."[8]

The demolition of Hull House also elicited high-profile responses. Famed labor organizer Bessie Hillman of the Amalgamated Clothing Workers wrote that she enthusiastically supported education but could not comprehend how tearing down a "hallowed and venerable" institution like Hull House justified this goal: "The institution is not only hallowed and venerable, it is sacred," she continued. "If it dies, a vital part of America dies."[9] Illinois senator Paul Douglas urged the university to retain Hull House in its "major form" as part of the new campus: "Hull-House and Lincoln's home are the two great inspiration centers in Illinois. It would be an act of vandalism—complete and unadulterated—to bulldoze it."[10] State senator Arthur R. Gottschalk called the impending demolition of Hull House a "terrible disservice to the people of Illinois and a tragic waste of money and opportunity."[11]

These letters, which represent the views of many different community stakeholders—from immediate Hull House neighbors to the larger national community—demonstrate that Hull

House's preservation engaged and motivated a broad audience. Four principal constituencies emerge from these letters: the Harrison-Halsted neighbors, the Chicago community, past residents of the Hull House Settlement, and the social work community. Each identified a different stake in Hull House's past and future. While each community called for Hull House's preservation, each also wanted different things preserved. From human rights and Addams's legacy to pre-Fire Chicago architecture, from community service and education to a place to meet friends, Hull House represented a multitude of things for these various constituents. Opinion regarding what to preserve was equally varied—from fine mantels to the entire, sprawling settlement complex.

Members of the Harrison-Halsted neighborhood, who intimately knew Hull House, called for the retention of Hull House as an active settlement house. The Debonairs, a teenage club at Hull House, wrote that Hull House was for them a place where friends could "gather," "be safe," and "mix with all different types of children." "We love this neighborhood and we love Hull-House," they proclaimed.[12] The Young Adults of Hull-House also pleaded for the retention of the Hull House Settlement in its original buildings and location, referring to it as their "second home."[13] The august St. Simon Golden Age Group requested that "'Hull-House stay where it is now" in memory of the work of "Miss Jane Addams" and her "co-workers." "How would you like to have something dear taken away from you?" they added. "Think it over."[14] An "old time friend" wrote that she hoped Hull House could be saved, adding that when she was a child she lived there. In her plea for the retention of the settlement, she referenced "happy" memories of Addams and recalled learning to sing, dance, and sew. She also boasted that famed jazz musician Benny Goodman "learned to play clarinet there."[15]

Other letters testified to Hull House's influence beyond the immediate Harrison-Halsted neighborhood. "From one who has lived on Chicago's Old West Side since 1893," Chicago resident Joseph Holland wrote, "I have heard nothing but goodness coming from Jane Addams Hull-House and her faithful helpers." "Instead of destroying this living and practical monument, improve and expand it," he continued. "It will serve to dignify the university."[16] Chicagoan Robert T. Constable similarly entreated that Hull House be "maintained and helped," writing that a nondenominational organization was essential for the people of Chicago.[17]

Past residents—many of whom were elderly—begged the university to retain at least the Hull House mansion to commemorate Jane Addams. Resident of Hull House from 1895 to 1898, ninety-six-year-old Ralph E. Blount wrote of his concern for the "future of the plant." "If it is desirable to tear down all the accessory buildings I should not object," he continued. "But the old residence housing Miss Addams' office and desk, the sitting room, dining room and chambers, must be kept as a memorial."[18] Another former Hull House worker wrote, "Will not even the original House be saved as a memorial? Is there not a public support to retain at least something of old Hull-House that so many of us loved?"[19] Past Hull House resident and prominent lawyer Robert Szold also pleaded for the retention of the original mansion. "Is it not possible that the campus of the University of Illinois be built without destroying this landmark?" he asked. "After all, the actual Hull-House building is not large."[20]

Members of sister agencies and social work programs from around the country emphasized the significance of Hull House as an institution, calling for its preservation as a living shrine or symbol of the settlement house movement. On the whole they cited Hull House's ongoing value and proposed keeping it as a training center for the National Federation of Settlements and Neighborhood Centers (NFSNC), which had opened at Hull House in 1960.[21] Anne Fried, executive director of Bridgeport, Connecticut's Hall Neighborhood House, wrote that Addams's spirit was "still alive at Hull-House" and pleaded that this "landmark" of great "spiritual and material significance" be left "untouched."[22] From Chattanooga, Tennessee, Reverend Lindon Peoples wondered why the university would not keep Hull House on campus "for students to observe how the proper social work is to be done."[23] Paul K. Weinandy, chairman of the Central New York Chapter of the National Association of Social Workers, imagined that "with the assistance of able architects, surely the building, or buildings, could be gracefully integrated into the design for new structures."[24]

Across these communities letter writers described their connection to the interiors of Hull House. Corinne S. Tsanoff, past president of the NFSNC, urged "the University of Illinois recognize the influence of the memories Hull-House recalls." She added that if it was not possible to preserve the mansion and its surroundings, then at least the "interiors of the main rooms," adding that "the paneling, woodwork, and mantels are beautiful in themselves" and "recall the lives and work of some of the most constructive women and men that America has produced."[25] A resident of Evanston, Illinois, and Navy Pier teacher, Norman Atwood argued for Hull House's preservation as a symbol of Addams and her work and also because of the "great beauty of the original house belonging to Mr. Hull." He extolled the virtues of the mansion's pre-Fire interiors, proclaiming:

> The original house of Mr. Hull is quite a magnificent piece of Victorian architecture. Those tall beautiful rooms, those carved white marble fireplaces, those intricately carved door and window frames, and that beautiful octagonal office of Jane Addams represent a fine period in American domestic architecture and are a *very* fine example of it. Since the center of Chicago was fire-swept, a house like that one is quite a rarity in the region and is not to be demolished without a thought.[26]

These letters illustrate that people not just within Chicago but also across the country were invested in the fate of Hull House. Driven by concerns about architecture and human rights, education and community service, fine mantels and sprawling complexes, the letters announced multiple stakes in Hull House's preservation. These letters also invite us to move beyond woodwork, furniture, and design to make words, ordeals, and recollections a basis of preservation. In these letters individuals recalled lives lived inside Hull House: and they recalled the lives of Addams and her cohorts, and they also recalled their own memories of gathering with friends, singing, dancing, and working. The letters draw our attention to Hull House's interior spaces, which supported such a diversity of experiences. Despite their passion, letter writers would discover that the ultimate decision of what to do with Hull House rested with the university, which had its own interests.

The University

According to University of Illinois president David Henry, the preservation of Hull House was a university decision. In a letter to the director of the School of Social Work, he explained that the decision to preserve was not a matter for the "lay person" or members of the community. "What architectural recognition can be given to the Hull-House site or to the conservation of any portion of Hull-House is now under study by the architect," he continued, adding, "This is a technical matter."[27] In June 1961 President Henry announced his intent to incorporate the original Hull House mansion into the design of the new campus. To save any more of the settlement, he reasoned, would "render the site unusable."[28] Hull House would be bulldozed to make way for the university; in its place officials "hinted" at a "bold" campus design, touting that "old beaten paths are not necessarily to be followed in setting up this new institution."[29] Master plan proposals showed a complex of concrete, granite, and brick that radiated from a central agora. It was clear that Hull House's "stained common brick" and "hodge-podge buildings" did not suit university plans for a modern urban campus.[30]

By 1963 only two of Hull House's thirteen structures remained: the original Hull House mansion and the settlement's dining hall (Figure 3). The university had begun restoring the Hull House mansion to what was believed to be its appearance as a mid-Victorian brick mansion replete with a hip roof, cupola, and a veranda that extended around the house.[31] Architect Walter Netsch, from Skidmore, Owings & Merrill, headed the design of the new campus; he claimed to be behind the choice to save the Hull House mansion and to return it to its 1856 appearance. "I saved Hull House—not the brick factory building, but I decided that the idea of Jane Addams should go back to the farmhouse she lived in," Netsch asserted in a 1995 interview. He also claimed to be behind the university's choice to save the craftsman-style dining hall building "because that was the building that Frank Lloyd Wright first gave his famous speech on 'The Art and Craft of the Machine,' in 1901."[32] With this statement he proposed yet another reason to preserve Hull House, one that was not named by members of its community.

The university committed to the mansion and dining hall but had no idea what to do with them. President Henry convened the Ad Hoc Committee to examine potential uses. A range of possibilities were considered, including headquarters for the NFSNC training center, administrative offices for the School of Social Work, headquarters for a social welfare research center, and honors program offices and a student center.[33] Mark Hale, a committee member and director of the University of Illinois's newly formed Jane Addams School of Social Work, expressed concerns, however, regarding the impact of these proposed uses on fund-raising for the restoration. The idea of a "shrine," he continued, "would be the best image to keep before the public. Any appeal such as this is based largely on sentiment. The very persons and organizations most likely to contribute money or memorabilia are also likely to be more interested in preserving the traditional aspects of Hull House than in some peripheral use, however, worthwhile."[34] To harness "public sentiment," jump-start fund-raising, and generate good "publicity for the University," the committee unanimously recommended to President Henry that "the restored Hull Mansion be devoted primarily to museum type displays of artifacts and memorabilia."[35]

The community drove calls to preserve Hull House, but ultimately the university decided which aspects of Hull House to preserve. President Henry sought to reduce the preservation of Hull House to simple terms—to make it a technical decision. He asserted that experts should decide what to preserve, not laypeople, despite the arbitrary logic behind Walter Netsch's self-proclaimed decision to keep the mansion and dining hall. Henry, who was trying to build a university and in many ways saw Hull House's preservation as an impediment, convened the Ad Hoc Advisory Committee to decide what to do with the mansion. In the process he bureaucratized Hull House's preservation, cut the community out, and attempted to transform Hull House into a publicity boon for the university, announcing the university's status as principal stakeholder. Physically, Hull House was also reduced to its simplest terms. Resurfaced with new brick, stripped of its sprawling additions, and restored to its architecturally pure suburban beginnings, the Hull House mansion was sanitized. Placed off axis to one of the main entrances and dwarfed by the brutalist structures that rose up behind it, the mansion's exterior did not challenge the monolithic campus plan (Figure 4).

Figure 3. Dining hall being relocated near Hull House mansion, circa 1963. 086 UA 90-999.0439, Photograph Subject Files, UIC ARCHIVES, University of Illinois at Chicago Library.

The Subcommittee on Memorabilia

Once the university decided that it was going to preserve Hull House, it put together a series of committees to oversee its interior restoration. In the process it continued the pattern of viewing the physical restoration of Hull House as a series of bureaucratic decisions rather than community decisions.[36] Specifically, the Subcommittee on Memorabilia was placed in charge of planning the interior restoration. Chaired by Mark Hale,

Figure 7. (*Above*) Restored southeast parlor of Jane Addams's Hull-House. 057-00-01 Chicago Circle Center (1968), UIC ARCHIVES, University of Illinois at Chicago Library.

Figure 8. (*Right*) Restored southwest parlor of Jane Addams's Hull-House. 057-00-01 Chicago Circle Center (1968), UIC ARCHIVES, University of Illinois at Chicago Library.

committee stripped the room down to its bare bones. Deprived of all but its fine woodwork—a product of prison labor during the time of Charles Hull—the room harmonized with the pre-Fire Chicago architecture of the mansion's restored exterior. Display cases were added that housed photographs and maps associated with Hull House and Addams. And a melodeon from Addams's childhood home, recently purchased from her niece, stood on one side of the room.[44]

The "concept of the restored Hull House as shrine to Jane Addams," which earlier the Ad Hoc Committee had identified as key for publicity, was reflected in the committee's restoration. The octagon room on the south side of the mansion became a memorial room for Addams and suggested the late 1930s in content and use. The octagon room had served as a memorial room for Addams from 1936, when she died, until 1943, when Russell Ballard became head resident, at which time he moved his office into this space. Historic photographs showed this memorial room "filled with pictures of her associates and her trophies."[45] The committee reintroduced these objects into the room alongside a bust of Addams, "placed on a pedestal and appropriately lighted," where it would be "the center of attention" (Figure 11).[46]

The Subcommittee on Memorabilia—composed of university directors and deans—oversaw the transformation of Hull House from a settlement house to a museum. This restoration was not an easy task; the committee inherited interiors dramatically transformed by demolition, along with a budget that did not allow for extensive restoration. Meeting minutes chart the committee's efforts to make the best of these circumstances. In response to space and budget limitations, the committee sidestepped a strict restoration in favor of resurrecting a historic "spirit." To curry "public sentiment," it created exhibits. And to further fund-raising campaigns, it emphasized the mansion's shrine-like qualities. But where the letters calling for Hull House to be saved stressed its richness, diversity, and multivalences—as a neighborhood center, a club house, a safe spot, a living monument to human welfare, a wonderful example of pre-Fire Chicago architecture—the committee reduced Hull House to a specific interpretation—a young Jane Addams and the idea of "gracious, cultured hospitality."

Preserving the Interior

In its publicity brochures, the university hailed the restored Hull House mansion "as a permanent reminder of the work of Jane Addams—for

Figure 9. Reception room and stairs before restoration. Hull-House Photograph collection, Special Collections, University of Illinois at Chicago Library.

Figure 10. Restored reception room of Jane Addams's Hull-House. 057-00-01 Chicago Circle Center (1968), UIC ARCHIVES, University of Illinois at Chicago Library.

people, everywhere."[47] Outside the university the restoration met with mixed reviews almost immediately. Not surprisingly, community members were critical of the restoration. Jessie Binford, who lived at the Hull House Settlement for sixty years, recounted that a "former neighbor, a boy born near Hull House," had remarked when he saw images of the restored Hull House, "But that isn't our Hull House."[48] The response from the preservation community was ambivalent. Hull House's National Register nomination claimed that Hull House was worthy of landmark status as an important historical site but also stressed that the architectural character of the restored mansion was a "contradiction," with the exterior of the house "restored to a good example of an Italianate house of ca. 1850, while on the interior it has been restored to its appearance when Jane Addams worked there after 1890."[49] Chicago's Landmark Commission also nominated the restored mansion, but in name only. Tellingly, the landmarking did not include a "mandatory ban on demolition." In defense of this decision, one commission member stated, "Hull House is a bastardized reconstruction to begin with."[50] Finally, Mary Lynn McCree Bryan, the first curator of the Jane Addams Hull-House Museum, judiciously observed that the museum's "well-organized exhibits and immaculately restored rooms," surrounded by "antiseptic" academic buildings, made it "impossible even for the most

Figure 11. Restored octagon room of Jane Addams's Hull-House. 057-00-01 Chicago Circle Center (1968), UIC ARCHIVES, University of Illinois at Chicago Library.

perceptive of visitors to appreciate the purpose and meaning of the Settlement." The restoration had successfully achieved a spirit of gracious living, but at the cost of cutting out the messiness of the settlement's history—its "dingy disarray" and the multitude of voices and experiences that it had housed throughout its life.[51]

Following Hull House's opening as a museum, McCree Bryan attempted to resurrect this history, to make a building that had lost its relevance relevant again. To accomplish this, she sought to reconnect the museum to its community. She recorded the stories of Hull House residents, collected and exhibited original artifacts, and published numerous monographs documenting the story of the settlement, its residents, and its neighbors. Subsequent directors would highlight issues of discrimination, civil liberties, and sexuality and reinvigorate traditional practices, like the settlement's communal dining experience with the Re-thinking Soup program, which brings people together for food and conversation. These contributions are important and point to some of the ways that historic interiors speak to multiple constituencies—how they capture, record, and sometimes stage multiplicity. These contributions also speak to the challenges of preserving interior spaces.

Hull House provides us with a valuable lens on interior preservation. In part, this is because it tells a story of loss and demolition. But its preservation also tells a story of opportunity. The community's words, ordeals, and recollections captured Hull House's interiors and how they shifted over time in response to their context and use. They remind us, as preservationists, that when we think about the preservation of interiors we need to look at interiors comprehensively—connected strongly not only to their physical structures but also to a larger social context. Interiors frequently change and evolve; they house multiple voices and experiences and evoke powerful feelings. How can we know what to preserve? How can we know what is meaningful? Perhaps we can start with the community, with the words of everyday stakeholders whose recollections help define the value of interior preservation.

AUTHOR BIOGRAPHY

Erin Cunningham is assistant professor in the Interior Design Department at the University of Florida. Her research focuses on the history and preservation of nineteenth- and twentieth-century interior spaces, including social settlement houses and public housing interiors.

NOTES

A version of this paper was originally presented at the Vernacular Architecture Forum in 2015. The author would like to thank the editors at *Buildings & Landscapes* for their thoughtful guidance in bringing this article to fruition.

1. Settlement houses emerged in the Progressive Era to help immigrants and low-income workers.

2. Dorothea Moore, "A Day at Hull-House," *American Journal of Sociology* 2 (March 1897): 629–42.

3. Eleanor Roosevelt, "My Day," November 19, 1937, Eleanor Roosevelt Papers Project, George Washington University, *https://www.gwu.edu/~erpapers/myday/displaydoc.cfm?_y=1937&_f=md054803*; Beatrice Webb, *Beatrice Webb's American Diary, 1898*, ed. David A. Shannon (Madison: University of Wisconsin Press, 1963), 107–9.

4. Mary Lynn McCree Bryan and Allen F. Davis, eds., *100 Years at Hull-House* (Bloomington: Indiana University Press, 1990), xii; Paul Gapp, "Decision Raises Questions," *Chicago Tribune*, April 7, 1974, 40.

5. For examples of scholarship on Hull House's histories and personalities, see Robyn Muncy, *Creating a Female Dominion in American Reform 1890–1935* (New York: Oxford University Press, 1991); Eleanor J. Stebner, *The Women of Hull House: A Study in Spirituality, Vocation, and Friendship* (New York: Albany State University of New York Press, 1997); Sharon Harr, "Location, Location, Location: Gender and the Archaeology of Urban Settlement," *Journal of Architectural Education* 55 (February 2002): 150–60; Sharon Harr, "The Hull House Settlement and the Study of the City," in *Embodied Utopias: Gender, Social Change, and the Modern Metropolis*, ed. Amy Bingaman, Lise Sanders, and Rebecca Zorach (London: Routledge, 2002): 99–115; Rivika S. Lissak, *Pluralism and Progressives: Hull House and the New Immigrants, 1890–1919* (Chicago: University of Chicago Press, 1989). This paper largely draws from the University of Illinois at Chicago's Special Collections (UIC Spec Coll), which

houses the Jane Addams Memorial Collection, including the Hull House Collection as well as the Hull House Oral History Collection. UIC's Special Collections also contain the university archives, which include documents from the chancellor, Auxiliary Services, and the Chicago Circle Center. It also draws from the Mark P. Hale Papers located in the University of Illinois Archives.

6. Alice Hamilton, letter to Mr. Ballard, March 22, 1961; Stanley Cantor, letter to Dear Sirs, February 25, 1961; Julius Zittler, letter to ?, n.d.; Thomas B. Stauffer, letter to the editor, *Saturday Review,* June 29, 1961; Bernard S. Houghton, letter to Mr. Williamson, March 30, 1961; Della Owen Drum, letter to Mr. Ballard, March 21, n.y., Hull House Collection, Box 9, Folder 51, UIC Spec Coll.

7. Louis Cirrincione, letter to Mr. Kenney Williamson, April 19, 1961, Hull House Collection, Box 9, Folder 51, UIC Spec Coll.

8. Earl Planty, letter to Russell Ballard, February 18, 1961, Hull House Collection, Box 9, Folder 51, UIC Spec Coll; John A. Leiser, "Barbarians?," *Chicago American,* September 6, 1961, Hull House Collection, Box 9, Folder 51, UIC Spec Coll.

9. Bessie Hillman, letter to Mayor Daley, March 17, 1961, Hull House Collection, Box 9, Folder 51, UIC Spec Coll.

10. Paul H. Douglas, letter to President David D. Henry, February 21, 1961, Hull House Collection, Box 9, Folder 51, UIC Spec Coll.

11. Arthur R. Gottschalk, letter to Trustees of the University of Illinois, February 14, 1961, Hull House Collection, Box 9, Folder 51, UIC Spec Coll.

12. The Debonairs, letter to Mayor Daley, March 17, 1961, Hull House Collection, Box 9, Folder 51, UIC Spec Coll.

13. The Young Adults of Hull-House, letter to Mayor Daley, February 14, 1961, Hull House Collection, Box 9, Folder 51, UIC Spec Coll.

14. St. Simon "Golden Age Group," letter to Dear Sirs, n.d., Hull House Collection, Box 9, Folder 51, UIC Spec Coll.

15. Just an old time friend, letter to Mr. Ballard, April 11, 1961, Hull House Collection, Box 9, Folder 51, UIC Spec Coll.

16. Joseph Holland, letter to Dear Sir, February 23, 1961, Hull House Collection, Box 9, Folder 51, UIC Spec Coll.

17. Robert T. Constable, letter to Dear Sir, March 28, 1961, Hull House Collection, Box 9, Folder 51, UIC Spec Coll.

18. Ralph E. Blount, letter to Hull-House, March 31, 1961, Hull House Collection, Box 9, Folder 51, UIC Spec Coll.

19. William Bacon, letter to Mr. Russell Ballard, March 19, 1961, Hull House Collection, Box 9, Folder 51, UIC Spec Coll.

20. Robert Szold, letter to President Henry, March 15, 1961, Hull House Collection, Box 9, Folder 51, UIC Spec Coll.

21. William H. Spitler, letter to Mr. Kenney Williamson, n.d.; Carl W. Lauterbach, letter to Kenney Williamson, April 7, 1961, Hull House Collection, Box 9, Folder 51, UIC Spec Coll.

22. Anne Fried, letter to Mr. Kenney Williamson, March 10, 1961, Hull House Collection, Box 9, Folder 51, UIC Spec Coll.

23. Reverend Lindon Peoples, Sr., letter to Matron, President or Manager, n.d., Hull House Collection, Box 9, Folder 51, UIC Spec Coll.

24. Paul K. Weinandy, letter to Dr. David D. Henry, February 23, 1961, Hull House Collection, Box 9, Folder 51, UIC Spec Coll.

25. Corinne S. Tsanoff, letter to Mr. Kenney Williamson, March 27, 1961, Hull House Collection, Box 9, Folder 51, UIC Spec Coll.

26. Norman R. Atwood, letter to Director, Hull House, March 20, 1961, Hull House Collection, Box 9, Folder 51, UIC Spec Coll.

27. David D. Henry, letter to Director Marietta Stevenson, April 28, 1961, Mark P. Hale Papers, Box 17, Folder 3, University of Illinois Archives.

28. Helen Fleming, "U. of I. Trustees Vote to Raze Other Buildings," *Chicago Daily News,* June 22, 1961.

29. "U. of I. Aides Promise Beautiful Campus Here," *Chicago Daily News,* February 11, 1961, History and Development, 1916–1975, Box 8, Folder 89, UIC University Archives.

30. "Plans for New U. of I. Campus Here Doom Historic Hull House," *Real Estate News Weekly,* September 22, 1961.

31. The exterior restoration was based on an 1896 painting of the Hull House mansion. Based on photographic and documentary evidence, this painting and the architect's restoration were historically incorrect. See Vince Michael, "Recovering the Layout of the

Hull House Complex," scholarly essay and image gallery, *Urban Experience in Chicago: Hull House and Its Neighborhoods, 1889–1963*, 2003, *http://hullhouse.uic.edu/hull/urbanexp/main.cgi?file=viewer*.ptt&mime=blank&doc=834&type=print.

32. Walter Netsch, "Oral History of Walter Netsch," by Betty J. Blum, Chicago Architects Oral History Project, Art Institute of Chicago, May 8 and June 5–28, 1997, 193–94, http://digital-libraries.saic.edu/cdm/ref/collection/caohp/id/19289.

33. The committee included C. E. Flynn, assistant to the president and university director of public information; Charles C. Caveny, assistant to the president; Robert B. Downs, dean of library administration; Mark P. Hale, director of the University of Illinois's newly formed Jane Addams' School of Social Work; and Allen S. Weller, dean of fine and applied arts.

34. Mark Hale, letter to Charles E. Flynn, October 22, 1961, Mark P. Hale Papers, Box 17, Folder 3, University of Illinois Archives.

35. Ad Hoc Committee to study Hull House, letter to President David D. Henry, November 1, 1962, Mark P. Hale Papers, Box 17, Folder 3, University of Illinois Archives.

36. The Hull House Committee oversaw the interior restoration of the mansion and dining hall. This committee was composed of three subcommittees: the Subcommittee on Memorabilia, the Subcommittee on Restoration, and the Subcommittee on Administration and Utilization. Hull House Committee, Subcommittee on Memorabilia, "Minutes of Meeting in Urbana," December 4, 1964, Box 2, Folder 25/26, University Library Archives, UIC Spec Coll.

37. Chaired by Mark Hale, director of the University of Illinois's newly formed Jane Addams' School of Social Work, the members of the Subcommittee on Memorabilia all worked for the University of Illinois and consisted of Allen S. Weller, dean of fine and applied arts; Frazer G. Poole, director of the University of Illinois Undergraduate Library; Leonard Currie, dean of the College of Art and Architecture; and Robert B. Downs, dean of library administration.

38. Physical Plant Department, University of Illinois, "Memorandum Concerning Policies Related to the Rehabilitation of Hull House," July 10, 1964, page 1, Mark P. Hale Papers, Box 17, Folder 5, University of Illinois Archives.

39. "Conclusions: Uses and Furnishings of Hull House," Hull-House Museum Archival Records, Box 8, Preservation of Hull House Folder, UIC Spec Coll, 5.

40. "Conclusions: Uses and Furnishings of Hull House," 5.

41. Hull House Memorabilia Committee, "As Jane Addams Saw Hull House," December 5, 1964, Mark P. Hale Papers, Box 17, Folder 5, University of Illinois Archives.

42. Hull House Committee, Subcommittee on Memorabilia, "Minutes of Meeting in Urbana," December 4, 1964, page 2, University Library Records, Box 2, Acc. 2006-25/26, University of Illinois at Chicago.

43. Physical Plant Department, "Memorandum Concerning Policies Related to the Rehabilitation of Hull House," 3.

44. "Founder's 1846 Melodeon Purchased among Restored Furniture Pieces," *The Chicagoan* (June 1967): 3.

45. Hull House Memorabilia Committee, "Suggestions: Uses and Furnishings of Hull House," 1964, Hull-House Museum Archive Records, Box 8, UIC Spec Coll.

46. Hull House Committee, Subcommittee on Memorabilia, "Minutes of Meeting in Urbana," December 4, 1964, page 1, University Library Collections Box 2, Acc. 2006-25/26. Sculpted by Lawrence Taylor for the Jane Addams's centennial, the bust was acquired from the Illinois State Historical Society in Springfield. See "Minutes of a Meeting of the Hull House Committee," Wednesday, March 9, 1966, University Library Collections, Box 046/09/01, Folder 2006-25/26.

47. "Jane Addams' Hull House," 1967, University Archives, Box 57, UIC Spec Coll.

48. Jessie Binford, letter to Mr. Hale, August 5, 1963, Mark P. Hale Papers, Box 17, Folder 3, University of Illinois Archives.

49. "Jane Addams' Hull House," National Register Nomination Form, 1964.

50. Paul Gapp, "Decision Raises Questions," *Chicago Tribune*, April 7, 1974, 40.

51. Bryan and Davis, *100 Years at Hull-House*, xii.

SARAH ROVANG

The Grid Comes Home

Wiring and Lighting the American Farmhouse

ABSTRACT

Established in 1935 under the New Deal, the Rural Electrification Administration (REA) brought affordable electricity to underserved agrarian populations throughout the United States. The arrival of electricity transformed everyday patterns of work and leisure on the American farm. No change was more immediately palpable than the clean, steady glow of electrical light. Many times brighter than the dirty kerosene lamps they replaced, electric lights became a sought-after commodity even among farm families unwilling to invest in other electrified conveniences. Between 1935 and the early 1950s, REA, along with other government agricultural agencies and for-profit corporations such as General Electric, published numerous advertisements and guides that promoted best practices in lighting and wiring. Seizing on rural enthusiasm for electric illumination, these publications promoted proper light as the first, critical step toward attaining an all-electric mode of living. These publications are vital in understanding changes to the spatial layout of the farm landscape in the mid-twentieth century. Through text, diagrams, illustrations, and photographs, wiring and lighting materials articulated a new approach to farm planning and rural space that foreshadowed many of the farm's architectural transformations after World War II.

On May 3, 1941, a group of Pennsylvania farm families gathered to celebrate what was termed the "Second Battle of Gettysburg": the arrival of electric power in rural parts of the state. Among the day's events was a mock funeral for a kerosene lantern. After the unfortunate lamp was laid to rest, a tombstone was placed at the burial site, which read: "Here lies a coal-oil lamp. Buried here . . . as a symbol of the drudgery and toil which its member-families bore far longer than was necessary or right but which, with the energization of their own power system are now abolished for all time" (Figure 1).[1] Recalling President Lincoln's eulogizing address at Gettysburg, this inscription suggested that rural electrification rivaled the Civil War battle in its potential to shape the everyday lives of many Americans, liberating rural people from menial labor and drudgery.

Over the preceding six years, the percentage of farms receiving central station electricity in the United States had climbed to well over 30 percent, up from 11 percent in 1935.[2] The agency in large part responsible for this dramatic increase in farm electrification and for hosting the festivities at Gettysburg was the Rural Electrification Administration (REA). Founded in 1935 under the New Deal, REA brought affordable electric power to rural areas by offering long-term, low-interest loans to farm cooperatives. Within its first decade of operation, REA had left an indelible mark on the American rural landscape, erecting thousands of miles of electrical lines and dozens of new generating facilities and cooperative offices. But for the rural families who used REA's power, perhaps no change was more visceral than the adoption of electric light. For

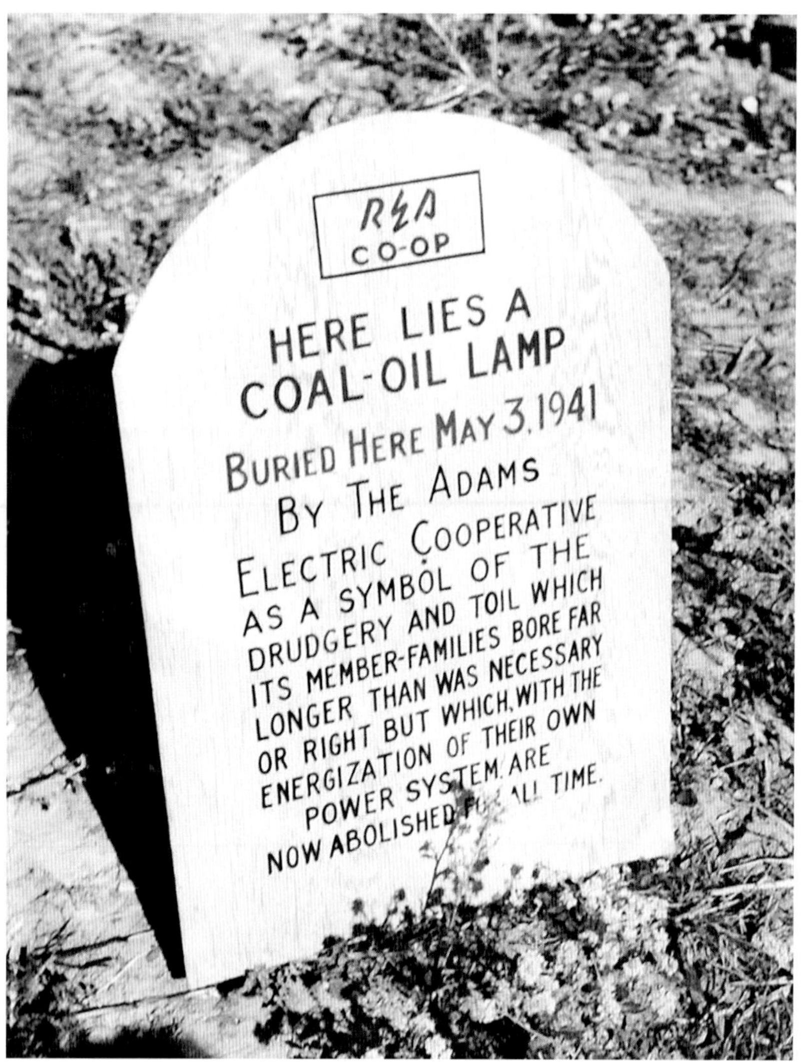

Figure 1. Kerosene Lantern Tombstone at Pennsylvania Rural Electrification Administration celebration, May 3, 1941. National Archives and Records Administration, Photographs of the Rural Electrification Administration, Folder 6 "Power Use in the Home," Negative no. 6298, National Archives Identifier 540048, HMS ID 221-P.

the majority of farm residents, who still burned kerosene as their primary light source during this period, electricity's clean, steady glow could save significant time by eliminating the need for scrubbing and maintaining kerosene lamps—one REA publication estimated 176 hours of labor saved annually per household.[3]

In order to communicate these benefits, REA disseminated a wide range of print media, much of which was produced in-house, but which also included publications from for-profit corporations such as General Electric and Westinghouse and other government agricultural organizations. Capitalizing on the near-universal appeal of electric illumination, these publications positioned the installation of proper lighting as a stepping stone to the acquisition of other appliances and machinery—the first component of an all-electric lifestyle. Unlike previous attempts to sell electric lighting to farm populations, much of this literature catered to a distinctly rural audience, calling attention to the unique functional requirements of farm lighting. These materials acknowledged the need for effective, task-oriented lighting on the farm, urging farmers to distinguish between diverse lighting situations in the house and across the rest of the farm.

Anticipating the purchase of further electrical implements and ensuring maximum efficiency for domestic and farm uses, this literature enjoined farmers to plan ahead for a unified program of proper wiring and lighting (Figures 2 and 3). The program was rooted in the abundant use of specialized electrical devices and lighting fixtures, encouraging the corresponding differentiation and specialization of spaces across the farm and among rooms within the farmhouse. Print materials articulated a new spatial logic of planning for electric wiring. This new way of conceptualizing the farm and the rural landscape writ large was based on an orthogonal grid, mimicking the idealized rectangular circuits that coursed through planning diagrams and illustrations.

REA's publications on lighting reached a broad audience. They circulated in the agency's monthly newsletter, with reprints in local newspapers, at farm shows such as REA's equipment tour, and at local cooperative buildings. Beyond disseminating these promotional and didactic materials, REA instituted new financing options that would put electric lighting in the economic grasp of many farm families.[4] REA's faith in the value of electric light extended beyond its ability to transform the physical landscape of the farm and patterns of buying. REA's slogan from the late 1930s, "If you put a light on every farm, you put a light in every heart," underscored the power of electric illumination to fundamentally alter farmers and their habits—the spark that could ignite the transformation of farm families into educated consumers and, by extension, into modernized farmers and homemakers.[5]

At least initially, REA's intentions rarely matched the lived reality of rural people, particu-

Figure 2. "When Wiring Plan Ahead," poster from *First Steps in Load Building*, Rural Electrification Administration, 1937. Office Files of Harlow S. Person, 1936–1953, Records of the Rural Electrification Administration, Record Group 221, National Archives Identifier 1872021, HMS ID A1 34.

Figure 3. "Plan Your Lighting for Better Seeing," poster from *First Steps in Load Building*, Rural Electrification Administration, 1937. Office Files of Harlow S. Person, 1936–1953, Records of the Rural Electrification Administration, Record Group 221, National Archives Identifier 1872021, HMS ID A1 34.

larly during the late Depression and wartime, when deprivation and rationing curtailed consumption. Nevertheless, the promotional and didactic literature distributed by the agency and its collaborators shaped the American farm landscape over time as these ubiquitous pamphlets, bulletins, and periodicals found their way into farm homes across the nation. In addition to transmitting practical knowledge about wiring or fixture choice, the prescriptive literature conveyed a vision of idealized rural life that by the post–World War II years began to seem less outlandish and more feasible for broader segments of the rural population, as the farmhouse shifted from being a hybrid space of work and recreation to a structure much more heavily centered around domesticity. Farm homes of the 1950s and 1960s experienced substantial material changes, such as the installation of electric kitchens, closets, and separate bedrooms for boys and girls and the decline of the outhouse in favor of in-home bathrooms.[6] Historian Jane Adams has attributed this transformation "from generalized structures to more specialized, efficiency-oriented homes" to farmers' exposure to routinized orderings of time and space during World War II through wage labor and factory work, in combination with the relative financial affluence of the postwar period.[7] Although these factors certainly contributed to the modernization of farms, interwar and immediate postwar materials designed to sell electric lighting and demonstrate proper wiring prefigured these physical changes to farmhouses by putting forth a new spatial logic for the farm grounded in the arrangements of circuits and permanent light fixtures. In pre–World War II print publications, REA and its contemporaries already imagined the farmhouse as part of an encompassing system of modernized agricultural efficiency and spatial specialization.

Planning for Wiring and Lighting

During the 1920s, American farm families dramatically accelerated the adoption of rural telephony by executing much of the wire stringing and installation themselves. This do-it-yourself mentality became a powerful way for agrarian populations to negotiate and modulate technological modernity.[8] In contrast to telephony, self-installation of electric wiring and lighting posed significant safety hazards to novice electricians. Farmers' interventions into wiring represented an intrusion on what was, at least in urban areas, an already established area of professional knowledge. REA urged its cooperative members to secure the services of a "competent electrical contractor" and to have the contractor's work inspected before delivering payment.[9] Despite the agency's hope that the majority of farm families would hire a specialist to do the wiring for them, the profusion of wiring guides suggests that REA was aware that many families either would attempt to install the wiring themselves or would want information in advance of their electrification.

This need to educate potential consumers extended from installing wiring to making lighting decisions. When approaching the particular problem of lighting the farm, specialists feared that uninformed farm families would be apt to replace kerosene lamps with single, unshaded bulbs suspended from the ceiling.[10] In order to avoid the menace of the bare bulb solution, REA warned against hastily tossing out kerosene lamps and installing electric ones before taking proper steps to plan ahead. In a 1941 pamphlet entitled *Get the Best from the Start,* REA reminded the reader, "Good lighting need not be expensive but it must be planned."[11] Planning ahead for lighting meant creating a sustainable strategy that would accommodate not only the few electric lights that farmers wanted now but also future purchases. This strategy necessitated a new way of visualizing the farm landscape and required farm families to think scientifically about the placement of light fixtures and outlets in the farmhouse, in outbuildings, and throughout the farmyard. Having ready access to electric light went hand in hand with convenient placement of outlets, ensuring that nocturnal tasks requiring other electrified devices might be sufficiently illuminated. For instance, an image from Sears, Roebuck & Co.'s *Electric Wiring for Home or Farm* showed a nighttime scene of a man using an electric saw in his farm workshop under the ample glow of three electric lamps (Figure 4).

Although rural reformers had called on farmers to adopt rational planning techniques since the nineteenth century, the 1920s witnessed an unprecedented shift toward agricultural industrialization at the national level.[12] This new understanding of agriculture was defined by an increased focus on efficient production at an expanded scale, facilitated by standardized processes that relied on specialized machines and techniques.[13] By the late interwar years, as American involvement in World War II grew increasingly inevitable and the vast mechanisms of national defense roared to life, "planning" became a kind of national watchword. As Andrew Shanken has argued, "War generalized and naturalized planning, putting the essentially specialist term . . . into wider circulation. Total war . . . made planning universal, linking individual acts of restraint with national and wartime planning."[14] The logic of planning suffused American culture from the most sprawling military operations and urban plans down to the smallest family farm. For REA, which provided power to a number of defense operations during World War II, planning ahead was linked not only to the exigencies of war but also to an imagined postwar future.[15] Echoing the imposing magnitude of "total war," REA's end goal was nothing less than total electrification, through which all American rural families would receive central station electric power and rely heavily on electricity in both agricultural production and domestic tasks.[16]

Although there was an ideological impetus

behind REA's promotion of total electrification, the agency's postwar plans were borne largely out of monetary constraints. The economics of REA's operation meant that the agency had a substantial financial stake in persuading farmers to use sustained, heavy electrical loads. Not originally envisioned as a cooperative lending scheme, REA had initially tried to work with existing electric utilities, loaning them money to subsidize the extension of lines to new rural customers. When these suppliers proved resistant, REA switched to a method of making loans directly to farming cooperatives, which defrayed construction costs by reaching a wider customer base and therefore allowed farmers to purchase electricity at wholesale rates.[17]

By the late 1930s, the cooperative system became the defining aspect of REA's business model, with the agency working to facilitate all aspects of cooperative building and management.[18] Under this nonprofit organization, the charges that members paid in their monthly bills went back to their cooperatives, financing electric service while also paying off the initial loans from REA. The more electricity cooperative members used, the higher their bills and, thus, the more quickly REA amortized its debts. Additionally, since REA cooperatives purchased the majority of their power at wholesale rates from established public or private electrical utilities, those utilities stood to benefit from their newly connected customers using more electricity. As Congress grew increasingly skeptical of New Deal programs, REA administrators were eager to prove that the cooperative lending plan was fiscally responsible and beneficial to the late-Depression economy. Load-building, or equipping farmers with an abundance of electric commodities and educating them on electricity's manifold uses, profited REA, its cooperatives, manufacturers of equipment and devices, and electric utilities.

The rhetoric of load-building even suffused REA's own generating facilities. Though most cooperatives bought power from nearby utilities, REA loans could also pay for the construction of new generating plants in instances where other power was unavailable for financial or geographic reasons.[19] REA power plants often anticipated future loads architecturally and were built to house more generating equipment than initially required. For example, at the REA generating facility for Clay Electric Cooperative in Keystone Heights, Florida, two diesel engines, each with a 150-kilowatt capacity, were installed upon the building's completion in 1939, but space was provided to house two additional engines later (Figures 5 and 6).[20] Responding to increased electrical demand, a new 473-kilowatt engine was installed in 1940.[21] This plant, which was housed in the same building as the cooperative's offices, encouraged members to witness these changes: the powerhouse side of the building featured floor-to-ceiling windows that revealed the process of power generation to members who came to pay bills or seek advice.

REA power plants' anticipation of load-building through the addition of space for more generators and increasingly powerful equipment was mirrored on farms (the consumer side of the equation), where future electrical needs could also be materially and architecturally planned. REA hoped that farmers would eventually invest in a panoply of electrified equipment, but it recognized that procurement of electrified goods (and the corresponding increases in electricity being used) would necessarily be gradual. Historian Charles Wetherell has described urban

Figure 4. Illustration from Sears, Roebuck and Co., *Electric Wiring for Home or Farm*, Chicago, first published 1947. Applications and Loans Division Office Files of George E. Dillon, Asst. Chief 1946–1953 (Correspondence), Record Group 221, Records of the Rural Electrification Administration, U.S. Department of Agriculture, National Archives Identifier 1872281, HMS ID A1 45: 4. The original caption read: "A welllighted, warm workshop, properly equipped with good tools, and an electric motor to furnish power for grinders and tools, is one of the most profitable farm investments you can make."

Figure 5. Clay Electric Cooperative, Keystone Heights, Florida, Roland Wank and Mario Bianculli, architects, 1939. National Archives and Records Administration, U.S. Department of Agriculture, Photographs of the Rural Electrification Administration, Folder "Cooperatives-Rural Electrification Administration," Negative no. 5598, National Archives Identifier 512795, HMS ID 16-G.

electrical modernization during the New Deal as a series of ascending tiers, each marked by the acquisition of key appliances. Based on meter readings in Riverside, California, during this period, Wetherell's model shows how after they purchased electric lights, families tended to invest in a radio, then a refrigerator, then an electric range or water heater.[22] In this tiered model, electric light became a necessary first link in this chain of predicted purchases.[23] Although Wetherell formulated this theory based on an urban situation, REA's surveys and the U.S. Housing Census of 1940 suggested that the same principles of staggered acquisition and usage applied in rural settings.[24]

Since lights were almost certainly the first electrified conveniences to be installed on farms, lighting presented unique possibilities in REA's load-building campaign. Unlike urban environments, which were almost universally electrified by the 1920s, farms still presented a virtual tabula rasa for the installation of lighting in the mid-1930s. REA's 1938 annual report extolled the possibilities of new rural wiring schemes, explaining, "The urban dweller, with a variety of obsolescent fixtures and lamps representing a considerable investment, is likely to acquire . . . improved equipment only gradually. The new user, on the other hand, starts with a clean slate and can therefore install the most modern lighting devices at the outset."[25] Taking advantage of the opportunity to install a comprehensive lighting scheme all at once rather than incrementally, both REA and corporate lighting promoters portrayed proper lighting as the essential preliminary step in adopting other electrified commodities.

Proper planning ensured that there were multiple lights and, thus, multiple convenience outlets in each room and outbuilding. REA's 1937 guide, *First Steps in Load Building,* included a chart entitled "Check Wiring Requirements Now—Save Costly Additions Later." Organized by each room and exterior space that required wiring on the farm, the first column detailed the recommended lighting situation, while the

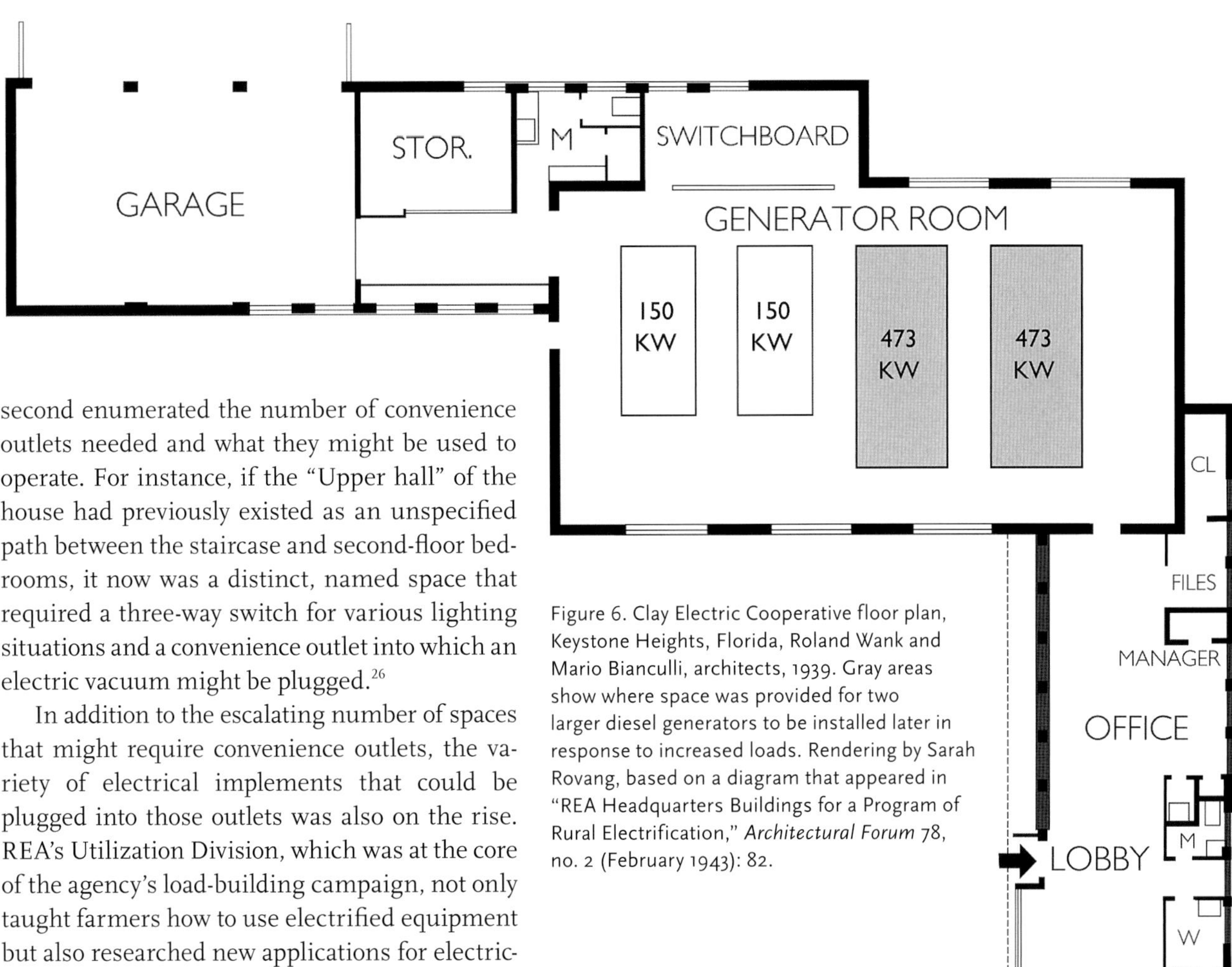

Figure 6. Clay Electric Cooperative floor plan, Keystone Heights, Florida, Roland Wank and Mario Bianculli, architects, 1939. Gray areas show where space was provided for two larger diesel generators to be installed later in response to increased loads. Rendering by Sarah Rovang, based on a diagram that appeared in "REA Headquarters Buildings for a Program of Rural Electrification," *Architectural Forum* 78, no. 2 (February 1943): 82.

second enumerated the number of convenience outlets needed and what they might be used to operate. For instance, if the "Upper hall" of the house had previously existed as an unspecified path between the staircase and second-floor bedrooms, it now was a distinct, named space that required a three-way switch for various lighting situations and a convenience outlet into which an electric vacuum might be plugged.[26]

In addition to the escalating number of spaces that might require convenience outlets, the variety of electrical implements that could be plugged into those outlets was also on the rise. REA's Utilization Division, which was at the core of the agency's load-building campaign, not only taught farmers how to use electrified equipment but also researched new applications for electricity in rural life. Additionally, REA collaborated with major equipment manufacturers through the New Deal's Electric Home and Farm Authority to design appliances and equipment uniquely suited to farm living.[27] Anticipation of new uses for electricity was frequently reflected in the advice given by wiring and lighting guides. For example, the 1946 booklet *Planning Your Farmstead Wiring and Lighting* showed an axonometric drawing of a barn meticulously rigged with numerous lights and convenience outlets. The text explained, "Power machinery will be increasingly important in the barn to save time and labor, and its source of electricity must be adequate to supply the power needed" (Figure 7).[28] As farming grew increasingly professionalized, government agricultural organizations urged farmers themselves to become researchers.[29] As one REA pamphlet advised, "The more you live with [electricity] the more you discover its innumerable services and economies."[30] By wiring for a sophisticated program of lighting, farmers concurrently equipped homes, yards, and outbuildings to handle increased electric loads made necessary by novel uses and inventions.

The adoption of lighting rarely spurred farm families to purchase other electrified goods, as REA had hoped. Oftentimes, only small appliances followed the initial investment, a far cry from the high-powered farm equipment, refrigerators, and electric ranges that filled the pages of lighting and wiring guides. More costly investments were often purchased over a number of years, as war gave way to greater peacetime prosperity and the practice of buying on credit gained in acceptance and popularity.[31] In 1939 market saturation of electric radios and irons among REA members topped 80 percent for each device. By contrast, only 25.6 percent owned a refrigerator, and 15.5 percent owned a vacuum cleaner.[32]

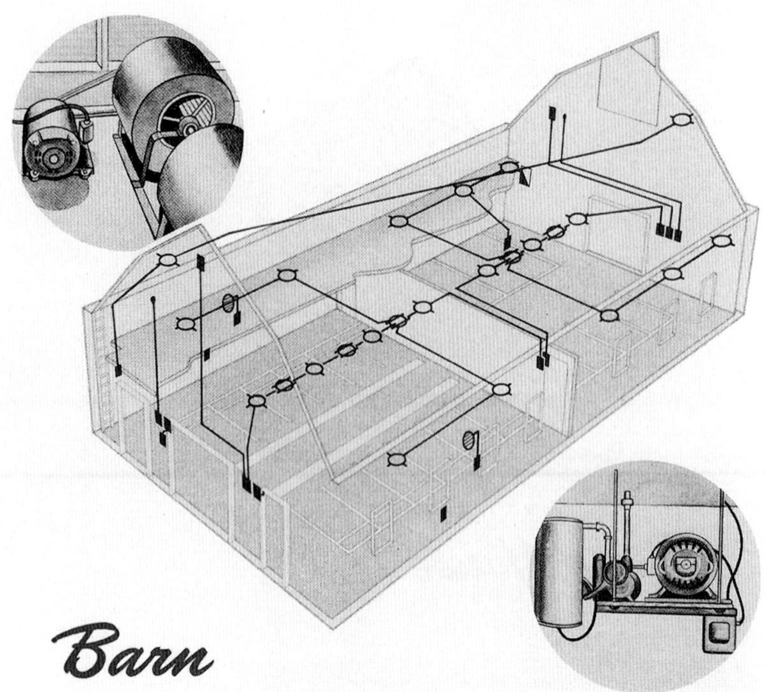

Figure 7. Barn schematic from *Planning Your Farmstead Wiring and Lighting*, Rural Electrification Administration, 1946. National Archives and Records Administration, Records of the Rural Electrification Administration, Record Group 221, Box 7, Folder "Motion Pictures REA Coop—Prac. Approach to Policy Making, Planning Your Farmstead Wiring and Lighting," National Archives Identifier 1938128, HMS ID A1 93A.

After lowering its rates to encourage more appliance and equipment sales, REA found that while overall rates of electricity consumption jumped, farm families still were not using their savings to buy large devices but were instead buying more small appliances and leaving lights on longer.[33]

Rather than recalcitrant attitudes toward new technology, these practices were often spurred by financial considerations, particularly in depression and wartime conditions. Although REA had a financing scheme for low-income members, all of the larger load-building items such as refrigerators and washing machines remained the purview of farmers who were already relatively well-off.[34] As historian Ronald Kline has argued, the minimum monthly electric bill became a kind of bottom line for some families, who occasionally reverted to the use of nonelectrified technologies such as kerosene lamps after reaching that baseline usage.[35] Despite REA's efforts to bury the lantern, many farmers still kept one or more on hand for power outages or found even more regular use for the "old coal-oil lamp."

As farmers continued to negotiate when and to what extent they incorporated electrical modernity into daily life, REA's attempts to build load by exhorting farmers to plan ahead rarely yielded the intended results. Perhaps more significant was the new role print materials imagined for American farmers. The visual language used to communicate the precepts of wiring and lighting cast farmers as planners as much as consumers of electrical goods and power. In doing so these prescriptive materials facilitated new ways of thinking about electrified space on the farm.

Planning on the Grid

More than merely calculating future electrical loads and predicting upcoming purchases, REA counseled its customers to consider the spatial implications of electrification. This spatial paradigm might be best understood as a scaled-down version of how REA's engineers envisioned electrification at a regional or even national level. The agency defined its electrification program in relation to previous practices of private electrical utilities. Before REA, local utilities would often "skim the cream" of a given area, selectively extending their lines to profitable rural industries or large farming operations.[36] The result was an uneven and sporadic allocation of electrical service with single lines cutting through the landscape. REA pioneered the concept of area coverage, which sought an even distribution of electric service across rural regions (Figure 8).[37]

REA imagined its systems as orthogonal, regularly spaced grids of poles and lines, in keeping with entrenched rectilinear understandings of the American landscape, such as those imagined in early land surveys and later imprinted through homesteading policies and the layout of rural counties. As historian David Nye has noted, "This conception of space assumed that in every unit a single social reality could be replicated, creating a society at once homogenous and made up of self-reliant parts."[38] Accordingly, REA translated the rationality of the evenly distributed power grid to the scale of the family farm (Figure 9). For REA the arrangement of spaces on the farm and in the farmhouse, like those on the larger rural landscape, should be rooted in the logic of electricity—as determined by the radius of light shed by electric bulbs and the necessary placement of convenience outlets (Figure 10).

By the late 1930s and early 1940s, this new

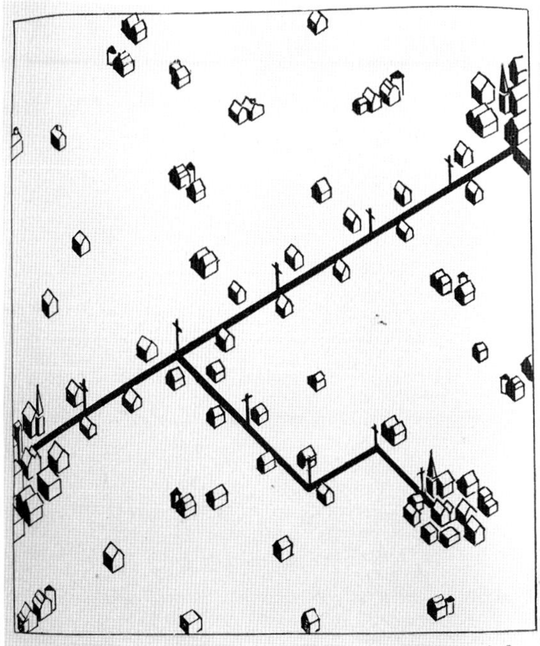

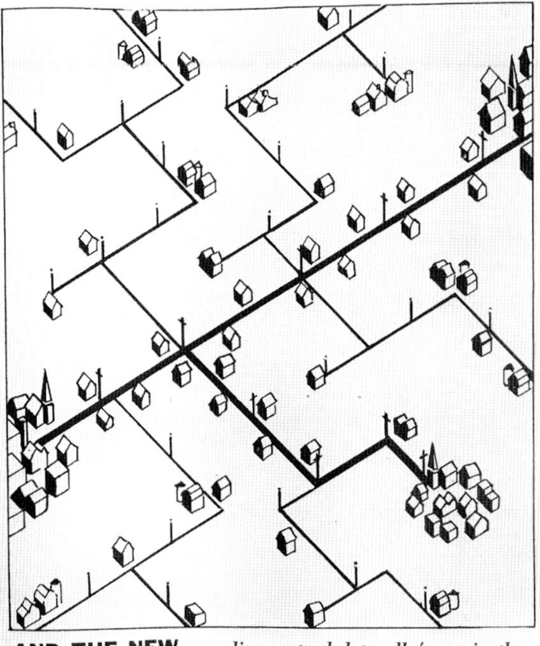

Figure 8. Diagram showing the principle of area coverage from "Why Area Coverage?" The original caption read: "The Old . . . power lines served only the 'cream' of the area—farms away from the highways left unserved [left]. And the New . . . lines extended to all farms in the area, on an 'area coverage' basis [right]." *Rural Electrification News* 10, no. 4 (December 1944): 3.

conception of electrified space on the farm had acquired its own set of visual conventions, which differed from those used to represent electricity and lighting to farmers in decades past. During the late 1920s, General Electric's guides typically showed the effects of electrification but not the methods or logic of its installation. In a brochure from 1927, one illustration included a panel representing life before electricity, showing a farmer carrying a single pail for milk and a kerosene lantern into a dark barn. Below, a larger panel depicted the same farmer toting two milk pails under the steady glow of new electric light, visually implying that this new technology had the potential to double farm efficiency (Figure 11).[39] In addition to illustrations such as this, this guide featured atmospheric nighttime photographs, depicting lighting fixtures entirely obscured by the brilliant haloes radiating from them. Cumulatively, these representations insinuated not only that electricity would lessen drudgery on the farm but that, on the whole, established traditions of rural life would persist. Lighting might extend working time in the barn, but milking was still done by hand rather than by machine. Prior to the massive uptick of rural electrification in the 1930s, many modernizing advances were presented as punctuations of modernity in otherwise conventional rural spaces.

Figure 9. "The Farm," Rural Electrification Administration poster, late 1930s. National Archives and Records Administration, Photographs of the Rural Electrification Administration, Folder 7 "Power Use in Schools: REA Posters and Exhibits," Negative no. 3347, National Archives Identifier 540048, HMS ID 221-P.

In contrast, General Electric's 1940 *Farm Wiring Handbook* imagined electricity as the primary organizing agent on the farm and across

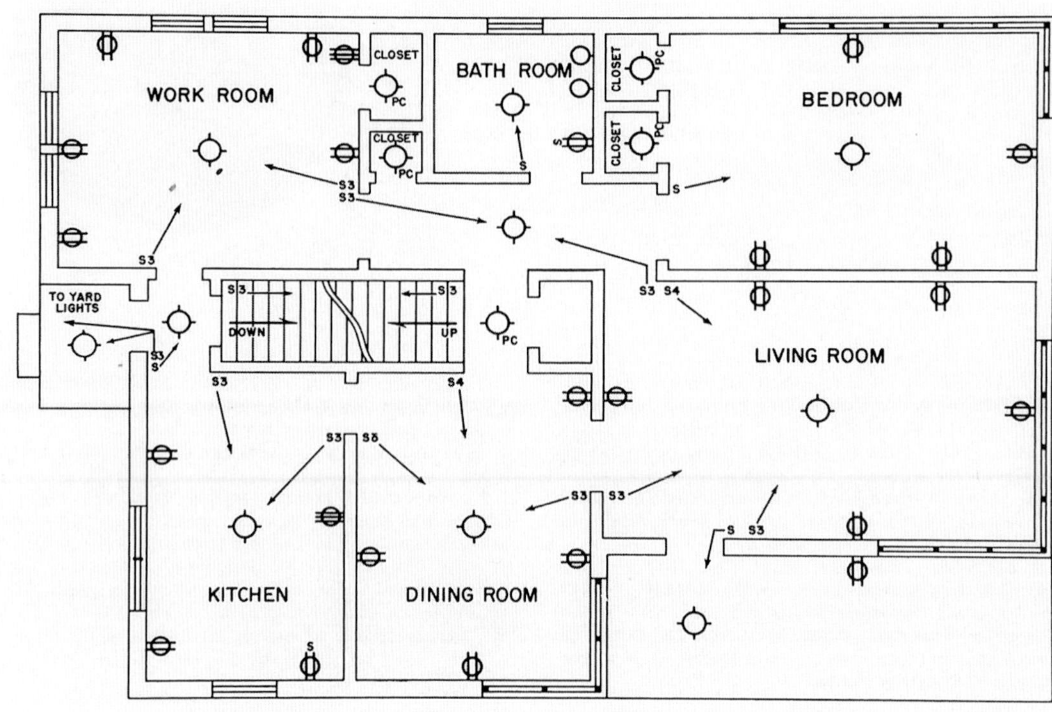

Figure 10. Floor plan from *Planning Your Farmstead Wiring and Lighting*, Rural Electrification Administration, 1946. National Archives and Records Administration, Records of the Rural Electrification Administration, Record Group 221, Box 7, Folder "Motion Pictures REA Coop—Prac. Approach to Policy Making, Planning Your Farmstead Wiring and Lighting," National Archives Identifier 1938128, HMS ID A1 93A.

Figure 11. "Good lighting means convenience, comfort, and safety," illustration showing the contrast of farm life before and after electric lighting. General Electric Company, *Farm Lighting*, edited by W. C. Brown, bulletin 53 (Cleveland, Ohio: National Lamp Works of General Electric Co, 1927), 4.

the rural landscape more broadly. Whereas earlier materials had artfully concealed the means by which electricity entered the farm and its buildings, this manual made the process central to the narrative, tracing the journey of electricity from towering high-voltage lines onto the family farm. One pair of diagrams compared this flow of electricity to a tree, with progressive step-downs in voltage represented as smaller and smaller branches—the organic growth of the tree transformed into an abstract grid of circuitry (Figure 12).[40] General Electric's 1945 *Farm Wiring Guide* illustrated this effect even more dramatically. Though intended for a lay audience, this booklet presented lines, poles, power feeders, and service entrance panels with precise technical detail. Circuit diagrams wove through every room and outbuilding—a farm environment specifically imagined and illustrated with electricity in mind (Figure 13).

This same shift toward more technical detail and numerous grid-like diagrams appeared in manuals and brochures produced by REA and its other corporate partners during the late 1930s and early 1940s, which similarly featured idealized farmyards effectively reorganized and clarified by the addition of electricity.[41] While the neat, orderly farms shown in these illustrations were more aspirational than reflective of reality, they demonstrated the effects of the electrical planning REA envisioned on the farm taken to their logical extreme—roads, fences, and buildings submitting to the spatial logic of wiring and lighting. In addition to providing sample diagrams of typical building organizations, some booklets even included gridded, blank pages where farmers could work out their own schematics.[42] By engaging farmers in the early stages of the design process (even if electrical contractors would be hired later on), rural electrification promoters laid the grid as the foundation of proper planning.

By reducing the farm to a series of circuit diagrams, electricity's promoters presented the agrarian landscape as a regularized and abstracted orthogonal space, continuous with the regional or, even, national infrastructure of electrification REA sought to construct. Yet the grid did not exist only to facilitate rationalization; it was also a tool to be mobilized in service of an increasingly specialized and consumption-driven farm layout. Concurrent with the establishment of REA, government agencies and private corporations increasingly acknowledged that electric lighting for the farm presented unique challenges when compared with lighting urban settings. The particular aesthetic, functional, and architectural issues of farm illumination shaped the written and visual language of promotional lighting publications.

Ideals and Realities in Marketing Light to the Farm

Though the translation of urban values onto rural people persisted during the New Deal as part of continuing and new agricultural reforms, manufacturers and government agencies also began to recognize the distinctive aspects of rural living.[43] During the early twentieth century, proponents of the country life movement had sought to improve rural living conditions. Many of these reformers were urbanites who believed that the struggles of agrarian life were social rather than economic, the result of geographic isolation and

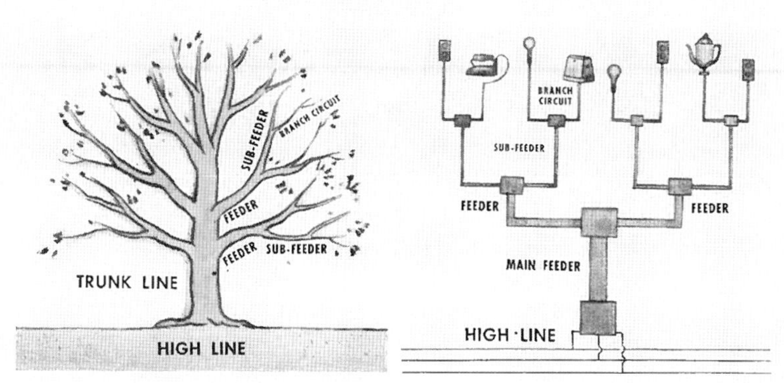

Figure 12. Diagram showing voltage drops necessary for the circuits that power appliances and lights from General Electric Company, *Farm Wiring Hand-book: A Guide for Planning Electrical Wiring on Farms* (Bridgeport, Conn., 1940), 4.

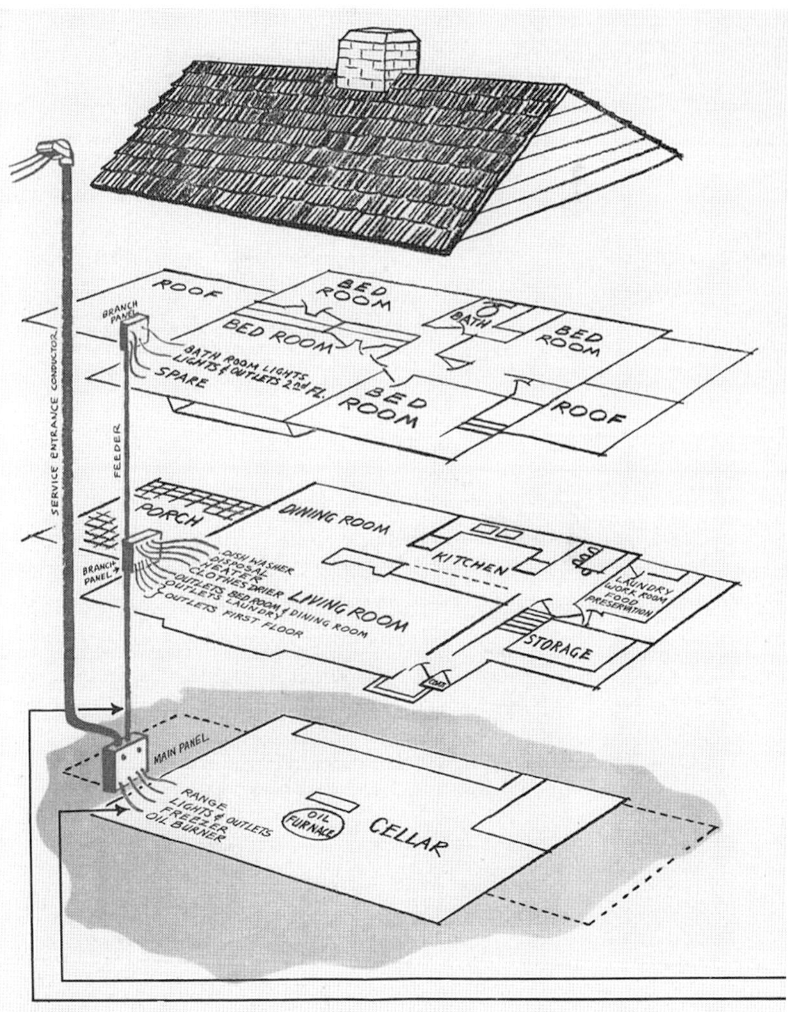

Figure 13. Diagram from General Electric, *GE Farm Wiring Guide*, 1945. Applications and Loans Division Office Files of George E. Dillon, Asst. Chief 1946–1953 (Correspondence), Record Group 221, Records of the Rural Electrification Administration, U.S. Department of Agriculture, National Archives Identifier 1872281, HMS ID A1 45: 44.

disintegrating rural institutions. Driven in part by concerns over food shortages and farm productivity, they urged the adoption of technological modernization, new business practices, and domestic management modeled after urban standards.[44] However, as major manufacturers such as General Electric and Westinghouse sought a more homespun, folksy appeal during the Depression years, the realization that rural consumers were not precisely comparable with their urban counterparts began to color the way that light and other electric devices were marketed toward agrarian populations.[45] A government survey in 1934 of over one hundred thousand farms nationwide had come to the conclusion that "the farmer's position and viewpoint is different from that of the industrialist and . . . the city domestic user. The selling approach to the farmer must also be different. It should be based upon the farmer's point of view."[46] This recognition that farmers represented a distinct market for electrified devices roughly coincided with the rise of the grid in materials on wiring and lighting, suggesting that the farm market also required a new visual paradigm. As REA's monthly member newsletter, *Rural Electrification News,* observed, lighting "manufacturers realized that in serving this rural market it is necessary to employ methods different from those which have been used in urban districts."[47]

One of the ways in which lighting promoters targeted rural consumers was by playing on the historical difficulties of lighting the farm. While many American urbanites had access to gas lighting prior to electricity, most farmers looking to electrify would be making a much greater leap in lighting technology. As a 1910 bulletin from the Pennsylvania State College Agricultural Experiment Station noted, "In the city, the householder finds his house already provided with means for gas lighting or electric lighting. . . . Neither of these can be had in the farm house, except in so few instances that they need not be considered. Practically, the kerosene lamp is the present means of lighting the farm house."[48] Although some wealthy agriculturalists had turned to Delco Light Plants and several alternative fuel sources for lamps were available (including gasoline, acetylene, and denatured alcohol), kerosene dominated farm lighting before the arrival of electricity.[49] Although kerosene lanterns provided some flexibility, owing to their portable nature, fire safety concerns effectively curtailed that freedom, prohibiting the placement of lamps near flammable materials.[50] In its promotion of electric lighting, REA capitalized on existing anxieties about kerosene, emphasizing not only its combustible nature but also its unhygienic aspects and the relatively scarce illumination provided by its use. Film director Joris Ivens's 1940 film for REA, *Power and the Land,* exploited the disadvantages of kerosene to dramatic cinematic effect, contrasting the antediluvian toil of cleaning lamps and trimming wicks with the cleanliness and convenience of electric light.[51]

REA materials also critiqued the use of kerosene lanterns as all-purpose lighting implements. A 1936 cartoon in *Rural Electrification News* found humor in the notion that someone could simply walk off with the family's primary light source, suggesting that kerosene lanterns' inadequacy at performing multiple lighting tasks at the same time outweighed the advantage of their portability (Figure 14).[52] For REA, having to relocate a nonelectric light source was a form of drudgery, one that could be eliminated by providing constant, evenly distributed electric light using a blend of permanent fixtures, table lamps, and floor lamps.

For many rural people, the even dispersion of high-quality electric light made a significant difference in everyday tasks, as suggested by interviews conducted as part of the Southern Oral History Program in the 1980s. Shirley Collier, whose North Carolina home was electrified in 1945, described how before electricity she and her many siblings would sit huddled around the fireplace to read. After the family installed electric lighting, however, "there was a big, whole room full of light. You could sit anywhere you wanted to. You could see just as well in one place as you could the other. I think it made a lot of difference."[53] Similarly, David Batemen, who was nine years old when his family received electricity in the late 1940s, reported that after using kerosene, "you could put one 60-watt light bulb in the center of the room and it just looked like it lit the whole place up so brightly."[54] The frequency with which interviewees remarked on this striking contrast between the dimmer, localized light of kerosene and the brilliant and enveloping illumination of electricity is understandable, as light bulbs were at least ten times brighter than lanterns.

For others, particularly adults, the upgrade to electric light in the home seemed less pressing. For example, H. E. Daughtry, a school teacher during the Depression, was perfectly content to grade papers at home by the light of a kerosene lantern, as he was young and had good eyesight. However, Daughtry was pleased that the bright, even electric lighting in the school lunchroom seemed to improve the health of his students.[55] Likewise, Mrs. W. D. Elliot declared that she was perfectly content using her three kerosene Aladdin lamps for light but that her young daughters "thought it was magic to stand in the lower hall and turn on the [newly installed electric] light in the upper hall."[56]

Many of the interviewees recalled having just a few electric lights in key places. Shirley Collier's family had one bulb in each of the public rooms of the house, but the only bedroom with electric light was that of her parents.[57] Such sparing use of electric lighting diverged markedly from the fastidiously planned lighting environment REA imagined, which depended heavily on farmers purchasing diverse fixtures and bulbs specially designed for productivity, safety, or creating a pleasant home atmosphere. One typical pamphlet featured forty-eight options, with a range of styles and budgets for the farmyard, house, and outbuildings.[58] Home extension agents from local agricultural schools also promoted task-oriented lighting, often providing on-site consultations to ensure that farm families were using sufficient light for various jobs in the house and on the farm (Figure 15). Trade organizations such as the Illuminating Engineering Society assisted REA in championing specialized lighting, disseminating technical statistics detailing how many foot-candles were needed for various activities and recommending that lights be placed at scientifically determined intervals to ensure illumination tailored to an array of settings and tasks. These guidelines, which were designed to ensure an illuminated interior environment that blended even, general lighting with more focused task lighting for sewing, reading, or dining, reinforced the concept of the farmhouse as part of the larger wiring grid. Though fixtures could be swapped out to modify or upgrade the lighting program, outlets became the fixed interstices that allowed for these modifications (Figure 16).

Lighting recommendations for the farmhouse drew on existing advertising strategies targeted at urban homeowners while emphasizing the special priorities of rural living. In the *Rural Electrification News*, "Illuminating Engineer" Lawrence C. Porter recommended that sixty-watt bulbs with reflectors be placed over the kitchen sink so that the farm wife would not have to work in "her own shadow," as she would using only a single, central bulb for illumination.[59] Similar advice could be found in General Electric's 1934 urbanite-oriented guidebook *The Electric Home,* which suggested a similar light placed over the range and the sink "to eliminate the annoyance of washing dishes in the shade."[60] While *The*

Figure 14. "Born Thirty Years Too Soon," cartoon by J. R. Williams, 1936. *Rural Electrification News* 1, no. 12 (July 1936): 24.

Figure 15. Using a light meter to measure adequate light for reading from Bureaus of Agricultural Chemistry and Engineering and Home Economics, *Electric Light for the Farmstead* (Washington, D.C.: U.S. Government Printing Office, 1940), 10. The original caption read: "This light meter for checking illumination in footcandles is placed in the location of the work for which the light is being tested. The lamp shown has a 10-inch diffusing bowl and uses a 100-200-300-watt, 3-way bulb. It provides adequate light for reading, writing, ordinary sewing on light cloth, and other tasks requiring close vision. If walls and ceilings are light in color, it also provides considerable general illumination."

Electric Home devoted the bulk of its sixty-page chapter on home lighting to style, atmosphere, and decorative effects, these aspects played a decidedly secondary role in farm literature. Even though rural reformers advocated the adoption of urbanizing features in the farmhouse, there was a simultaneous and perhaps contradictory recognition that (sub)urban and farm dwellings functioned differently.

David Weaver, a rural housing advocate in North Carolina and onetime REA employee, concisely summarized the divergences between urban and rural homes, maintaining that the farmhouse must not only serve the basic function of shelter but also act as "the center of business for the farm" while taking on "some of the aspects of a factory or processing plant." And compared with urban settings, which offered a variety of options outside the home for nighttime recreation, in rural areas the farmhouse functioned as the farm family's primary site for leisure and recreation.[61] These unique functional requirements had particular ramifications for certain spaces in the house—for example, in the kitchen, where "raw foods . . . are converted into edible products or preserved for future consumption," and in the living room, where due to the amount of time spent there, "every factor having to do with good lighting and comfort should be incorporated."[62]

Writing in 1940, Weaver proposed the farmhouse as a space that mingled productive tasks and leisure but where work and recreation were increasingly segregated into distinct spaces. This distinction between spaces, facilitated and reinforced by a new, specialized program of lighting, presaged the eventual shift toward the domestic, consumption-oriented farmhouse of the 1950s and 1960s.[63] In 1938 REA collaborated with lighting manufacturers to produce three variously priced sets, each of nine fixtures associated with six different rooms in the house (Figure 17).[64] Though the ornateness of the fixtures varied among the three sets, the shape and function of the globular porch lights, pendant dining room lights, and ceiling-mounted kitchen lights remained constant. The price differential between the cheapest and most expensive set was only two dollars, signaling a belief that farmers neither needed nor desired the elaborate, atmospheric lighting environments advertised to urban audiences.

When rural people adopted new lighting programs, whether by buying a complete lighting set from REA or by purchasing lights from multiple dealers over a period of time, the fixtures entered preexisting homes and farms that had previously been shaped by other technologies and associated practices. For example, Lena Boyce, another Southern Oral History interviewee, had maintained a level of cleanliness in her kitchen that she found perfectly acceptable in indirect sunlight or by kerosene lamp. When electricity arrived, however, she was horrified to discover that her kitchen walls "looked so dirty."[65] REA recognized that electric light would impact other material aspects of the rural home and through print publications and architectural examples attempted to preempt and shape the aesthetic and design choices farm families made in the wake of electric light.

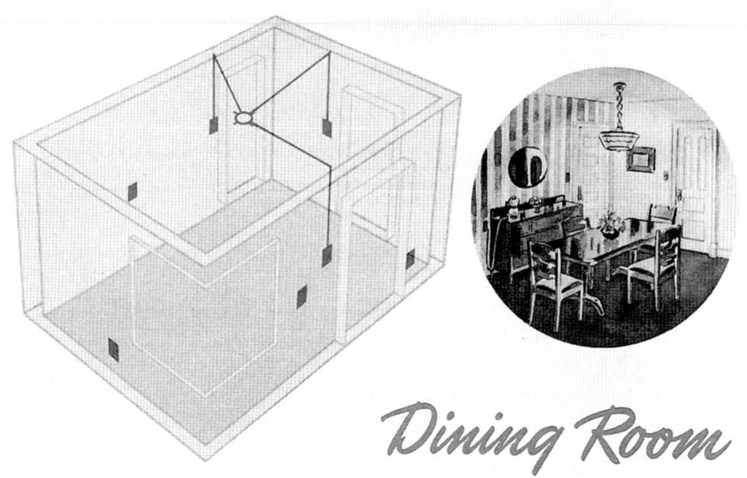

Figure 16. Dining Room schematic from *Planning Your Farmstead Wiring and Lighting,* Rural Electrification Administration, 1946. National Archives and Records Administration, Records of the Rural Electrification Administration, Record Group 221, Box 7, Folder "Motion Pictures REA Coop—Prac. Approach to Policy Making, Planning Your Farmstead Wiring and Lighting," National Archives Identifier 1938128, HMS ID A1 93A.

Architectural Changes to the Modern Farm

While the representation, marketing, and sale of electric lighting programs to rural consumers encouraged a new way of planning, one that emphasized the spatial importance of the orthogonal grid, the material changes that REA envisioned accompanying this shift were often relatively superficial, geared more toward basic interior renovations than significant structural changes. Urban lighting promoters had long extolled electrical illumination as the key to transforming the interior environment, culminating in the Light for Living and Live Better Electrically campaigns of the 1950s.[66] For rural audiences, lighting was shown to both heighten farm productivity and encourage the renovation and redecoration of the farmhouse. While most farmers did not tear down buildings and start over to accommodate electricity, the process of electric retrofitting often led to tangible and significant material changes to the farmhouse and outbuildings. Historian Ronald Tobey has argued in relation to urban electrification that "electrical modernization usually required rewiring dwellings, reconfiguring rooms . . . changing the architectural arrangement of living and working in the house. Electrical modernization . . . led to the whole renovation of the home to bring the quality of living in it up to the electrical standard."[67] In the agrarian context, the goal of achieving such an "electrical standard" was subsumed into preexisting concerns over rural housing.

The 1940 U.S. Housing Census revealed that rural dwellings were, on the whole, much older than urban residences and that a majority were badly in need of significant repairs.[68] Rural reformers hoped that lighting could spur necessary refurbishments to the farmhouse beyond those merely connected to electricity. As General Electric home lighting specialist Helen McKinlay noted, "The psychological effect [of electric lighting] is evident on every hand—homes boasting of recent paint, rooms freshly papered, windows brightly curtained, or repairs given attention that have long been overlooked."[69] Such changes were not only noted but encouraged. A 1941 lighting guide implored farm families to paint walls with flat-finish, light-colored paint to promote an even diffusion of reflected light.[70]

The interior changes that accompanied electric light often mirrored other cultural transformations that long had been promoted by government agricultural organizations. These included professionalizing the occupations of the farmer and farm wife and embracing middle-class urban standards of taste, cleanliness, and decor. Agricultural agents during the late interwar period urged farmers to maintain meticulous records of crop production, feed allocation, and fertilizer distribution. Fittingly, the cover of the 1940 booklet *Electric Light for the Farmstead,* by the Bureaus of Agricultural Chemistry and Engineering and Home Economics, showed a farmer assiduously maintaining his records under the glow of a "table study and reading lamp" giving "semi-indirect light . . . for reading, writing, studying, or drawing."[71]

In the frequent images of nighttime recreation on the farm that appear in wiring and lighting guides, family members are nearly always shown reading under electric lights or listening to the radio, suggesting that the members of the farm family had been transformed into consumers of mainstream modern media. They imply

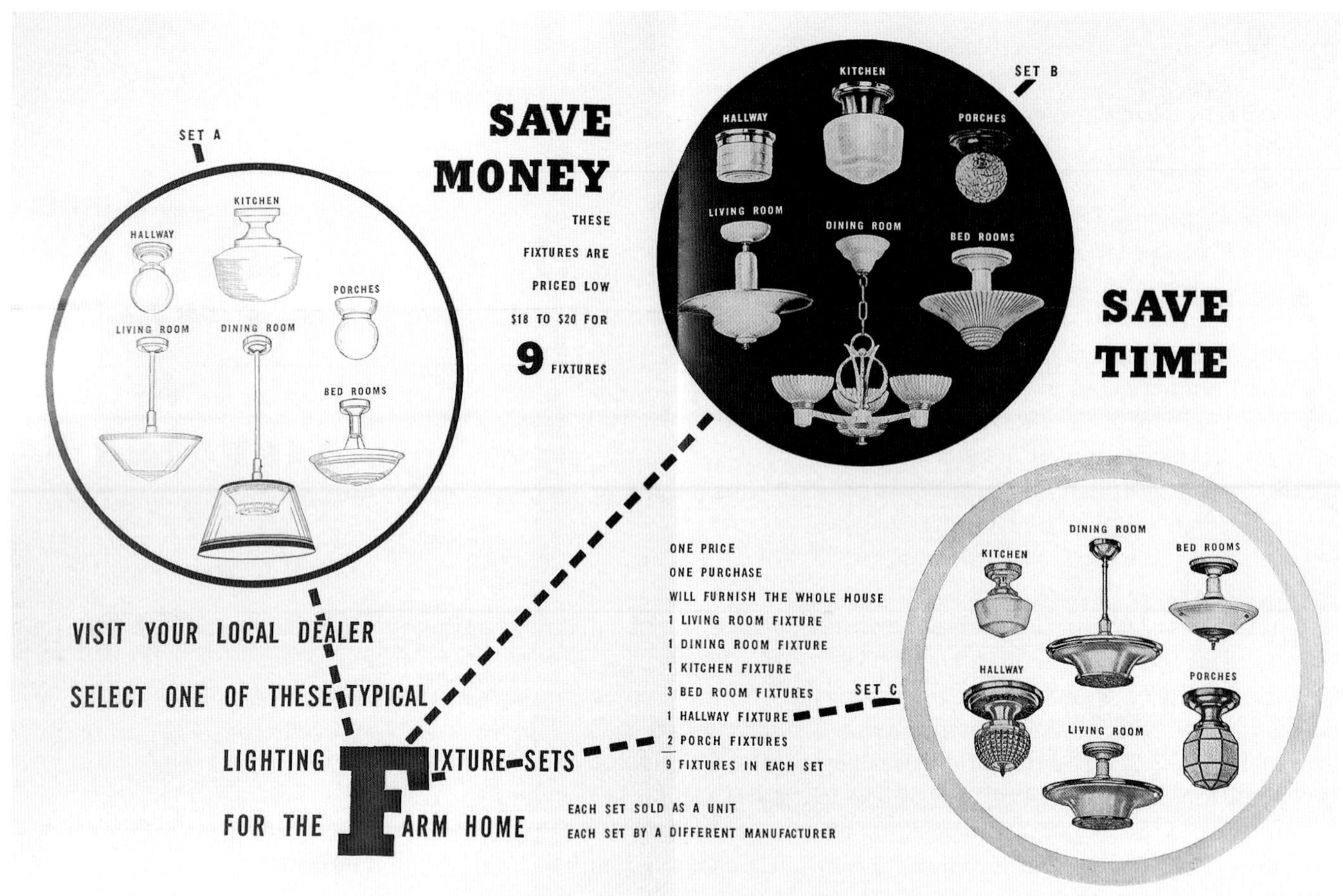

Figure 17. Fixture sets from *Ask to See the Low Cost Lighting Fixture Sets for the Farm Home*, Rural Electrification Administration, U.S. Government Printing Office, 1938. National Archives and Records Administration, Records of the Rural Electrification Administration, Record Group 221, Box 2, Folder "Adm. Repts. 1947—Bldg. Elec. Equip. for the Farm, Ask to See," National Archives Identifier 1938128, HMS ID A1 93A.

that by listening to radio broadcasts and reading print publications, farm families could assimilate into a national mass culture, dismantling the cultural rifts that had previously divided city and country.[72] Significantly, the literature these images depicted farm folks reading, such as the newsletter published by the local REA electrical cooperative, was often related to electricity (Figure 18). In this way, lighting became a critical element for accessing further information about electricity in the print media. Though materials aimed at urban audiences similarly expounded the "relationship between light and sight," pushing adequate, high-quality light to reduce eyestrain and protect eyesight, media aimed at farm people spoke to the expanded array of productive and recreational activities that electric light could aid on the farm.

The cultural changes facilitated by electric light frequently reinforced the gendered distribution of work. Experts enjoined farm women to bring the values of scientific efficiency and electrical modernization into the home, particularly the kitchen. In a 1941 guide contrasting poorly planned lighting with a better alternative, the farm wife in the "before" panel had to suffice with a lone bulb hung from the ceiling by an exposed wire. The process of installing new lighting, the "after" picture reveals, also provided an opportunity to redo the hazardous wiring of the electric iron. Perhaps even more striking, the space depicted is entirely new—the focus is on the other modernizing changes, such as the farm wife's clothing, the cabinetry, and the electric stove, rather than the lighting and wiring, which recede to the background (Figure 19).[73] As one official of the U.S. Public Health Service wrote in the *Rural Electrification News*, "Proper lighting . . . is no solemn pronunciamento of aesthetics or architecture. It is a fact, a fact that insists upon being built into a modern home, like pantry shelves or ample closets."[74]

For REA the modernity of electric lighting was related more to function than to architectural style, as exemplified by the agency's one venture into designing domestic architecture. In late 1938 REA hired Roland Wank, lead architect of the Tennessee Valley Authority, as an architectural consultant. In addition to designing the generating plant at Keystone Heights, Florida, one of Wank's first projects was revising the design of a pair of identical houses for the operators of two REA-financed power plants in Iowa. Like lighthouse keepers, the plant operators were to be always nearby and on call; an alarm system would be wired into their houses, and the operators would be alerted in the case of any system malfunction. Additionally, the houses would serve as models for the ideal electrified home. Equipped with all the latest electrical devices, these dwellings would be suitable for entertaining members of REA cooperatives.[75]

In March 1939 the engineering firm Young & Stanley, Inc., which had been originally hired to design the two Iowa generating facilities, provided REA and Wank with preliminary sketches for these dwellings. The approximately 950-square-foot design, which had received the approval of the local electric cooperative board, was two stories in height, with three bedrooms and an attached single-car garage (Figure 20). The simple, flat-roofed structure featured large windows with horizontal mullions that rounded the corners of the house. The exterior was to be concrete block; the interior would be finished with clay tiles.[76] Early in the design process, one REA engineer had suggested that the houses be of a "suitable appearance to harmonize satisfactorily with the plant building."[77] Young & Stanley's plan abided by this suggestion, using concrete construction and a slab concrete foundation that resembled those used at the two Iowa generating plants—a structural move that brought the power plant aesthetic into the home in a very literal way (Figure 21).

Wank returned the drawings with a number of surprising suggestions pertaining to the layout, structure, and appearance of the houses. A staunch proponent of REA power plants and cooperative headquarters that explicitly reflected the modernity of electricity through the use of modern materials and forms, Wank discouraged the adoption of similar idioms in the case of the operators' houses. In order to economize, Wank suggested the engineers employ simplified wood frame construction and a pitched roof, noting, "A design can be thoroughly modern without necessarily using a flat roof."[78] Wank also encouraged the engineers to maximize and properly arrange the storage spaces on the first and second floors, "in view of the possibility that members' wives might be conducted through the service portions of the house."[79] Although drawings of Wank's revised plan have not survived, the written specifications for the houses called for standard balloon frame construction with sloping, galvanized roofs.[80] Instead of placing the emphasis on an outwardly modern appearance, Wank's

Figure 18. Woman reading the newsletter of a local REA cooperative, circa 1940. National Archives and Records Administration, U.S. Department of Agriculture, Photographs of the Rural Electrification Administration, Folder "Wiring and Lighting: Lamps," Negative no. 11,698, National Archives Identifier 512795, HMS ID 16-G.

Poor kitchen arrangement. No outlets for appliances.

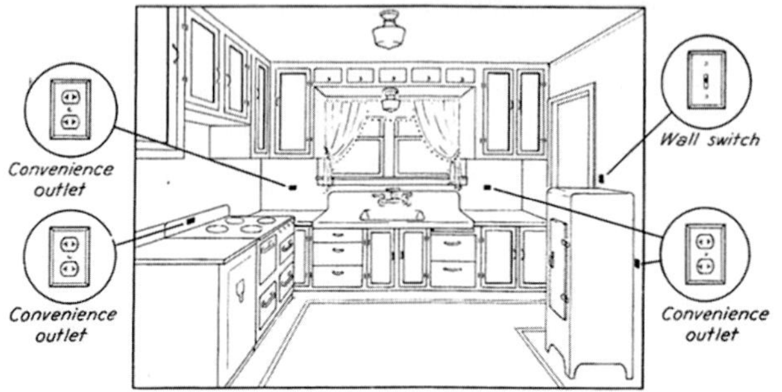

Good kitchen arrangement. See diagram above for location of outlets.

Figure 19. Kitchen arrangements before and after planning for electric lighting in W. J. R. Browder and Lillian L. Keller, *Planning for Electricity on Tennessee Farms* (Knoxville: Agricultural Extension Service, University of Tennessee, 1940), 13.

specifications paid much greater attention to the electric wiring hidden inside the houses' walls. As model all-electric houses built from the ground up, they would each feature an electric doorbell, three-way switches for the hall and garage, and a total of thirty convenience outlets, including two weatherproof ones for the porch. All spaces in the houses, including closets and bathrooms, would possess entry outlets for ceiling or bracket light fixtures.[81]

Wank began with the amenities needed in a "modern home of moderate standards" and worked the design from there, focusing less on an overall vision than on the provision of the correct light and storage for each distinct space in the homes.[82] Interestingly, the architectural specifications for the houses indicated that light fixtures and electric appliances would not be included with the structures. Instead, Wank listed the possible equipment that the operators' families might choose to install, including an "electric range, refrigerator, washing machine," and "ironer."[83] The enumeration of distinct required spaces and the specialized lighting and appliances necessitated by each mirrored the method of planning ahead that REA advocated for its rural clients. By envisioning the houses as parts of an electrical grid into which escalating tiers of other electrical devices might be plugged, the operators' houses served as models for load-building, grounded in technological functionality and the spatialized potential for modernization.

Though REA planned to include operators' houses with many of its generating plants, wartime materials restrictions and lack of funding largely curtailed the program. Archival evidence suggests that in addition to the two houses constructed in Iowa, only four more were erected at the Tri-State Power Cooperative plant near Genoa, Wisconsin.[84] REA's attempt to architecturally manifest the fully electrified and well-lit rural home thus reached only a small population of nearby farmers and cooperative members. Print materials were—and would remain in the postwar period—the more effective way of communicating electricity's promise for the rural home to a mass audience.

Planning for a Postwar World

From the mid-1930s through the late 1940s, REA, along with corporate partners and other farm-related government agencies, including the U.S. Department of Agriculture, extension services, and the Tennessee Valley Authority, nurtured incipient rural enthusiasm for electric light.[85] Through pamphlets, wiring guides, magazine advertisements, and even REA's own nascent architecture program, farm families were exposed to the latest fixtures and most

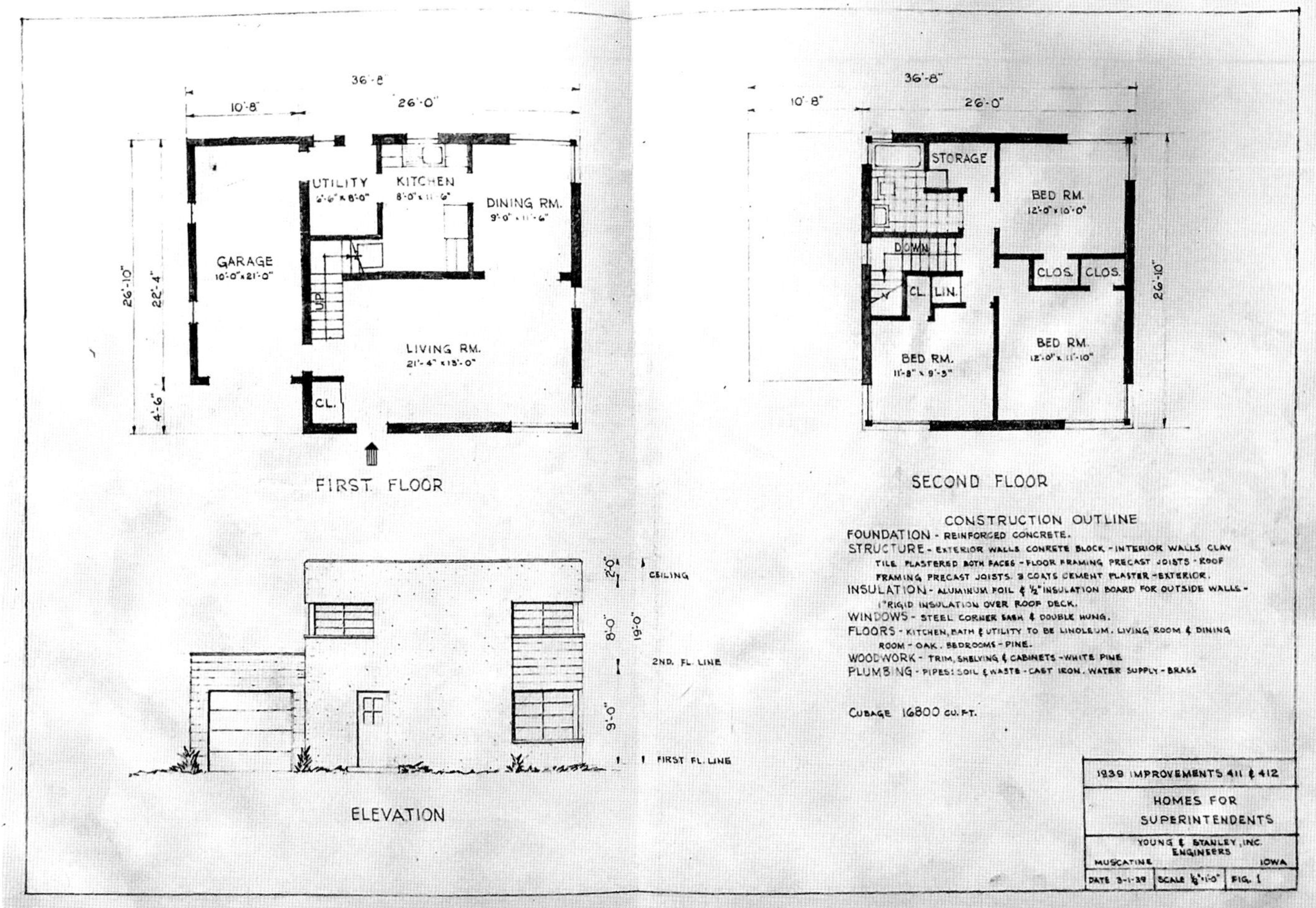

Figure 20. Young and Stanley, Inc., Engineers, "1939 Improvements 411 & 412, Homes for Superintendents." Office of Economic & Community Development, Regional Studies Dept. General Correspondence 1940–1948, Box 95, 8558 R 21 County Power Building, Record Group 142 Records of the Tennessee Valley Authority at the National Archives at Atlanta, Morrow, Georgia.

cutting-edge advances in lighting design. From the struggles of the Depression years to the prosperous immediate postwar period, these materials capitalized on rural desires for electrical light, showing the adoption of light as a stepping stone to other electric appliances and machinery on the farm. By situating electric lighting as part of an "all-electric" lifestyle, light was co-opted into the rhetoric of an industrialized farming system that required substantial capital to invest in an array of modern technologies.[86]

Lighting was part of the initial electric retrofitting process, since the installation of outdoor yard lights and indoor ceiling fixtures and wall sconces often accompanied the wiring process. Though REA hoped that the installation of good lighting would segue into the purchase of many other electrified devices, the agency recognized that these procurements would be necessarily gradual. A proper wiring job at the outset eased the acquisition of further electrified devices by providing numerous convenience outlets to power future purchases. Additionally, by showing electric lights on the farm not as a series of isolated, random fixtures bought in succession but as a well-planned and harmonized lighting program, electrification promoters encouraged the spread of rational planning techniques and the use of highly specialized electrified equipment beyond illumination.

In planning for this program of electric wiring and lighting, REA asked farmers to imagine the farm as an orthogonal, modular space that would anticipate the total electrical modernization of the farmstead. The spatial logic of rural electrification reified and confirmed already established understandings of the American rural landscape as a grid marked by the right-angled layouts of rural townships and the ubiquitous construction of balloon-frame houses.[87] This

Figure 21. REA Power Plant in Hampton, Iowa (now REA Power Plant Museum of the Franklin County Historical Society), 1939. Photograph by Sarah Rovang, June 10, 2011.

logic was not necessarily architectural or structural but instead conceptual, shaping how the imagined space of the electrified rural landscape was presented to farmers during the late 1930s and 1940s. Notably, this time period bridges World War II, suggesting a continuity rather than a harsh break in the modernizing, industrializing changes to the farm; wartime mobilization accelerated processes that had already been set in motion by the late–New Deal period.

In this new spatial system, which encompassed the house, the yard, and farm outbuildings, each distinct space possessed the potential to use electricity to save labor and increase quality of life. While in some ways the farmhouse was viewed as continuous with the rest of the farm in terms of its subjugation to the grid, electricity paradoxically enabled the mental distancing of the farmhouse from the rest of the farm in terms of expected functionality and aesthetics. Indeed, the increasing number of specialized rooms featured in lighting and wiring guides anticipated the recommendations of postwar farmhouse remodeling literature. The USDA's 1947 booklet *Your Farmhouse . . . How to Plan Remodeling,* for example, documented the Hubbard family's process of adding closets, a designated office, an entryway, a workroom, and an indoor bathroom to their preexisting farmhouse. Electricity was a critical part of the plan: "Fortunate is the home owner whose house has a good wiring plan and plenty of outlets for electrical equipment. All through the planning for remodeling, the Hubbards kept this point in mind."[88]

It is ironic that family farms such as the Hubbards' diminished significantly during the 1950s and 1960s as the Green Revolution expedited farm consolidation and factory farming practices, thanks largely to the continued modernizing advances touted by REA and related agencies. Though REA could hardly have foreseen the apotheosis of industrial agriculture, the consumer-oriented materials produced in its first years are nevertheless important and undervalued artifacts of a time when putting a light on every farm did seem "to put a light in every heart." For a fleeting moment, the specialization, rational planning, and efficiency promised in the glimmer of electric light seemed to spell salvation for the family farm and continued solvency for agrarian America.

AUTHOR BIOGRAPHY

Sarah Rovang received her PhD from Brown University in 2016 in the history of art and architecture. Her dissertation, "Modernization and Architecture under the Rural Electrification Administration, 1935–1945," addresses the relationship between technology, agrarian life, and architecture during the late–New Deal period and World War II.

NOTES

1. Photograph of Kerosene Lantern Tombstone at Pennsylvania Rural Electrification Administration celebration, May 3, 1941, National Archives and Records Administration, Photographs of the Rural Electrification Administration, Folder 6 "Power Use in the Home," Negative no. 6298, National Archives Identifier 540048, HMS-ID 221-P.

2. *Graphic Summary of the REA Program,* Rural Electrification Administration, 1951, Correspondence, 1946–1953, Record Group 221, Records of the Rural Electrification Administration, Applications and Loans Division, U.S. Department of Agriculture, National Archives Identifier 1872281, HMS ID A1 45, figure 23; and "Rural Electrification in Various Countries,"

Rural Electrification News 1, no. 8 (April 1936): 7. This statistic includes farms receiving power from public and private utilities as well as through the few electric cooperatives that existed prior to the founding of REA. In comparison, contemporary rates in some western European countries such as France, Germany, and Holland topped 90 percent.

3. Louisan Mamer, "Electricity Pays Its Way," Rural Electrification Administration memo, March 11, 1952, Correspondence, 1937–1953, Record Group 221, Records of the Rural Electrification Administration, Engineering Division, U.S. Department of Agriculture, National Archives Identifier 1919487, HMS ID A1 55A, 10.

4. In 1937 the agency established a program that made additional loans to cooperatives to help individual farms afford wiring, lighting, and plumbing. These loans would finance the necessary materials and pay for a wiring contractor to install lights and wiring according to preapproved REA plans. See "First Steps in Load Building," Rural Electrification Administration, 1937, Office Files of Harlow S. Person, 1936–1953, Records of the Rural Electrification Administration, Record Group 221, National Archives Identifier 1872021, HMS ID A1 34, n.p.

5. Harry Slattery and Jack Levin, "Rural Electrification for the Millions," unpublished manuscript, circa 1941, Judson King Papers, Library of Congress Manuscripts and Archives Division, 86.

6. Jane Adams, *The Transformation of Rural Life: Southern Illinois, 1890–1990* (Chapel Hill: University of North Carolina Press, 1994), 210–11.

7. Adams, *The Transformation of Rural Life,* 213.

8. Ronald R. Kline, *Consumers in the Country: Technology and Social Change in Rural America* (Baltimore, Md.: Johns Hopkins University Press, 2000), 30–41.

9. *Wiring Your Farm and Home,* Rural Electrification Administration, 1939, News Releases, Bulletins, and Other Records, 1935–1953, Records of the Rural Electrification Administration, Record Group 221, National Archives Identifier 1938128, HMS ID A1 93A.

10. Writing for *Rural Electrification News,* an illuminating engineer from General Electric exclaimed, "How often we see a bedroom with a single lamp in the center of the ceiling!" Lawrence C. Porter, "Good Lighting Inside and Outside the Farmhouse," *Rural Electrification News* 3, no. 1 (September 1937): 4.

11. *Get the Best from the Start: Good Lighting Need Not Be Expensive but It Must Be Planned,* Rural Electrification Administration, U.S. Government Printing Office, 1941, News Releases, Bulletins, Reports, and Other Records, 1935–1953, Record Group 221, Records of the Rural Electrification Administration, U.S. Department of Agriculture, National Archives Identifier 1938128, HMS ID A1 93A.

12. Deborah Fitzgerald, *Every Farm a Factory: The Industrial Ideal in American Agriculture* (New Haven, Conn.: Yale University Press, 2003), 8.

13. Fitzgerald, *Every Farm a Factory,* 22–23.

14. Andrew M. Shanken, *194X: Architecture, Planning, and Consumer Culture on the American Home Front* (Minneapolis: University of Minnesota Press, 2009), 2.

15. "Power Makes More Power for National Defense," *Rural Electrification News* 6, no. 3 (November 1940): 3–7.

16. REA discouraged farmers from using alternative sources of energy for cooking and heating, contending it was more efficient to use electricity exclusively rather than the liquid petroleum gas or other fossil fuels that many farmers favored during this period. See file "Farm Consumption of Liquified Petroleum Gas," Correspondence 1946–1953, Record Group 221, Records of the Rural Electrification Administration, U.S. Department of Agriculture, National Archives Identifier 1872281, HMS ID A1 45.

17. For more on REA's lending history, see D. Clayton Brown, *Electricity for Rural America: The Fight for the REA* (Westport, Conn.: Greenwood Press, 1980).

18. *A Guide for Members of REA Cooperatives,* Rural Electrification Administration, U.S. Government Printing Office, 1939, News Releases, Bulletins, Reports, and Other Records, 1935–1953, Record Group 221, Records of the Rural Electrification Administration, U.S. Department of Agriculture, National Archives Identifier 1938128, HMS ID A1 93A.

19. Delbert Clark, "New York Times Reviews REA Program," *Rural Electrification News* 5, no. 9 (June 1940): 19.

20. "REA Co-Op Dedicates New Generating Plant and Office of Exceptional Design," *Rural Electrification News* 5, no. 3 (November 1939): 8–9. By 1944 REA had constructed over fifty generating facilities nationwide. See Guy W. Thaxton, "REA Projects Which Have Constructed and Acquired Generating Plants,"

internal REA memo, April 25, 1944, Office Files of Harry Slattery, 1939–1944, Record Group 221, Records of the Rural Electrification Administration, U.S. Department of Agriculture, National Archives Identifier 1818425, HMS ID A1 18.

21. Progress Bulletin, Florida 14 Clay, February 8, 1940, Project Case Files and Office Files of Harry Slattery, 1939–1945, Record Group 221, Records of the Rural Electrification Administration, U.S. Department of Agriculture, National Archives Identifier 1817936, HMS ID A1 8.

22. Charles Wetherell, "Political Paths to Electrical Modernization" in *Technology as Freedom: The New Deal and the Electrical Modernization of the American Home,* ed. Ronald C. Tobey (Berkeley: University of California Press, 1996), 166.

23. "How Power Serves Farmers on 46 REA Projects," *Rural Electrification News* 3, no. 11 (July 1938): 3–4.

24. "More Appliance Buying," *Rural Electrification News* 4, no. 5 (January 1939): 10–11.

25. Rural Electrification Administration, *1938 Report of Rural Electrification Administration* (Washington, D.C.: U.S. Government Printing Office, 1939), 14.

26. *First Steps in Load Building,* Rural Electrification Administration, 1937, Office Files of Harlow S. Person, 1936–1953, Record Group 221, Records of the Rural Electrification Administration, U.S. Department of Agriculture, National Archives Identifier 1872021, HMS ID A1 34, n.p.

27. Gregory B. Field, "'Electricity for All': The Electric Home and Farm Authority and the Politics of Mass Consumption, 1932–1935," *Business History Review* 64, no. 1 (April 1, 1990): 51. However, not all of these products were commercially successful. As Field's article describes, General Electric's chest refrigerator, with its top-opening design, turned out to be a significant hassle for farm families.

28. *Planning Your Farmstead Wiring and Lighting,* Rural Electrification Administration, Misc. Publication no. 597, 1946, News Releases, Bulletins, Reports, and Other Records, 1935–1953, Record Group 221, Records of the Rural Electrification Administration, U.S. Department of Agriculture, National Archives Identifier 1938128, HMS ID A1 93A, 21.

29. See C. J. Hurd, "The Cooperative Approach to Rural Electrification Education and Research," *Rural Electrification News* 5, no. 9 (May 1940): 5–8.

30. "Dollars in Your Pocket: Adequate Wiring—Now Saves Dollars, Time, Labor—Later," *Rural Electrification News* 2, no. 12 (August 1937): 8.

31. In concert with the Electric Home and Farm Authority (EFHA), REA hoped to promote credit buying plans to farming populations by adding installment payments for items such as refrigerators to monthly electric bills. See Field, "'Electricity for All,'" 32–60.

32. "More Appliance Buying," 11.

33. *Graphic Summary of the REA Program,* fig. 10.

34. Brown, *Electricity for Rural America,* 70. This financing scheme was called the "Arkansas Plan" and offered wiring at the rate of ten dollars for a two-room house. Participants could also buy an iron for three dollars and a radio for seven.

35. Kline, *Consumers in the Country,* 197–98.

36. Slattery and Levin, "Rural Electrification for the Millions," 9.

37. "Area Electrification," *Rural Electrification News* 2, no. 5 (January 1937): 10–11.

38. David E. Nye, *America as Second Creation: Technology and Narratives of New Beginnings* (Cambridge, Mass.: MIT Press, 2003), 26.

39. General Electric Company, *Farm Lighting,* ed. W. C. Brown, bulletin 53 (Cleveland, Ohio: National Lamp Works of General Electric Co, 1927), 4.

40. General Electric Company, *Farm Wiring Handbook: A Guide for Planning Electrical Wiring on Farms* (Bridgeport, Conn., 1940), 4.

41. Wartime planning and militarization during the buildup to World War II were undoubtedly partially responsible for this newly regimented approach to rural space, though USDA and other agencies had urged the efficient layout of farms in prior decades as part of an overarching drive to accelerate food production. See David B. Danbom, *The Resisted Revolution: Urban America and the Industrialization of Agriculture, 1900–1930* (Ames: Iowa State University Press, 1979); and Fitzgerald, *Every Farm a Factory.*

42. General Electric, *GE Farm Wiring Guide,* 1945, Correspondence, 1946–1953, Record Group 221, Records of the Rural Electrification Administration, Applications and Loans Division, U.S. Department of Agriculture, National Archives Identifier 1872281, HMS ID A1 45.

43. This increased interest in the distinctiveness of rural life might be attributed to what historian William Stott has termed the "documentary impulse," a

national tendency during the New Deal to observe, record, and share information about the qualities and characteristics of regions, peoples, and economic conditions in the United States. See William Stott, *Documentary Expression and Thirties America* (New York: Oxford University Press, 1973).

44. Danbom, *The Resisted Revolution*, 62.

45. Roland Marchand, *Creating the Corporate Soul: The Rise of Public Relations and Corporate Imagery in American Big Business* (Berkeley: University of California Press, 1998), 214.

46. George Wallace Kable, *Report on C.W.A. National Survey of Rural Electrification* (Washington, D.C., 1934), 63.

47. "Lighting Fixture Combinations Made Available to REA Projects," *Rural Electrification News* 3, no. 9 (May 1938): 22.

48. I. Thornton Osmond, "The Lighting of Farm Houses," *Bulletin of Pennsylvania State College, Agricultural Experiment Station*, no. 103 (State College: Pennsylvania State College Agricultural Experiment Station, 1910), 3.

49. For more history of the Delco Light Plant, which used a gasoline generator to charge large, wet-cell storage batteries, see D. Clayton Brown, "North Carolina Rural Electrification: Precedent of the REA," *North Carolina Historical Review* 59, no. 2 (April 1982): 109–24.

50. U.S. Department of Agriculture, "Safe Use and Storage of Gasoline and Kerosene on the Farm," *Farmers' Bulletin* 1678 (1945), 3–4. This bulletin warns against placing kerosene lamps near curtains, the edges of tables, cooking stoves, cobwebs, and other combustible material.

51. *Power and the Land*, directed by Joris Ivens for the Rural Electrification Administration (United States: RKO Radio Picture, 1940), 38 min.

52. J. R. Williams, "Born Thirty Years Too Soon," *Rural Electrification News* 1, no. 12 (August 1936): 24.

53. Renate Dahlin, transcript of Southern Oral History Program interview with Shirley Collier (D-0007), June 4, 1984, UNC Center for the Study of the American South, http://dc.lib.unc.edu/cdm/compoundobject/collection/sohp/id/10629/rec/10.

54. As Batemen noted, however, this effect appeared to diminish with time: "It seems like this day with a 60-watt bulb it's not nearly that light." Larry Johnson, transcript of Southern Oral History Program interview with David Batemen (D-0003), circa 1983/84, UNC Center for the Study of the American South, http://dc.lib.unc.edu/cdm/compoundobject/collection/sohp/id/10623/rec/2.

55. Larry Johnson, transcript of Southern Oral History Program interview with H. E. Daughtry (D-0011), circa 1983/84, UNC Center for the Study of the American South, http://dc.lib.unc.edu/cdm/compoundobject/collection/sohp/id/10659/rec/1.

56. Larry Johnson, transcript of Southern Oral History Program interview with Mrs. W. D. Elliott (D-0015), circa 1983/84, UNC Center for the Study of the American South, http://dc.lib.unc.edu/cdm/compoundobject/collection/sohp/id/10647/rec/2.

57. Renate Dahlin, transcript of Southern Oral History Program interview with Shirley Collier (D-0007), June 4, 1984.

58. *Lighting Equipment for the Farm and Farm Home*, Rural Electrification Administration, 1938, News Releases, Bulletins, Reports, and Other Records, 1935–1953, Record Group 221, Records of the Rural Electrification Administration, U.S. Department of Agriculture, National Archives Identifier 1938128, HMS ID A1 93A.

59. Porter, "Good Lighting Inside and Outside the Farmhouse," 3.

60. Edwin Stoddard Lincoln and Paul Smith, *The Electric Home: A Standard Ready Reference Book* (New York: The Electric Home Publishing Company, 1934), 109.

61. David S. Weaver, *Agricultural Engineering and the Rural Housing Problem* (Raleigh, N.C.: Department of Agricultural Engineering, North Carolina State College, 1940), 1.

62. Weaver, *Agricultural Engineering and the Rural Housing Problem*, 2.

63. Adams, *The Transformation of Rural Life*, 213.

64. *Ask to See the Low Cost Lighting Fixture Sets for the Farm Home*, Rural Electrification Administration, U.S. Government Printing Office, 1938, News Releases, Bulletins, Reports, and Other Records, 1935–1953, Record Group 221, Records of the Rural Electrification Administration, U.S. Department of Agriculture, National Archives Identifier 1938128, HMS ID A1 93A.

65. Sue Beal, transcript of Southern Oral History Program interview with Lena Boyce (D-0005), October 16, 1984, UNC Center for the Study of the American

South, http://dc.lib.unc.edu/cdm/compoundobject/collection/sohp/id/10597/rec/2.

66. See Margaret Maile Petty, "Threats and Promises: The Marketing and Promotion of Electric Lighting to Women in the United States, 1880s–1960s," *West 86th* 21, no. 1 (Spring–Summer 2014): 17–18.

67. Tobey, *Technology as Freedom,* 139.

68. In 1940, 33.9 percent of farmhouses needed major repairs; 65.2 percent of these were built before 1920, and an estimated 90 percent of farms possessed at least one structure that needed to be significantly repaired or replaced. See U.S. Census Bureau, "Table 5a. Percent Distribution by Year Built for All Dwelling Units by Occupancy and Tenure, for the United States, by Regions, Urban and Rural, 1940," in "United States Summary: General Characteristics of Housing" from *Sixteenth Census of the United States: 1940* (Washington, D.C., 1940), 13.

69. Helen K. McKinlay, "Good Lighting Systems on Farms Bring Benefits to Entire Family," *Rural Electrification News* 3, no. 5 (November 1938): 7.

70. W. J. R. Browder and Lillian L. Keller, *Planning for Electricity on Tennessee Farms* (Knoxville: Agricultural Extension Service, University of Tennessee, 1940), 10.

71. Bureaus of Agricultural Chemistry and Engineering and Home Economics, *Electric Light for the Farmstead* (Washington, D.C.: U.S. Government Printing Office, 1940), 23.

72. For an analysis of how farm families actually negotiated or resisted this assimilation, see Kline, *Consumers in the Country,* 127.

73. Browder and Keller, *Planning for Electricity on Tennessee Farms,* 13.

74. J. M. Dalla Valle, "Good Light—Good Health," *Rural Electrification News* 4, no. 2 (October 1938): 3–4.

75. Franklin Wood to Administrator John Carmody, October 14, 1938, Iowa 48G Pocahontas Engineering Files, 1939 1938, Record Group 221, Records of the Rural Electrification Administration, U.S. Department of Agriculture, National Archives Identifier 1812914, HMS ID A17.

76. Young and Stanley, Inc., Engineers, "1939 Improvements 411 & 412, Homes for Superintendents," Office of Economic & Community Development, Regional Studies Department General Correspondence, 1940–1948, Records of the Tennessee Valley Authority.

77. Wood to Carmody, October 14, 1938.

78. Roland Wank to W. B. Phillips, April 18, 1939, Office of Economic & Community Development, Regional Studies Department General Correspondence, 1940–1948, Records of the Tennessee Valley Authority.

79. Wank to Phillips, April 18, 1939.

80. Roland Wank, *Outline Specification for Operator's Residences at Hampton and Pocahontas, Iowa,* Rural Electrification Administration, June 1, 1939, Office of Economic & Community Development, Regional Studies Department General Correspondence, 1940–1948, Records of the Tennessee Valley Authority, 1.

81. Wank, *Outline Specification for Operator's Residences,* 3.

82. Wank to Phillips, April 18, 1939.

83. Wank, *Outline Specification for Operator's Residences,* 3.

84. F. L. Glazier and Roland Wank, *Tri-State Power Cooperative, La Crosse, Wisconsin, Wisconsin R9056G1 Crawford, Proposal, Specifications, and Contract, Operators Cottages,* 1940, Office of Economic & Community Development, Regional Studies Department General Correspondence, 1940–1948, 97S 91 Rural Electrification Administration, Record Group 142, Records of the Tennessee Valley Authority.

85. David E. Nye, *Electrifying America: Social Meanings of a New Technology, 1880–1940* (Cambridge, Mass: MIT Press, 1990), 318.

86. See Fitzgerald, *Every Farm a Factory,* 8, 17.

87. For more on the modernization of the farm through balloon-frame construction, see Fred W. Peterson, *Homes in the Heartland: Balloon Frame Farmhouses of the Upper Midwest, 1850–1920* (Lawrence: University Press of Kansas, 1992).

88. U.S. Department of Agriculture, *Your Farmhouse . . . How to Plan Remodeling,* Miscellaneous Publication No. 619, 1947, https://archive.org/details/yourfarmhousehow619unit.

NATHANIEL ROBERT WALKER

American Crossroads

General Motors' Midcentury Campaign to Promote Modernist Urban Design in Hometown U.S.A.

ABSTRACT

Norman Bel Geddes's *Futurama* exhibit was a national sensation, but it was only one component of a larger effort by General Motors to promote highway-centric urban design to the citizenry of North America. Historians of architecture and planning have neglected most of this effort, focusing on the important roles of designers and governments in highway creation while downplaying the powerful voices of corporations. GM's engagement with urbanism began in the wake of the 1933–34 Century of Progress Exposition in Chicago when it capitalized on the success of its fair exhibit by launching the Parade of Progress, a roadshow that took visions of America's high-tech future to towns all across the continent. Millions saw this "miniature world's fair on wheels." The subsequent success of the *Futurama* in 1939 reinvigorated the parade, and several schemes were concocted to add the *Futurama* to the roadshow. World War II interrupted these efforts, but victory eventually brought the Parade of Progress back to the highways and byways of America, with renewed emphasis on the importance of urban demolition and highway construction for any community that hoped to enter the promised land of scientific progress. From Palm Beach to Portland, from Pasadena to Providence, the General Motors Parade of Progress spread the "gospel of research," pleading with Americans to plow freeways through the hearts of their old-fashioned towns and embrace the car as a necessity of daily life. The dramatic rise of state support for urban and suburban highways in the mid-1950s suggests the message was heard.

By the 1940s the General Motors Corporation had acquired a popular reputation for visionary urban design. Best remembered today is the company's collaboration with industrial designer Norman Bel Geddes to create the *Futurama,* an enormous mechanized diorama of the United States as it might appear in the not-too-distant future. This spectacular display of miniature landscapes, knit together with broad highways coursing with model automobiles, was the most popular exhibit of the 1939–40 New York World's Fair.[1] It was seen by millions of people and discussed by millions more, and it has been the focus of a number of thoughtful analyses, including Adnan Morshed's recent book *Impossible Heights* and the 2012 traveling exhibition *Norman Bel Geddes Designs America.*[2]

Most studies of General Motors' *Futurama* spotlight its glamorous designer, but there is a great deal to learn by turning to the company that sponsored Bel Geddes's work. The *Futurama* was not GM's first foray into urban design, nor was it the last. Indeed, the *Futurama* was merely one episode—and not even the most widely seen one—in a large-scale, sustained marketing campaign by General Motors to promote highway-centric urban reforms directly to the citizens of North America. The bulk of this campaign consisted of small-scale architecture and urban design exhibits that were taken to cities and towns across the continent in an intimate but nonetheless sensational roadshow entitled the Parade of Progress (Figure 1). This "miniature world's fair on wheels" ran intermittently from 1936 to 1956. It stopped in hundreds of communities in a quest to capture the imaginations of the American people with provocative demonstrations of "scientific" futurity, several of which prescribed both modernist aesthetics and automotive functionality for towns and cities.

At the heart of this campaign was a desire—publically articulated by one of GM's top executives—to remake the North American landscape so that the automobile was elevated to a required necessity of daily life, alongside housing, clothing, and food. It was believed the consumption entailed by nonstop motoring, together with the economic activity generated by the destruction and re-creation of American towns and cities, would contribute to widespread and self-perpetuating prosperity by generating insatiable demand for industrial products, especially cars. This ambition meant that it would never be enough to simply build rural highways connecting cities to one another. American highways would have to be cut through the civic and commercial cores of communities, utterly and permanently transforming them. It was precisely this kind of urban automobile infrastructure the Federal Aid Highway Act of 1956 made possible, and it cannot be a coincidence that, after appealing off and on to the North American buying and voting public for two decades, GM's urban design campaign came to a close immediately after this act was passed.

Historians of architecture have largely neglected the conversation that transpired between General Motors and the North American public, perhaps because no famous architects directed it. Broader studies on midcentury highway design and construction in general have also underemphasized GM's role, instead foregrounding planning professionals and government

Figure 1. Press photograph of the Parade of Progress issued by General Motors, circa 1953. Copyright 2014 General Motors LLC. Used with permission, GM Media Archive (image number POP3 0620).

agencies and their efforts to formulate, promote, finance, and implement highway projects.[3] General Motors was, however, capable of competing with any design professional and even the state for the attention and confidence of the American public, broadcasting its vision for the future form of Main Street with the same continental corporate infrastructure and marketing prowess that had filled the existing Main Street with its automobiles. Consequently, GM's conversation with the American people was of such a breadth and intensity that it is indispensable to understanding mid-twentieth-century popular concepts of urban modernity in America. The core message of General Motors' urban design exhibits was clear: if any community hoped to enter the imminent future of scientific progress and economic prosperity, it would have to be drastically transformed to embrace high-speed motoring. The costs of action in terms of both demolition and construction would be high, but the costs of inaction would be higher still: obsolescence.

To Make People Dissatisfied

In early 1929, when the American economy still seemed sound, the editor of the magazine *Advertising and Selling* praised Charles F. Kettering (1876–1958), the outspoken and charismatic vice president in charge of research for General Motors, for plainly confessing that his principal job was "to make people dissatisfied with what they already have."[4] Less than a year later, the Great Depression began to shake confidence in the virtues of a consumer-driven capitalist economy. Kettering and his fellow GM executives perceived their company was under dire threat, not only from a reduced demand for automobiles but also from an increasing public perception that the mechanization of corporate industry was making workers redundant even as it saturated the market with cheap products.[5] General Motors responded by crafting and disseminating an empowering message of hope: corporations would restore the promise of prosperity broken by the crash, and they would do so by conquering the frontiers of science to create new products that would stimulate consumption and thereby put more Americans back to work.[6]

Central to this proposal for economic redemption through consumption was the replacement of the ideal of product durability with that of planned obsolescence, a concept promoted before the Depression by Alfred P. Sloan (1875–1966), president of General Motors, as "dynamic obsolescence."[7] Whereas old economic common sense dictated that "you must wear out everything you have before you can get anything new," Kettering countered that "any world that tries to run on a wearing-out basis is not a fit place in which to live." Useful or not, products were to be discarded as soon as newer and better products were available, Kettering declared, and until the energizing power of obsolescence was fully embraced by businesses and their accountants, "we will have depressions over and over again, because that's nature's way of clearing a stomach that has been overloaded."[8] General Motors would do its part to avoid such economic indigestion by continually developing new and improved products; meanwhile, the American people would do their part by purchasing them.

The reach of "dynamic obsolescence" extended beyond automobiles to include the towns and landscapes through which they were driven. GM was not alone in prescribing creative destruction as a stimulant for America's cities; indeed, by the 1930s the term "obsolescence" had "become ubiquitous in the fields of real estate, finance, and city planning," condemning even sturdy and unblemished buildings, and sometimes whole neighborhoods, to an early demise as a glad concession to the economic dynamism that would replace them with something new.[9] A broad "cult of the new" had become an increasingly dominant feature of American consumer culture since the close of the nineteenth century, as many manufacturers, merchants, and advertisers deliberately worked to produce "a new consumer consciousness," opening the average American's "imagination and emotion to desire."[10] The key to success in the ruthlessly competitive, high-volume, low-margin world of industrial corporate capitalism was to escape the confines of a limited and quickly sated market by proactively expanding that market, increasing and inflaming people's natural acquisitiveness, not least by perpetually brandishing the prestige and promise of the new.

Kettering had another proposal for the American consumer that, together with "dynamic obsolescence," painted a rosy picture for the future of the automobile industry. In 1932 he and fellow GM engineer Allen Orth published a small book to promote the upcoming 1933–34 Century of Progress Exposition in Chicago. Tellingly entitled *The New Necessity: The Culmination of a Century of Progress in Transportation*, the book opened with a declaration that Americans should see the car not merely as a luxury but rather as "a worthy candidate for a position along side that of food, clothing and shelter as—the new necessity."[11] For the automobile to join the ranks of basic human requirements, adjustments would need to be made in the infrastructure of daily life, especially in cities, where walking and the electric streetcar were still important modes of transport. Kettering and his fellow General Motors executives would soon suggest the required reforms, showing the way forward to universal daily automobile use and, consequently, to total automobile dependence.

GM's message to the American people first coalesced at the company's large pavilion at the Century of Progress (Figure 2). Here, Sloan and Kettering both gave widely publicized speeches promising unending progress through scientific industry, so long as Americans avoided falling behind in the global march of history by becoming "satisfied with a static position."[12] Visitors to the pavilion were welcomed into a large moderne entrance chamber called the Hall of Progress, which featured an exhibition of the company's contributions to the automotive industry. Beyond was a small area dedicated to research containing "startling" novelty displays designed to "thrill" fairgoers: "Imagine playing music on a light beam—or seeing colors in a stone with the help of a violet ray!"[13] These were essentially technological gimmicks conceived by Kettering to identify GM with scientific progress and help restore public confidence in the future of industrial capitalism.[14]

Figure 2. Postcard of Albert Kahn's GM pavilion at the 1933–34 Century of Progress Exposition in Chicago. Collection of Nathaniel Walker.

Most of the pavilion was taken up with the more prosaic display of a real, working automobile assembly line. This was hardly a novel idea; the Ford Motor Company had set up a car assembly line as the centerpiece of its award-winning exhibition at the 1915 Panama–Pacific International Exposition in San Francisco.[15] GM's decision to duplicate this performance in Depression-era Chicago, however, was probably calculated as something more than a mere demonstration of technological wizardry. Instead, it was likely conceived to help bridge the widening gulf between the giant corporation and the disenchanted public. Indeed, the need for large American companies to reconnect with their estranged consumers on a visceral level would soon become a GM mantra.

After the Century of Progress drew to a close in late 1934, Kettering convinced his fellow executives to make the most of their public relations investment by taking GM's narrative of industrial progress and prosperity directly to American communities in the form of a roadshow.[16] The small technological gimmicks in the research zone of the world's fair pavilion would easily be converted into mobile exhibits, and rousing lectures could be delivered in a manner similar to political campaign speeches or the sermons of big tent revivals. Christened the Parade of Progress, Sloan billed the roadshow as a "circus of science" and a "world's fair on wheels" designed "especially for that vast portion of the population living in smaller towns."[17] Newspapers heralded the launching of the parade, paying special attention to the dramatic fleet of thirty-three-foot-long, gleaming, red-and-silver streamlined buses that GM built to carry its message across the nation: "highway leviathans" that were themselves "portents of the future."[18] "Industry," Sloan explained, "because of its very size has seemed to be something apart and remote from the life of the average man . . . [the parade will] bring industry to the people."[19] To facilitate this rapprochement, admission to the Parade of Progress would be free of charge. The company strove to banish even a whiff of commercialism as every opportunity was taken to emphasize this was "not an automobile show!" (Figure 3). GM insisted it was producing a scientific, educational event, and newspaper editors seemed persuaded, announcing the parade offered the nation nothing less than "a heartening look at evidence of its present progress and an inspiring glimpse of the continued advancement which the future holds."[20]

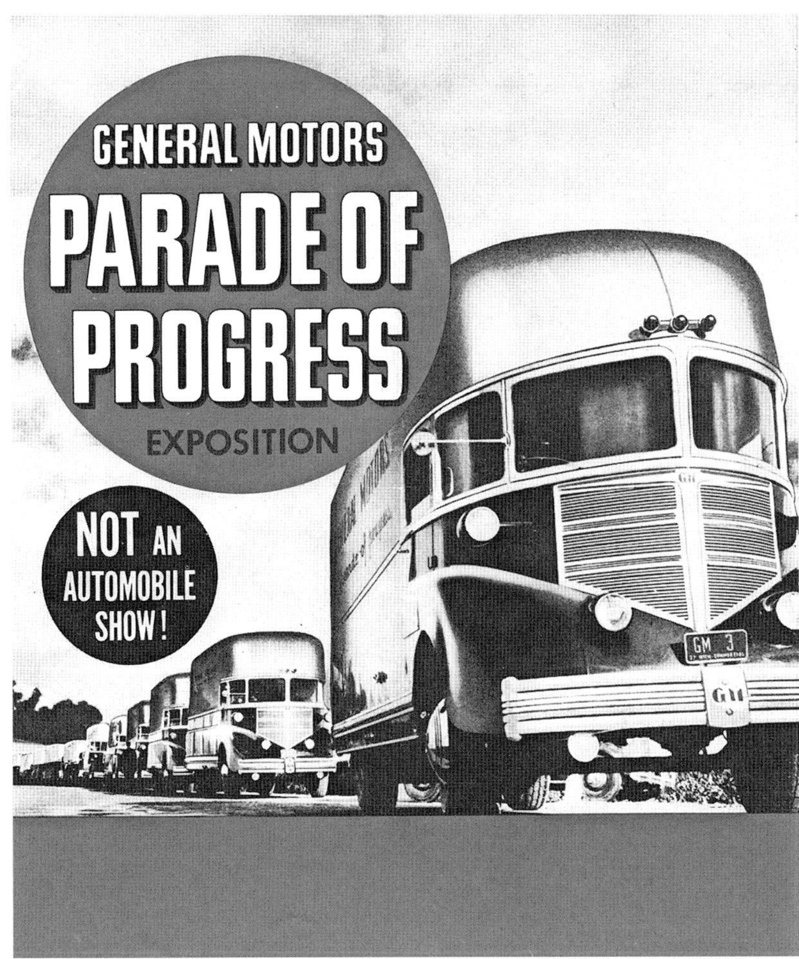

Figure 3. *General Motors Parade of Progress Exposition* promotional brochure, circa 1938. Collection of Nathaniel Walker.

In early 1936 the Parade of Progress, with roughly forty young men on staff, began the journey from Detroit to Florida, where the caravan officially debuted in Miami on February 15. The physical configuration of the show remained consistent for three years; the streamliners and accompanying passenger vehicles were arranged to form a court in front of a large silver tent (Figure 4). This tent, spacious enough for about 1,200 people, hosted lectures on industrial progress as well as displays of technological novelty such as induction cooking and magnetic levitation. Historians Roland Marchand and Michael L. Smith argued these ostensibly scientific performances were in reality very much akin to circus acts or magic shows.[21] Outside the tent the sleek, glistening bodies of the streamliners were opened up and linked together by canvas enclosures to house smaller exhibits for more intimate groups of people. Many of these displays were drawn from the research zone of the Chicago pavilion, but some were newly created for the caravan.

Figure 4. Promotional postcard for the Parade of Progress exhibition, circa 1936. Collection of Nathaniel Walker.

Two of the new displays engaged with domestic architecture and one addressed urban design. A heavy coal-burning stove on which work "was a chore indeed" was contrasted with the "clean and bright and decorative" stainless steel of the electrified, ventilated modern kitchen, where "Science Frees Women from Drudgery."[22] A living room display focused on aesthetics, pitching the art deco streamlining of "a new design for living" against the late-Victorian parlor; the cause of the apparent evolution in furniture design and wall décor was attributed not to a shift in fashion or a rise in affluence but rather to technological and cultural progress: "What has transformed the stuffy, ornate and drab American parlor of a few decades ago into the gracious and simple beauty of today? Industry has joined science with art. Science has found new metals, new fabrics and now colors, and Art has found new ways to use them."[23]

The Parade of Progress's urban design exhibit was primarily dedicated to transportation infrastructure, but aesthetics were also deployed to sharpen its message (Figure 5). Echoing the before-and-after rhetoric of the domestic interior

Figure 5. Contrasting cities of today (*top*) and yesterday (*bottom*) in the *General Motors Parade of Progress Souvenir Edition* promotional brochure, circa 1936. Collection of Nathaniel Walker.

displays, two mechanized cityscape dioramas were presented, one of 1900 and one of 1936. In the city of 1900, buggies and trolleys plodded through the city grid, whereas in 1936 motorcars and streamlined diesel trains flowed on and along an urban freeway at a rapid pace unencumbered by intersections. The appearance of the architecture in each diorama heightened the contrast between old and new; the smaller, wooden-and-brick, ornate mixed-use streetscape of 1900 was pitched against the gleaming high-rise business district of 1936, with many of its simple, streamlined masses broken by horizontal ribbon windows and, in one instance, capped by a rooftop airstrip. This didactic display was understandably described in one newspaper as a comparison not only between old and new modes of travel but also between past and future eras of living—as a presentation of "The City of Yesterday and That of Tomorrow."[24]

After a number of stops in Florida, the parade rolled up the East Coast, following the springtime weather. Then it turned west and traversed the continent coast-to-coast multiple times over the next three years, stopping in well over two hundred towns. When the caravan arrived at a destination, it would usually begin by parading down Main Street, often with a local high school band or drum squad leading the way, before stopping in front of city hall to take a photograph with the mayor and other local dignitaries. These civic events had been coordinated and promoted beforehand by an advance team of GM employees working with local GM dealers, who booked advertising space in the local press and mailed out postcards to drum up interest (Figure 6). After the caravan rolled down Main Street, it typically set up in a high school football field or, occasionally, on the town square. The huge, shining, streamlined "highway leviathans" would have inevitably stood out sharply against backgrounds of leafy bungalow neighborhoods and Depression-era dime stores.

The Parade of Progress was celebrated as "mystifying, exciting, moving" by local newspapers, whose owners and employees were doubtlessly grateful for the advertising revenue GM provided.[25] The *Tuscaloosa News* declared,

Figure 6. Promotional postcard for the Parade of Progress exhibition in Charleston, South Carolina's Marion Square, 1938. Collection of Nathaniel Walker.

"This is a dark hour for the world, but the person who can witness this Parade of Progress and still not have a glow of pride in the ingenuity of man and a renewed faith in what he can accomplish in the years to come . . . is a pessimist without imagination."[26] This was not mere genuflecting; the sheer number of visitors confirms there was true public hunger for the caravan's entertaining and uplifting message. By the time the first Parade of Progress wrapped up at the end of 1939, over eight million Americans had seen it; this represented 37 percent of the population of the towns visited by the show and over 6 percent of all Americans.[27] Additionally, the parade had been to Cuba, Canada, and Mexico, where a phenomenal extended showing in Mexico City had attracted almost half a million people.[28]

In an attempt to consolidate the interest and goodwill of the public, General Motors ran an advertisement in newspapers everywhere the caravan visited a day or two after the show had moved on. "We hope we set a boy to dreaming," it read (Figure 7). The parade director reported back to Detroit that it was "a most effective way of crystallizing the imprint of General Motors on the community."[29] The notion of a boy filled with longing for future progress after witnessing the "miracle" of induction cooking or soaking up the vision of an uninterrupted urban freeway clearly resonated with Kettering's ambition to fill American hearts and minds with an insatiable hunger for new and improved industrial products. The sentimental vision offered by the ad was importantly

Figure 7. "We Hope We Set a Boy to Dreaming," follow-up advertisement for the General Motors Parade of Progress, 1938–39. Copyright 2014 General Motors LLC. Used with permission, GM Media Archive.

OUR Parade of Progress has come and gone.

The big silver trucks have packed up their shows and disappeared over the far horizon.

We enjoyed our stay and your hospitality; we hope that you enjoyed the things we had to show you.

If it gave you a clearer understanding of how General Motors links Science and Industry in the service of human needs, we are grateful.

We hope it accomplished one more thing: that somewhere in your city we have set a young boy to dreaming!

As we see our job, General Motors is not concerned alone with making good cars or fine products for today.

We are even more vitally concerned with preparing better cars for tomorrow and with providing even greater conveniences for future households.

For in so doing—in performing this task faithfully—we believe we are contributing toward a better country and a richer and more satisfactory future for our sons and daughters.

The real hope for continued progress lies in the spirit of individual initiative—in the methods and processes yet to be perfected and the discoveries still to be made.

That's why we hope that among the crowds who visited our exposition there were youngsters who found their imaginations stirred, who caught the glimmerings of a vision, who started in pursuit of that vision by turning to their home chemistry sets, their construction toys, their tool kits and workbenches.

The first purpose of the Parade of Progress is to interest, to enlighten, to entertain.

Through that purpose we hope to make clear the processes through which industry performs its share of the world's work.

But parades must sooner or later all reach their end. Progress is something that can never halt.

That is why we hope that somewhere we set a boy to dreaming—and set him on a road of usefulness and service to himself, his country and his fellow men.

GM GENERAL MOTORS

GENERAL MOTORS

one of active, empowering participation rather than mere passive consumption. The world of tomorrow would be a joint enterprise—the product of corporate research labs whose ideal partners were not board members or stockholders but rather a nation of youthful, heroically dissatisfied, dreaming white males.

Enter the *Futurama*

The next stop for GM's message was the 1939–40 New York World's Fair, where the company built an enormous pavilion for one of the most ambitious industrial expositions the world had ever seen.[30] The theme of the fair was "Building the World of Tomorrow," and it dovetailed perfectly with GM's ongoing efforts to broadcast its prophecy of progress and prosperity. The discourse on urban freeways had evolved in recent years as local governments had proposed and built projects in a handful of cities, including the West Side Elevated Highway and the Henry Hudson Parkway, both in New York. These could only enhance the apparent viability of GM's vision.

The future of urban freeways took center stage in the company's new exhibit. To create it GM utilized the services of famous industrial designer Norman Bel Geddes (1893–1958), who in recent years had emerged as an "authority on future trends."[31] His 1932 book *Horizons* had helped popularize the futuristic streamline moderne style so powerfully manifested in the Parade of Progress buses.[32] In 1936 Bel Geddes had been commissioned to design, build, and photograph a model of a futuristic city of skyscrapers and high-speed motorways for a Shell Motor Oil advertising campaign published in *Life, Collier's,* and the *Saturday Evening Post* (Figure 8). This project played the leading role in securing Bel Geddes the contract to design the GM exhibit in New York.

Although scholars have discussed the city model that Bel Geddes developed for Shell, none have situated it in the context of corporate-sponsored urban highway promotion and the inextricably linked notion of "dynamic obsolescence."[33] Bel Geddes's vision for the future was radical, but it was nonetheless both presented and received as a practical prediction of imminent developments in urban design as they might unfold by 1960. Photographs of the meticulously detailed model used dramatic lighting and the smoke of sulfur bombs to create a compelling sense of atmosphere and depth. The design process was equally detailed, with team members considering everything from automobile breakdowns to snow removal.[34] The degree of difference between the model and the present city of the 1930s was extensively debated—should the future city be an evolution or a revolution? Some staff members pointed out how baroque radial city plans, such as that of Washington, D.C., or Detroit, were efficient movers of street traffic, but Bel Geddes tersely countered, in a gesture toward revolution, "This type of plan is obsolete now."[35] At the same time, Bel Geddes felt ambivalent about the idea of existing cities being penetrated by the biggest roads. Limited-access express boulevards superimposed over old city grids were certainly desirable, but he believed that twelve-lane superhighways should probably be limited to city peripheries.[36] This may seem a minor distinction today, but it would later put a degree of distance between Bel Geddes's work and GM's view of the ideal future city.

While designing the Shell model, Bel Geddes consulted with Miller McClintock (1894–1960), leader of the Harvard Bureau of Street Traffic Research. McClintock had been an advocate of mitigating the dominance of the automobile in city streets until the Studebaker Corporation began funding his research.[37] Quickly evolving into a fervent believer in the importance of high-speed urban motoring, he was so pleased with Bel Geddes's city model that he presented it to the National Planning Conference in Detroit in 1937 and called for its implementation. If Americans hoped to realize "the full benefits of the automotive revolution," McClintock declared, then "the nation must discard its useless street and highway system, designing and rebuilding roadways so that traffic may move swiftly, unimpeded and safely."[38]

Dozens of newspapers across the country covered the Shell model, with a number of them making reference to McClintock's endorsement.[39] A glowing article in *Architectural Forum* cited it as the inspiration for a Harlem redevelopment

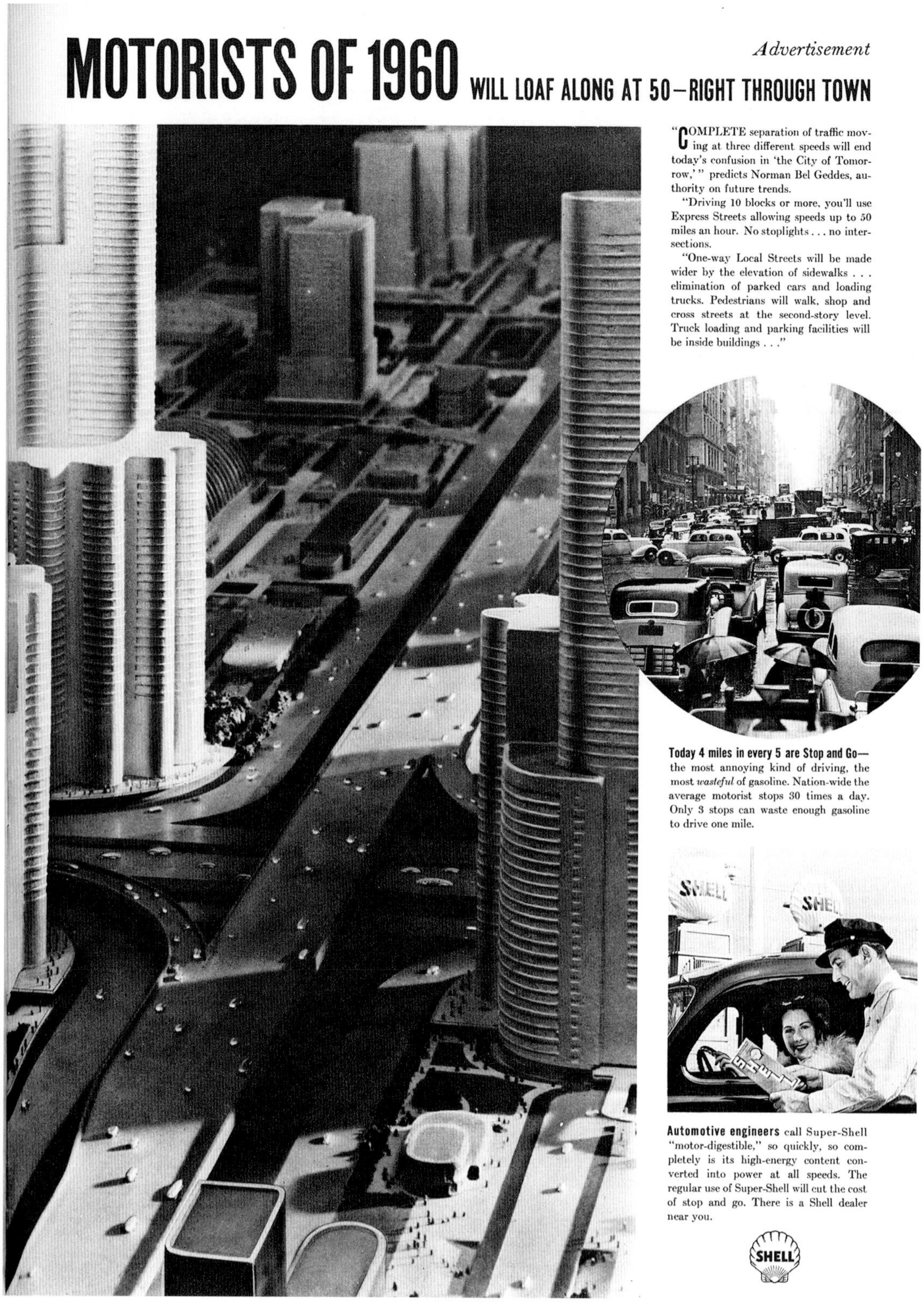
MOTORISTS OF 1960 WILL LOAF ALONG AT 50—RIGHT THROUGH TOWN
Advertisement
"COMPLETE separation of traffic moving at three different speeds will end today's confusion in 'the City of Tomorrow,'" predicts Norman Bel Geddes, authority on future trends.
"Driving 10 blocks or more, you'll use Express Streets allowing speeds up to 50 miles an hour. No stoplights . . . no intersections.
"One-way Local Streets will be made wider by the elevation of sidewalks . . . elimination of parked cars and loading trucks. Pedestrians will walk, shop and cross streets at the second-story level. Truck loading and parking facilities will be inside buildings . . ."
Today 4 miles in every 5 are Stop and Go—the most annoying kind of driving, the most wasteful of gasoline. Nation-wide the average motorist stops 30 times a day. Only 3 stops can waste enough gasoline to drive one mile.
SHELL
Automotive engineers call Super-Shell "motor-digestible," so quickly, so completely is its high-energy content converted into power at all speeds. The regular use of Super-Shell will cut the cost of stop and go. There is a Shell dealer near you.
SHELL

Figure 8. Shell Motor Oil advertisement featuring Norman Bel Geddes's city of tomorrow, *Life Magazine*, October 11, 1937. Collection of Nathaniel Walker.

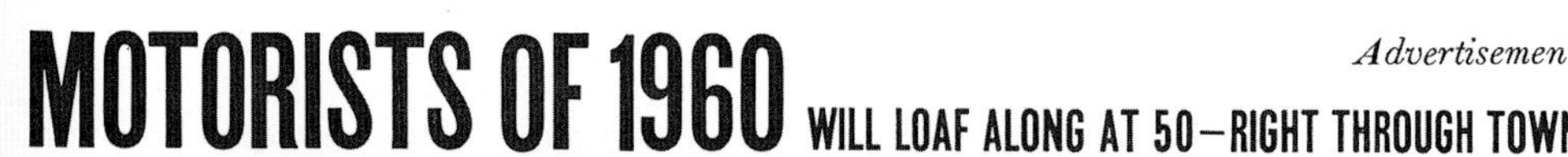

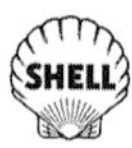

scheme by New York's Uptown Chamber of Commerce, and the *Daily News* asked Bel Geddes to turn his eye to the future of Brooklyn.[40] Robert Moses (1888–1981), New York's famous transportation planner, entered into discussion with Bel Geddes about the vision, sending a few men to take a look at the physical model and stating he wished to see it himself.[41] It is unclear if he ever did, but regardless, the project had clearly attracted serious attention in the world of urban planning as well as in the popular press.

Flush with success, Bel Geddes approached GM with a proposal to develop his urban vision into an enormous diorama for its New York World's Fair pavilion. The company equivocated, and Bel Geddes shopped his idea to other automotive corporations, but eventually GM agreed to the scheme.[42] To enhance the project's legitimacy, Bel Geddes and GM discussed setting up a puppet think tank called Traffic Forecasts to act as the official designer of the diorama. For all its praise from the public, the federal government had ultimately dismissed the Shell model as an advertising gimmick; this disturbed GM's public relations chief, as he was "most of all interested" in Washington's reception.[43] The company ultimately abandoned the idea of a puppet consultant, perhaps because Bel Geddes was by that time sufficiently respected to play the role of disinterested expert, but the proposal speaks to both the seriousness of GM's urban reform ambitions and its wariness of the taint of commercialism, so evident in its marketing for the Parade of Progress.

GM and Bel Geddes made natural partners. The Shell model resonated on many levels with the Parade of Progress city dioramas; both revealed a future in which high-speed, limited-access freeways were plowed through the hearts of cities, transforming "obsolete" downtowns and neighborhoods into shining central business districts. These similarities seem to have been borne out of a common set of design influences. As Morshed explained, Bel Geddes had absorbed Frank Lloyd Wright's Broadacre City, Le Corbusier's *Ville Contemporaine,* Hugh Ferriss's *Metropolis of Tomorrow,* Harvey Wiley Corbett's highway visions, and probably the prophecies of H. G. Wells while researching his urban design work.[44] In a lecture Kettering delivered to the annual meeting of the American Society of Civil Engineers in Detroit in July 1937, he described a few different predictions regarding the future of urban design that sound very much like the work of Le Corbusier and Wright, although he did not mention the architects by name.[45] Importantly, every design proposal Kettering cited used roads not only to facilitate transport but also to significantly reduce urban density. He believed this was inherently good: "Man has an inborn feeling for open spaces and a plot of ground. We have a number of indications that the trend is away from cities and back to smaller communities."[46] That such changes would require the wholesale demolition of existing towns was absolutely desirable: "We have a lot of things that we ought to tear down and throw away," Kettering argued. "We ought to rebuild this country and make it better than we did the first time."[47]

The General Motors *Futurama* was ultimately an expanded and mechanized version of the Shell model, featuring huge, high-speed, limited-access freeways coursing through rural landscapes and a radiantly modern city (Figure 9). Unlike the Shell model, the *Futurama* was designed to be experienced in person, and indeed it was Bel Geddes's ingenious method of revealing

Figure 9. City of tomorrow and surrounding landscape in the *Futurama*, circa 1939. From Folder 405.1, Photo Box 12, Job 405: Futurama Caravan, Norman Bel Geddes Collection, Harry Ransom Center, University of Texas at Austin. Image courtesy of the Edith Lutyens and Norman Bel Geddes Foundation.

the diorama to the audience that seems to have left the greatest impression on its millions of visitors. He transformed what would have normally been an overwhelming mass-culture experience into the simulation of an empowering personal journey by placing pairs of visitors in the enveloping arms of a dark, soft loveseat and then whisking them around the model while playing an individually timed audio recording that gently explained the vision before them. This "private traveling opera box," as the *New York Times* described it, gave visitors their "own private show" (Figure 10).[48] The personal nature of this journey was reinforced when the ride came to an end and visitors stepped out into a life-sized version of one of the model's urban intersections, receiving a button that declared, "I Have Seen the Future." The active agent in this moment of arrival was not GM or the glamorous Bel Geddes but the visitor, who had, it was doubtlessly hoped, been set furiously to dreaming as a result.

Figure 10. Woman experiencing the *Futurama* exhibit, circa 1939. Copyright 2014 General Motors LLC. Used with permission, GM Media Archive (image number 148519).

This was not the only time Bel Geddes worked to transform a large event into an intimate one, bridging the gap between spectacle and spectator. He first made a name for himself in 1924 by designing a stage set for *The Miracle*, pulling audience members into the play by transforming an entire theater into an incense-filled medieval cathedral with pews for chairs.[49] In the Amusement Area of the 1939–40 New York World's Fair, some distance from the GM pavilion, Bel Geddes also designed an adult exhibit called *Crystal Lassies*, which placed a single dancing woman in a chamber of one-way mirrors, multiplying her seminude form into infinity from all directions while simultaneously masking viewers from each other and themselves. This gave "each spectator . . . the illusion of being the only onlooker" and thereby transmuted a very public striptease into a voyeuristic peepshow.[50] Bel Geddes was, in short, a master of stagecraft. His talent for collapsing the distance between a performance and its audience was a natural fit with General Motors' longstanding desires to "bring industry to the people," restoring consumers' confidence and goodwill. It was also an ideal technique for eliciting an audience's emotions and, thus, potentially engaging with their personal hopes and dreams.

R. L. Duffus, critic for the *New York Times*, expressed frustration at the power of the *Futurama* to infiltrate the minds of the public: "Maybe we would enjoy [Bel Geddes's] kind of United States and maybe we would be terrified by it or wonder what was gained by going to so many places at such speeds. But the crowd is almost silent, wholly fascinated. Despite all disappointments these Fair-goers still worship the future."[51] The public was not alone; in a turn of events that surely thrilled GM, Bel Geddes was invited by President Roosevelt to the White House for a special summit on future traffic programs.[52] Robert Moses, however, was less complimentary about the *Futurama*, despite his previous flirtations with the Shell model.[53] He publically criticized as "bunk" Bel Geddes's belief that the largest superhighways should be kept to open countryside rather than driven through the hearts of cities.[54] Bel Geddes responded by willfully maintaining his position in a book he published in 1940 to capitalize on the success of the *Futurama,* entitled *Magic Motorways.*[55] GM would soon purge such ambivalence from its urban design campaign by turning away from Bel Geddes and instead enlisting Moses to help develop future exhibits.

With or without twelve-lane superhighways, however, the city envisioned in the *Futurama* was a high-speed, limited-access freeway advocate's dream, designed in unquestionable resonance with Kettering's stated ambitions for the American city. With the candor permitted only by a closed-door office meeting, one of Bel Geddes's employees argued in 1940 that the urban vision of the *Futurama* had captured the patronage of General Motors for one reason only: "It was selling to the public, without their knowing it, the importance of the automobile in daily use."[56]

On the Road Again

Understandably, both GM and Bel Geddes desired to merge the sensational *Futurama* with a new and improved Parade of Progress. Kettering and many of his fellow GM associates had hoped from the beginning that the New York World's Fair display would be recycled, receiving an "indefinite exhibit life long after the Fair was over" by being "transported and exhibited, as a unit, about the country."[57] The sheer size of the *Futurama* model and the complex machinery engaged in its exhibition presented major obstacles. Nonetheless, while the *Futurama* was still thrilling fairgoers, Sloan asked Bel Geddes to propose some ways that the exhibit could be preserved indefinitely or placed on tour.[58] After a few months of brainstorming and research, Bel Geddes revealed "A Presentation of Various Plans for Continuing the Use of the Futurama following the Close of the World's Fair."[59] These included, among other schemes, touring the *Futurama* along the country's coasts and inland waterways via a giant boat, installing it in a permanent new eye-catching GM building in Manhattan, constructing a new Parade of Progress roadshow headlined by a miniature *Futurama,* and, last but far from least, building the *Futurama* into the hull of a zeppelin and thus taking it on a spectacular airborne tour of America.

The Bel Geddes team was particularly excited about the zeppelin concept and did everything they could to sell it to GM, including securing statements of feasibility from the Goodyear Aircraft Corporation and the U.S. Navy.[60] Paul Garrett, director of publicity for General Motors, was convinced early: "The . . . Caravan and Permanent Display Building . . . are anti-climaxes. This dirigible idea goes the Futurama one better."[61] Other General Motors executives were concerned about safety.[62] Sloan was drawn to the more down-to-earth caravan idea, which Bel Geddes had beautifully presented with photographs of detailed models (Figures 11 and 12). As these images

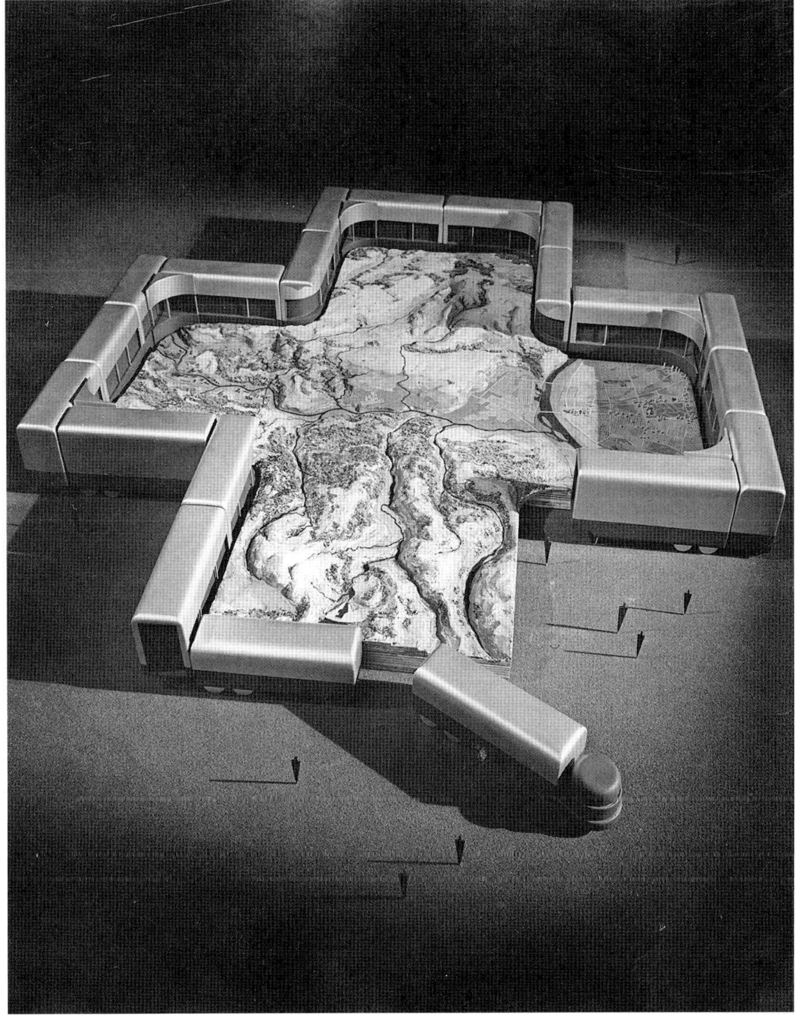

Figure 11. Proposal for a mobile *Futurama* model, to be assembled on a performance site and surrounded by truck trailers converted into observatory walkways, 1940. From Folder 405.1, Photo Box 12, Job 405: Futurama Caravan, Norman Bel Geddes Collection, Harry Ransom Center, University of Texas at Austin. Image courtesy of the Edith Lutyens and Norman Bel Geddes Foundation.

Figure 12. Proposal for the *Futurama* as a roadshow, in the vein of the Parade of Progress, 1940. From Folder 405.1, Photo Box 12, Job 405: Futurama Caravan, Norman Bel Geddes Collection, Harry Ransom Center, University of Texas at Austin. Image courtesy of the Edith Lutyens and Norman Bel Geddes Foundation.

reveal, the caravan would have operated much like the original Parade of Progress, as a fleet of trucks hauling a roadshow around the country. Most of these trucks would have carried sections of a much-reduced *Futurama* model that would be assembled and then surrounded by empty truck trailers converted into covered walkways. The model would be protected from the elements by a dramatic suspended tent, and other trucks featuring smaller exhibits would gather in front. Bel Geddes, perhaps in an attempt to steer GM toward the airship concept, was rather up front about the problems this mobile *Futurama* could face, including maintenance issues and visitor bottlenecks due to the lack of moving chairs.[63]

In the end General Motors decided against all of Bel Geddes's proposals, deciding instead to keep the format of the Parade of Progress more or less as it had been since 1936, while enhancing its futuristic aesthetics and adding new content. For the 1941 caravan, the old tent was replaced with a new, conspicuously high-tech affair large enough for 1,500 people. Called the Aer-O-Dome, it was itself a work of modern architecture, described in GM's promotional material as "a silver dirigible balloon hangar," perhaps owing something to Bel Geddes's airship proposal (Figure 13). It consisted of a frame of aluminum "airplane-alloy" ribs within which the "aluminum impregnated plastic" fabric of the tent was suspended, so that no supports were visible from the inside.[64]

More dramatic was the change made to the caravan vehicle fleet. GM converted the old streamliners into red-and-silver buses called Futurliners (Figure 14).[65] The twelve Futurliners each housed two sixteen-foot-long exhibits in their massive steel-and-aluminum bodies, with side hatches that opened upward to present the displays, no setup required. A long, thin slice of roof rose up from their backs on a single column to reveal banks of fluorescent lights. Their bullet-nosed front ends with glass canopies were deliberately designed to evoke "a Flying Fortress," and their "pilot's compartment" was finished like "a swank private airliner."[66] These vehicles spoke the language of scientific progress with the vigor of aircraft.

The old Parade of Progress exhibits were spruced up considerably, and new ones were added. The induction egg-frying trick was retained and combined with an electric ice cream maker, while the modern kitchen and living room displays were renovated to include a mock television and other cutting edge advances (Figure 15). Bel Geddes's work was initially included in the new parade, albeit in a form considerably less spectacular than he had hoped: "One of the most popular exhibits is 'Futurama Highlights.' . . . These sections are only a part of the mammoth original, [but] they give a comprehensive idea of the smash hit of the New York World's Fair."[67] As one employee of the 1941 Parade of Progress later recollected, "Everybody couldn't get to the New York World's Fair to see the Futurama, but [GM] took parts of the Futurama and put it in vehicles and drove it all over the country so people could see it in their own little home towns."[68]

A new urban design exhibit was also created. Entitled *Our American Crossroads,* it was as complex as clockwork, with multiple electric motors driving many moving parts (Figure 16). Construction had to be outsourced from Kettering's research division to the H. B. Stubbs exhibit company. It would prove to be one of the most popular and enduring exhibits GM ever produced, far outlasting *Futurama Highlights*. Whereas the original 1936 Parade of Progress urban exhibit had consisted of two separate city models, one old and one futuristic, *Our American Crossroads* used machinery and an audio recording by actor Parker Fennelly to brilliantly combine three epochs into a single model that, over fourteen minutes, mechanically evolved from old to new before the viewer's eyes.

The exhibit performance began with the tiny, backwards village of Pleasant Corners in the year 1900.[69] Dirt roads linked a general store, a blacksmith's shop, a humble schoolhouse, a quaint church, and a thin scattering of Victorian farmhouses. Its scarce citizens were described as either very old or very bored. Then, primitive motorcars slowly began to trickle into town, confounding the sleepy villagers. The exhibit's large dirt road mechanically flipped over to be replaced with a paved one, courtesy of the state government. The trickle of motorcars became a quick and steady stream. The local economy shuddered to life, and old buildings were rotated out for enlarged and improved versions. Houses popped up as commuters moved to the area, abandoning city neighborhoods for a subdivided piece of former farmland. A bank, a playhouse, and new shops all rotated into view. By 1920 the formerly bucolic place had become a full-fledged town, all courtesy of the paved road and automobiles that connected it to the larger world. Then, that road rotated yet again to reveal a four-lane, high-speed freeway. The pace of change quickened. The buildings, until now mostly traditional in style, were flipped out for modernist specimens, with flat roofs, large streamlined masses, and horizontal and corner windows. A motor inn made a conspicuous debut. The cars in the display were by this point whizzing past quite quickly, and there could be no question Pleasant Corners

Figure 13. 1941 Parade of Progress with the aluminum-framed Aer-O-Dome, 1941. Detail from a photograph by Stuart Blond in Notebook 2, Box 3, courtesy of the GM Futurliner Restoration Project Archive at the National Auto and Truck Museum. Copyright 2014 General Motors LLC. Used with permission, GM Media Archive.

Figure 14. New fleet of Parade of Progress vehicles called Futurliners, circa 1940. Photograph by Joel Dirnberger, Folder 6A, Box 3, GM Futurliner Restoration Project Archive at the National Auto and Truck Museum. Copyright 2014 General Motors LLC. Used with permission, GM Media Archive.

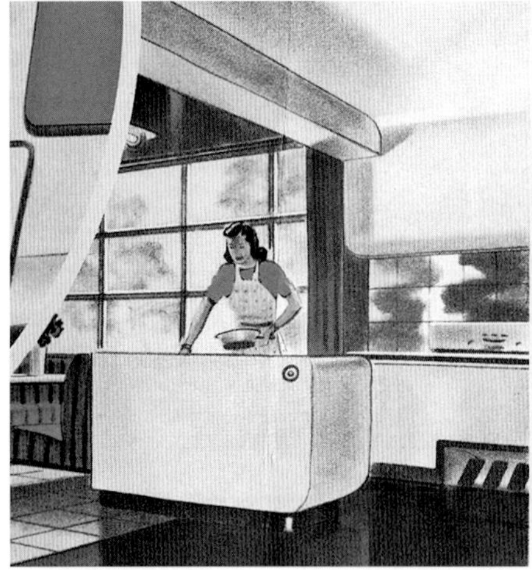

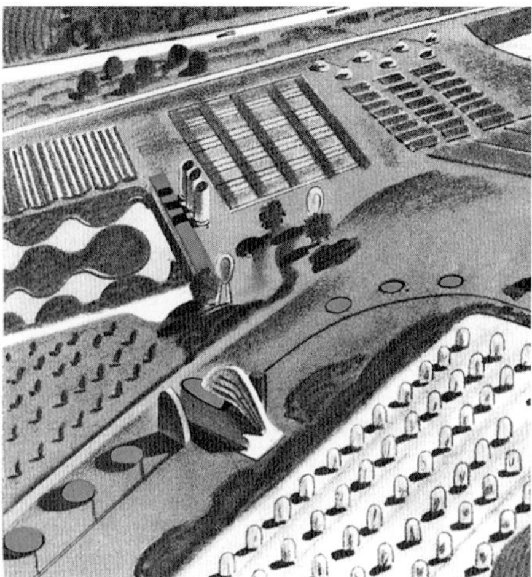

Figure 15. Domestic kitchen, living room, and *Futurama Highlights* exhibits as shown in the *General Motors New Parade of Progress: Souvenir Edition* promotional brochure, 1941. Collection of Nathaniel Walker.

had become a suburban dynamo, with no end to progress in sight. Anyone resisting the required advances had been proved an old fool. Main Street had become a roaring highway, and obsolescence had been overcome.

With *American Crossroads* in tow, the new Parade of Progress went out to "spread the gospel of research."[70] When the caravan debuted in Miami on February 26, 1941, Kettering himself was the main speaker. A reporter asked the roadshow's director, J. M. Jerpe, which displays were proving the most popular; he cited "our demonstration of how a water glass can be broken by waves of amplified sound and a piece of wood sawed in two by a rapidly rotating paper disc" as well as *Futurama Highlights*.[71]

As the caravan rolled across the continent, however, a new emphasis would emerge to displace the *Futurama*: national defense.[72] The growing global emergency of World War II prompted

Figure 16. *Our American Crossroads* mechanized exhibit of an isolated village transforming into a bustling suburb thanks to highway projects and motorcars. Official GM press release photograph taken in Portland, Oregon, 1956. Collection of Nathaniel Walker.

General Motors to substantially alter the parade, presenting the Aer-O-Dome as a potential military structure and emphasizing industry's potential to produce not only cars but also "machine guns, shells, cartridge cases, tank tracks."[73] By the fall of 1941, the exhibit listing still included *Our American Crossroads*, but *Futurama Highlights* had been dropped.[74] Nonetheless, the caravan's core message of progress through industrial research was still reaching audiences. *Kansas Business Magazine* urged employers to send their workers to the Parade of Progress in Wichita because it would "renew their faith in the American way of life."[75] A writer for the *Decatur Review* expressed wide-eyed enthusiasm for GM's vision of the future and made an urgent call for progress in Decatur:

> Research missionaries from the General Motor's [*sic*] Company came to our town this week. They found us about as far behind the times in the things that make up our household equipment as the missionaries of the early church found the hottentots. They showed us that technologically we are at least 100 years behind the times. . . . These missionaries were not trying to convert us to anything by word of mouth. They were trying to show us things that are rightfully a part of our inheritance. Things that we must have pretty soon or not at all.[76]

Such "hottentots" were clearly pained by the contrast between GM's vision of the future and their own rather average hometowns. Nonetheless, four million of them crowded under the tent of the revamped Parade of Progress in 1941, roughly 40 percent more than in any previous year. Some shows were simply phenomenal; at the parade's four-day stay in St. Louis, one hundred thousand people came out.[77] Caravan organizers were proud to report back to Detroit that the 1941 roadshow had been set up almost exclusively "in parks, on school and college campuses or on similar pieces of public or institutional property," including, on one glorious occasion, the state capitol lawn in Des Moines.[78] The Parade of Progress would, however, soon come to a halt. After the bombing of Pearl Harbor, GM retooled for armament production, and the men of the caravan went to war. The Futurliners and the Aer-O-Dome were mothballed.

Kettering was stoic about the interruption of his campaign. At the 1944 annual meeting of the American Automobile Association, he poetically described the country's emerging car culture as a "very broad highway" along which everyone had been quite happily advancing until "Hitler slipped in and blew up a bridge." Once the bridge was repaired by victory, however, the road would be rejoined, and progress would resume.[79] He had good reason to be optimistic. Already by the mid-1930s, growth in car ownership had shaken loose of the Depression, reaching new heights by 1940. During that same period, Kettering had watched millions of Americans thrill to corporate-sponsored visions of urban reforms that would make the country more dependent on automobiles. At the start of GM's Depression-era public relations campaign, he had called for Americans to embrace cars as a "new necessity" of daily life. By 1946 he felt confident this had been achieved: "Today the automobile takes its place alongside food, shelter, and clothing as the fourth American necessity. It is the new American way of life! From the cradle to the grave we are all dependent on automobile transportation."[80] With this among his many trophies, Kettering retired from his position as director of research at General Motors in 1947.

Progress along the postwar highway of car culture did not, however, pick up quite as quickly as GM hoped. Despite the increase in American car ownership and notwithstanding a growing consensus that the United States needed, in Kettering's words, a "long-range highway program which will assure the country of sound highway policies at national, state, and local levels," by the close of the 1940s, major highway reforms were still a dream.[81] In 1952 GM decided to resurrect the Parade of Progress, making only a few changes from the 1941 version. These included the installation of opaque roofs on the Futurliner driver compartments to mitigate heat gain and the addition of a number of new exhibits (Figure 17). The caravan debuted in Kettering's hometown of Dayton, Ohio. Vice President Garrett gave the keynote lecture; gone was the reassuring talk of overcoming adversity, and in its place

Figure 19. *Out of the Muddle,* part one, a mechanized exhibit revealing the opportunities brought to the population of a small town by the construction of large highway projects and an automobile suburb, circa 1954. Copyright 2014 General Motors LLC. Used with permission, GM Media Archive (image number POP4-0376).

different city rose from the back of the diorama: "There it is—a glimpse of the city of tomorrow. Space, light, room to move, room to breath feature in this city of the future." A huge motorway surrounded by "trees and flowers and grass" bisected the city. Buildings were large, simple modernist slabs, evocative of the 1952 United Nations Building by Le Corbusier and others; dispersed across the highway-cloven land, they offered not the slightest gesture toward ground-level pedestrian life.

This futuristic vision was admiringly described as a "dream city" by a number of reporters.[92] Today, it is perhaps best understood as a corporate-vernacular rendition of the automobile-centric modernist planning theories espoused in works such as *The Athens Charter,* published in 1943. A side-by-side visual comparison of the "dream city" and the old downtown in the lower register of the exhibit makes it clear the latter would have to be either abandoned or totally demolished for the former to take shape. The mild scruples of Bel Geddes regarding urban superhighways had been ousted. In both parts one and two of *Out of the Muddle,* the new ideal presented was a revolutionary change in traffic circulation as well as in the essential nature of building; the grid and its coordination in scale to the human foot were gone, and in their place rose a sprawling suburban landscape of far-flung houses and towers set in manicured parks. Here, the "fourth American necessity" would always be required for the most basic participation in economic and social life.

In early July 1956, a Parade of Progress employee told a reporter in Washington State he would soon have a respite from the road, if only a brief one: "After the Spokane show," he said, "we take the 40-odd vehicles back to Detroit, to start [the parade] all over again."[93] After it returned home to the Motor City, however, the Parade of Progress was canceled. The official reason was

Figure 20. *Out of the Muddle,* part two, focusing on the need for traffic reforms and highway construction in the center of a large city, circa 1954. In the upper register of the display is the climax of the mechanized exhibit, a modernist "dream city." Photograph by Tony Gagliardi, Box 1, GM Futurliner Restoration Project Archive at the National Auto and Truck Museum. Copyright 2014 General Motors LLC. Used with permission, GM Media Archive.

that public interest had been waning due to the advent of television.[94] This is not, however, a satisfactory explanation. For the three years the postwar parade had been operating—from the summer of 1953 to the summer of 1956—it had attracted 8,067,448 people.[95] This was hardly worse than the original parade that ran from 1936 to 1939, which had been considered a phenomenal success. If a drop in visitor interest cannot explain the sudden demise of the Parade of Progress, what might? In June 1956, Congress passed the Federal Aid Highway Act, allocating more than $30 billion for interstate motorways. Unlike every previous highway bill passed by Congress, this one included money for both road construction and for eminent-domain building seizure and neighborhood clearance, making inner-city highways possible. President Eisenhower signed the bill on June 29, and within a week GM's "miniature world's fair on wheels" was packed up for the last time.

In the twenty years spanning its launch in 1936 and its permanent termination in 1956, 20.5 million people saw the Parade of Progress. At least 19.5 million of these were citizens of the United States. Barring repeat visitors, of which there were probably at least a few, this figure represents approximately one in every eight Americans. In 1962, when GM and Robert Moses together unveiled a small preview of the company's 1964 world's fair exhibit at the Waldorf-Astoria, the *New York Times* explained that "a large and curious crowd" had gathered to see it because "many of the marvelous prophesies made by General Motors' Futurama at the New York World's Fair in 1939–40 have turned out to be true."[96] GM did not merely predict the future; the company worked tirelessly to shape it. General Motors was never the only party promoting autocentric urban reforms in the United States, and it was certainly not the first, but it was among the most powerful, enjoying a reach into average American communities arguably greater than that of any given professional architect or planner. More than Frank Lloyd Wright or Le Corbusier, whose work GM emulated in its displays, and even more than Norman Bel Geddes or Robert Moses, whose work it directly sponsored and promoted, GM was strategically positioned to capture the imaginations of everyday Americans—to affect their perceptions of their hometowns and their expectations and hopes for the future of the same. The company exhausted tremendous resources "to set a boy to dreaming" for a new, modern, high-tech, and high-speed alternative to the "obsolete" sidewalks along Main Street. The company's goal was not only the government-sponsored creation of new roads but also to put the people perpetually and compulsorily on them. Only comprehensive change in the way Americans inhabited the continent could transform the automobile into what it is today: "the fourth American necessity."

AUTHOR BIOGRAPHY

Nathaniel R. Walker is assistant professor of architectural history in the Art and Architectural History Department of the College of Charleston. His research focuses on the intersections of urban public space, aesthetics, utopian dreams of modernity and progress, and social and political power networks. He is author of "Savannah's Lost Squares: Progress *versus* Beauty in the Depression-era South," in the *Journal of the Society of Architectural Historians*; "Sister Cities: Corporate Destiny in the Metropolis Utopias of King Camp Gillette, Fritz Lang, and Thea von Harbou," in *Traditional Dwellings and Settlements Review*; "Babylon Electrified: Oriental Hybridity as Futurism in Victorian Utopian Architecture," in *Revival: Memories, Identities, Utopias*; and "Lost in the City of Light: Dystopia and Utopia in the Wake of Haussmann's Paris," in *Utopian Studies*.

NOTES

This essay began as a research paper in a seminar on "Miniature Worlds" taught at Brown University in the Fall of 2009 by Professor Ipek Türeli. I thank her, as well as Professor Dietrich Neumann, who helped me refine my argument for presentation at a graduate student symposium at the Harvard Graduate School of Design the next year. My research was helped considerably by the General Motors Archive, the archive at Kettering University, the Harry Ransom Center at the University of Texas at Austin, and the generous leaders of the Futurliner Restoration Project, who put me in touch with a number of original employees of the Parade of Progress, including Bob Krantz, Jim Genzel, and Vic Garske, all of whom I thank for their time and their kindness. I am indebted to the National Auto and Truck Museum and the Historic Vehicle Association, which provided me with access to the Futurliner Restoration Project Archive when it was being temporarily stored in Washington, D.C., in support of the Futurliner's entry into the new National Historic Vehicle Register. I thank the organizers and participants of the Ninth Savannah Symposium at the Savannah College of Art and Design, where my research was presented in something close to its final form and very graciously received, and Professor Louis Nelson, who after that symposium helped me refine the paper. I thank the anonymous reviewers who critiqued my study; their detailed comments and suggestions were extremely helpful. Finally, I thank the editors of this journal for their insightful contributions; I am sure this essay would have been much weaker without their excellent advice.

1. "General Motors Exhibit Best Liked," *Atlanta Constitution*, May 17, 1939, 16.

2. Adnan Morshed, *Impossible Heights: Skyscrapers, Flight, and the Master Builder* (Minneapolis: University of Minnesota Press, 2015); Donald Albrecht, ed., *Norman Bel Geddes Designs America* (New York: Abrams, 2012). See also Robert W. Rydell and Laura Burd Schiavo, eds., *Designing Tomorrow: America's World's Fairs of the 1930s* (New Haven, Conn.: Yale University Press, 2010); Adnan Morshed, "The Aesthetics of Ascension in Norman Bel Geddes's Futurama," *Journal of the Society of Architectural Historians* 63, no. 1 (March 2004): 74–99; Paul Mason Fotsch, "The Building of a Superhighway Future at the New York World's Fair," *Cultural Critique* 48 (Spring 2001): 65–97; Jeffrey L. Meikle, *Twentieth Century Limited: Industrial Design in America, 1925–1939*, 2nd ed. (Philadelphia: Temple University Press, 2001), 189–210; Christina Cogdell, "The Futurama Recontextualized:

Norman Bel Geddes's Eugenic 'World of Tomorrow,'" *American Quarterly* 52, no. 2 (June 2000): 193–245; David Gelernter, *1939: The Lost World of the Fair* (New York: Free Press, 1995); Robert W. Rydell, *World of Fairs: The Century-of-Progress Expositions* (Chicago: University of Chicago Press, 1993).

3. Studies on the evolution of highway culture include, among others, Joseph F. C. DiMento and Cliff Ellis, *Changing Lanes: Visions and Histories of Urban Freeways* (Cambridge, Mass.: MIT Press, 2013); Christopher W. Wells, *Car Country: An Environmental History* (Seattle: University of Washington Press, 2012); Mark H. Rose and Raymond A. Mohl, *Interstate: Highway Politics and Policy since 1939*, 3rd ed. (Knoxville: University of Tennessee Press, 2012); Ted Shelton, "Automobile Utopias and Traditional Urban Infrastructure: Visions of the Coming Conflict, 1925–1940," *Traditional Dwellings and Settlements Review*, 22, no. 2 (Spring 2011): 63–76.

4. *Advertising and Selling* 12 (January 9, 1929): 29; also quoted in Roland Marchand and Michael L. Smith, "Corporate Science on Display," in *Scientific Authority and Twentieth-Century America*, ed. Ronald G. Walter (Baltimore, Md.: Johns Hopkins University Press, 1997), 153.

5. "Address of Mr. Charles F. Kettering, Vice-President, in Charge of Research, of the General Motors Corporation. Guest Speaker at the Twenty-Second Annual Convention of the United States Chamber of Commerce at The New Willard Hotel, Washington, D.C.," May 2, 1934, 5, 9–10, Folder 6/7, Kettering Office Files, Kettering Papers, Kettering University Archive (hereafter referred to as KOF). See also Alfred P. Sloan Jr., Charles F. Kettering, et al., "Science and Industry in the Coming Century," *Scientific Monthly* 39, no. 1 (July 1934): 71. For a broad, contextualized discussion of GM's Depression-era public relations struggles, see Marchand and Smith, "Corporate Science on Display," 148–82.

6. Charles F. Kettering and Beverly Smith, "Ten Paths to Fame and Fortune," *American Magazine* 124, no. 6 (December 1937): 14–15, 119–124; Charles F. Kettering, "The World Ahead: What a Research Engineer Thinks a Manufacturer Is (Portion of an Address before the National Association of Manufacturers)," *Printer's Ink Monthly* 42 (February 1941): 12, 61–62; "Address of Mr. Charles F. Kettering, Vice-President, in Charge of Research, of the General Motors Corporation," KOF. See also Marchand and Smith, "Corporate Science on Display," 155–56.

7. For a discussion of the history of "planned obsolescence" or "dynamic obsolescence" see Giles Slade, *Made to Break: Technology and Obsolescence in America* (Cambridge, Mass.: Harvard University Press, 2006).

8. Charles F. Kettering, "Change and Progress," speech to the Merchant Association in New York City, November 1935, 2, Folder 6/33, KOF.

9. Daniel M. Abramson, "Boston's West End: Urban Obsolescence in Mid-Twentieth-Century America," in *Governing by Design: Architecture, Economy, and Politics in the Twentieth Century*, by Aggregate Architectural History Collaborative (Pittsburgh, Pa.: University of Pittsburgh Press, 2012), 55; for more on architectural and urban obsolescence, see Daniel M. Abramson, *Obsolescence: An Architectural History* (Chicago: University of Chicago Press, 2016).

10. William Leach, *Land of Desire: Merchants, Power, and the Rise of a New American Culture* (New York: Vintage Books, 1994), 4–5, 37. For more on this topic, see also Adrian Forty, *Objects of Desire: Design and Society since 1750* (New Haven, Conn.: Thames and Hudson, 1992); for an alternative argument that asserts consumer agency, see Regina Lee Blaszczyk, *Imagining Consumers: Design and Innovation from Wedgwood to Corning* (Baltimore, Md.: Johns Hopkins University Press, 2002).

11. Charles Franklin Kettering and Allen Orth, *The New Necessity: The Culmination of a Century of Progress in Transportation* (Baltimore, Md.: Williams & Wilkins Company and its Associates in Cooperation with The Century of Progress Exposition, 1932), x.

12. Sloan, Kettering, et al., "Science and Industry in the Coming Century," 67.

13. *The General Motors Exhibit at a Century of Progress 1934*, exhibition brochure, collection of Nathaniel Walker.

14. Marchand and Smith, "Corporate Science on Display," 153.

15. For an eyewitness description of Ford's exhibit, see James A. Buchanan, ed., *History of the Panama–Pacific International Exposition* (San Francisco: Pan-Pacific Press Association, 1915), 416.

16. Marchand and Smith, "Corporate Science on Display," 153; see also Roland Marchand, *Creating the Corporate Soul: The Rise of Public Relations and*

Corporate Imagery in American Big Business (Berkeley: University of California Press, 1998), 283–91.

17. "'Circus of Science' to Tour America," *Prescott Evening Courier,* January 28, 1936, 11.

18. For reference to the streamliners as "highway leviathans," see, for example, "Parade Fleet Uses Largest Trucks of Kind," *Miami Daily News,* February 19, 1936, 10. For reference to these streamliners as "portents of the future," see "'Circus of Science' to Tour America," 11.

19. "'Circus of Science' to Tour America," 11.

20. "'Circus of Science' to Tour America," 11.

21. Marchand and Smith, "Corporate Science on Display," 148–82.

22. *General Motors Parade of Progress: Souvenir Edition,* promotional brochure, circa 1936, collection of Nathaniel Walker.

23. *General Motors Parade of Progress: Souvenir Edition,* circa 1936.

24. "Science Marvels Are on Display at Local Show" and "The City of Yesterday and That of Tomorrow," *The Independent* (St. Petersburg, Florida), February 23, 1939, 3.

25. "Parade of Progress Arrives This Morning," *Palm Beach Post,* March 2, 1936, 1.

26. "Parade of Progress," *Tuscaloosa News,* December 8, 1939, 4.

27. "Eleventh Operating Report of the Parade of Progress: June 1–December 31, 1939," in Folder 87-11.2-271f, Box 93, KOF.

28. "Eighth Operating Report of the Parade of Progress: January 1 to July 13," 1938, in Folder 87-11.2-271c, Box 93, KOF.

29. "Eighth Operating Report of the Parade of Progress," 7.

30. For data on the size of the New York World's Fair, see "Facts about the New York World's Fair 1939," published by the Department of Feature Publicity, New York World's Fair 1939, Folder 3, Box 38, Yale University Century of Progress Collection.

31. "This Is the City of Tomorrow," Shell Motor Oil advertisement in *Life Magazine,* July 5, 1937, 54–55.

32. Norman Bel Geddes, *Horizons* (Boston: Little, Brown, 1932); Jeffrey L. Meikle, "'A Few Years Ahead': Defining a Modernism with Popular Appeal," in *Norman Bel Geddes Designs America,* 121–22.

33. Morshed, *Impossible Heights,* 192–96; Sandy Isenstadt, "The Future Is Here: Norman Bel Geddes and the Theater of Time," in *Norman Bel Geddes Designs America,* 142–44; Morshed, "The Aesthetics of Ascension in Norman Bel Geddes's Futurama," 87–89; Meikle, *Twentieth Century Limited,* 189–210; and Meikle, *The City of Tomorrow: Model 1937* (London: Pentagram Design, 1984).

34. See Folder 356.2 Shell Oil Advertising Campaign, Meeting Minutes Nov–Dec 1936, and Folder 356.3 Details for J. Walter Thompson Co.—Shell Ads—1-18-37, Box 18, Job 356: Shell Oil Advertising Campaign, Norman Bel Geddes Collection, Harry Ransom Center, University of Texas (hereafter referred to as NBGC).

35. "Notes of Meeting with Mr. Geddes—November 12, 1936," 2, Folder 356.2 Shell Oil Advertising Campaign, Meeting Minutes Nov-Dec 1936, Box 18, Job 356: Shell Oil Advertising Campaign, NBGC.

36. "Notes of Meeting with Mr. Geddes—November 10, 1936," 2, and "Notes of Meeting with Mr. Geddes—November 12, 1936," 5–10, Folder 356.2 Shell Oil Advertising Campaign, Meeting Minutes Nov–Dec 1936, Box 18, Job 356: Shell Oil Advertising Campaign, NBGC.

37. For a discussion of the different career phases of Miller McClintock in the context of the rise of traffic planning as a discipline in the United States, see Peter D. Norton, *Fighting Traffic: The Dawn of the Motor Age in the American City* (Cambridge, Mass.: MIT Press, 2008).

38. "Designs Future Traffic Lanes," *New York Sun,* June 1, 1937; clipping available in Folder 356.7 Record Copy Book Shell Clippings 1937, Box 18a, Job 356: Shell Oil Advertising Campaign, NBGC.

39. See numerous clippings in Folder 356.7 Record Copy Book Shell Clippings 1937, Box 18a, Job 356: Shell Oil Advertising Campaign, NBGC.

40. "Future of Uptown Area to Be Theme of Dinner," *New York Herald-Tribune,* April 10, 1938, and "Owners Rally to Win Back Harlem Charm," *New York American,* April 27, 1938, clippings available in Folder 356.8 Shell Oil Ad Campaign Clippings 1937–1938, Box 18a, Job 356: Shell Oil Advertising Campaign, NBGC; "City 1960, Norman Bel Geddes, Designer," *Architectural Forum* 67 (July 1937): 57–62; Letter from Brendan Jones, "Questions for Mr. Norman Bel Geddes on Future of Brooklyn—1960, or as Far Ahead

as He Cares to Predict," Brooklyn Desk, *Daily News*, Folder 356.6 Publicity Writing, Box 18, Job 356: Shell Oil Advertising Campaign, NBGC.

41. For correspondence between the office and associates of Robert Moses and Norman Bel Geddes, see Folder 356.1 Shell Oil Ad Campaign Correspondence, Agreements 1936–1937, Box 18, Job 356: Shell Oil Advertising Campaign, NBGC.

42. It is often reported that GM was seriously thinking about duplicating its assembly line exhibit from the *Century of Progress* exhibition. This is true, but even in mid-1937 Kettering and other GM executives were inclined to think they needed something that would be "more entertaining, educational, less costly, and would blend into the theme of the Fair more effectively" than the old show—and there was also the "obvious" issue of repeating themselves in two major fairs; see Technical Exhibits Department, Research Division, "Some Technical Suggestions Relative to the New York World Fair 1939," July 1, 1937, 5, Folder 87-11.2-343, Box 104, KOF. For the negotiations between GM and Geddes running up to their agreement to partner on the *Futurama*, see correspondence in Folder 381.4 GM—NYWF, Folder 381.2 GM Building Agreement May 3, 1938, and Folder 381.3 Proposal to Client April 1938—Condensed June 1938, Box 9a, Job 381: General Motors Building at the New York World's Fair, NBGC.

43. "Minutes of Promotional Meeting," January 27, 1938, 3, Folder 381.4 GM—NYWF, and "This Proposed Exhibit for the General Motors Corporation . . . ," Folder 381.3 Proposal to Client April 1938—Condensed June 1938, Box 9a, Job 381: General Motors Building at the New York World's Fair, NBGC.

44. Morshed, *Impossible Heights*, 155, 193.

45. Charles F. Kettering, "Motor Vehicles and Highways of the Future," an address given before the American Society of Civil Engineers in Detroit, July 21, 1937, 6, B4/149, Kettering Library, Kettering Papers, Kettering University Archive (hereafter referred to as KL).

46. Kettering, "Motor Vehicles and Highways of the Future," 5.

47. Kettering, "Motor Vehicles and Highways of the Future," 3.

48. For the reference to the opera box, see "'Futurama' at Fair Is Viewed in Test," *New York Times*, April 16, 1939, 3; for the reference to a "private show," see the interview with a fairgoer in Gelernter, *1939*, 22.

49. Albert A. Hopkins, "A Theater without a Stage: The Whole Building Given over to the Play with Audience Part of the Scenery," *Scientific American* 130, no. 4 (April 1924): 228–29.

50. George Herrick, "She Dances . . . She Shivers . . . She Shakes, and It's All Done by a Lot of Mirrors: How One Girl Replaces a Thousand," *Glass Digest* 18, no. 8 (August 1939): 8.

51. R. L. Duffus, "The Beginning of a World, Not the End," *New York Times*, July 2, 1939, SM1.

52. Meyer Berger, "At the World's Fair," *New York Times*, July 26, 1939, 14; for more on this, see Albrecht, "Introduction," in *Norman Bel Geddes Designs America*, 23–24.

53. For a comparison of the work of Robert Moses and Norman Bel Geddes and a discussion of their disagreement, see Paul Mason Fotsch, "The Building of a Superhighway Future at the New York World's Fair," *Cultural Critique* no. 48 (Spring 2001): 71–73; and Meikle, *Twentieth Century Limited*, 208–9.

54. "Moses Envisages Future Highways," *New York Times*, January 21, 1940, 11.

55. For a discussion of Bel Geddes's ambivalence toward urban highways as articulated in *Magic Motorways*, see DiMento and Ellis, *Changing Lanes*, 48–50.

56. "Minutes of Meeting: General Motors Corp.," February 15, 1940, Folder 405.1 GM-Futurama Caravan, Minutes of Meetings, Box 25, Job 405: Futurama Caravan, NBGC.

57. Technical Exhibits Department, Research Division, "Some Technical Suggestions Relative to the New York World Fair 1939," July 1, 1937, 13, Folder 87-11.2-343, Box 104, KOF.

58. "Minutes of Meeting: General Motors Futurama Caravan," March 26, 1940, 1, Folder 405.2 Futurama Caravan (Futurama Airship), Box 25, Job 405: Futurama Caravan, NBGC.

59. Norman Bel Geddes and Company, Inc., "A Presentation of Various Plans for Continuing the Use of the Futurama following the Close of the World's Fair: Futurama Caravan," April 1940, Folder 381.59, Box 19e, Job 381: General Motors Building at the New York World's Fair, NBGC.

60. See letter from Captain Garland Fulton, U.S. Navy, May 10, 1940, and "Minutes of Meeting: Results

of Meeting with Goodyear Engineers on Using Airship for Futurama," May 13, 1940, Folder 405.2 Futurama Caravan (Futurama Airship), Box 25, Job 405: Futurama Caravan, NBGC.

61. "Minutes of Meeting: General Motors Futurama Caravan," March 26, 1940, Folder 405.2 Futurama Caravan (Futurama Airship), Box 25, Job 405: Futurama Caravan, NBGC.

62. "Minutes of Meeting: Perpetuation of Futurama after the World's Fair," April 26, 1940, Folder 405.2 Futurama Caravan (Futurama Airship), Box 25, Job 405: Futurama Caravan, NBGC.

63. Norman Bel Geddes and Company, Inc., "A Presentation of Various Plans for Continuing the Use of the Futurama following the Close of the World's Fair: Futurama Caravan," April 1940, 25, Folder 381.59, Box 19e, Job 381: General Motors Building at the New York World's Fair, NBGC.

64. *General Motors New Parade of Progress: Souvenir Edition,* promotional brochure, 1941, collection of Nathaniel Walker.

65. It is not always mentioned that the streamliners were recycled into the Futurliners—instead it is often assumed that the former were scrapped and the latter built from scratch. For explicit reference to their conversion, refer to "For Immediate Release," June 1941, Parade of Progress press release, digitally catalogued as GM_NR_06201941.pdf in the General Motors Archive.

66. "The Body of the Month," *Commercial Car Journal* 61, no. 1 (March 1941): 32.

67. *General Motors New Parade of Progress: Souvenir Edition,* 1941.

68. Bob Krantz, staff member on the Parade of Progress in 1941, interview with the author on November 8, 2009.

69. *Our American Crossroads* transcript, March 20, 1953, the General Motors Archive. This is the only Futurliner exhibit to survive to the present day. After being retired from the Parade of Progress, it was shown on television and then installed at the Chicago Museum of Science and Industry. In 2001 it was taken to the GM Heritage Center north of Detroit, where it remains today, in something less than working order. One can find videos of the exhibit in motion on the Internet, including the GM Heritage Center website at "Our American Crossroads," GM Heritage Center, *https://www.gmheritagecenter.com/videos/1940/Our_American_Crossroads.html.*

70. "The Science Caravans of the General Motors Corporation," in "Scientific Events," *Science* 92, no. 2400 (December 27, 1940): 598.

71. "'Progress Expo Attracts 40,000 First Four Days," *Miami Daily News,* March 2, 1941, 4D.

72. "Thirteenth Operating Report of the Parade of Progress: February 26–September 30, 1941," 4, from the POP 1940-WWII section of Notebook 1, Box 2, GM Futurliner Restoration Project Archive at the National Auto and Truck Museum (hereafter referred to as FRPA). Marked as from Folder 87-11.5-26, KOF.

73. "Thirteenth Operating Report of the Parade of Progress: February 26–September 30, 1941," 5.

74. "Thirteenth Operating Report of the Parade of Progress: February 26–September 30, 1941," 4.

75. "'Parade of Progress' Tells of Industrial Future," *Kansas Business Magazine,* October 1941, 8, clipping available in Folder 87-11.2-271g, Box 93, KOF.

76. "About Town," *Decatur Review,* May 30, 1941, 4.

77. "'Scientific Circus' Seen by 51,000 at St. Louis in One Day," *Cape Girardeau Southeast Missourian,* evening ed., May 14, 1941, 7.

78. "Thirteenth Operating Report of the Parade of Progress: February 26–September 30, 1941," 1–2.

79. Charles F. Kettering, "Annual Meeting of the Delegates of the American Automobile Association," November 11, 1944, 58, Speech 9/5, KL.

80. Charles F. Kettering, "The New American Way of Life," in *Transportation—A Measurement of Civilization: Light, Life, Man, the George Westinghouse Centennial Forum,* vol. 2 (New York: Whittlesey House, McGraw-Hill Book Company, 1946), 95.

81. Kettering, "Annual Meeting of the Delegates of the American Automobile Association."

82. John D. M. White, "A Caravan of Science," *Automobile Topics* 53, no. 6 (June 1953): 4–5.

83. "Progress Parade: 7,500 Tour Exposition Opening Day," *Shreveport Times,* April 15, 1955, 4C.

84. "Second Quarter Sidelights," *GM Shareholders' Quarterly* (June 30, 1953), 14–15.

85. "For Release," July 8, 1954, Parade of Progress press release, digitally catalogued as GM_NR_07071954.pdf in the General Motors Archive, 2; see also "At Parade of Progress: Muddled Traffic Magically Unbefuddled in Model City," *Shreveport Times,* April 17, 1955, 3F.

86. "Out of the Muddle—Part I" transcript, August 26, 1954, 1, the General Motors Archive.

87. "Out of the Muddle—Part I," 1–2.

88. "Out of the Muddle—Part I," 3.

89. "Out of the Muddle—Part I," 5.

90. "Out of the Muddle—Part II" transcript, August 26, 1954, 1, the General Motors Archive.

91. "Out of the Muddle—Part II," 5.

92. "Mobile Exhibit Shows Auto Research Ideas," *Milwaukee Sentinel,* November 23, 1954, 5, part 3; "Science Show Will Open Here Soon," *American-Statesman,* March 6, 1955, B7, clipping available in Tom Van Voorhis Scrapbook, FRPA.

93. "GM 'Parade' Lures Crowd," *Spokane Daily Chronicle,* July 2, 1956, 11.

94. Bill Williams, "GM's Parade of Progress," *Special-Interest Autos* 39 (March–April 1977): 33.

95. Bruce G. Overbey, Director, Parade of Progress, "City Showing Summary," from the Folder Postwar Parade, Box 2, FRPA.

96. Gay Talese, "G.M. Unveils Futurama, 1964, But Crystal Ball Stays Covered," *New York Times,* May 9, 1962, 43.

MIKE CHRISTENSON

Research Notes: The Photographic Construction of Urban Renewal in Fargo, North Dakota

The federally subsidized urban renewal program had its roots in three major federal housing acts, those of 1937, 1949, and 1954. The Housing Act of 1937 defined a slum as "any area where dwellings predominate which, by reason of dilapidation, overcrowding, faulty arrangement or design, lack of ventilation, light or sanitation facilities, or any combination of these factors, are detrimental to safety, health, or morals."[1] Responding to a call in President Harry S. Truman's 1949 State of the Union address, Congress passed the Housing Act of 1949, Title I of which authorized the use of federal funds for what it termed slum clearance.[2] The 1949 act defined an approach to identifying and rebuilding "blighted or deteriorated" areas of cities that differed from previous efforts in two significant ways. Prior to 1949 slum clearance was a fundamentally local effort, accomplished largely or entirely without federal funding (with the exception of a small number of New Deal programs). In addition, early programs had generally failed to gain the participation of private developers. The Housing Act of 1949 explicitly enabled cities, with federal help, to purchase already-developed areas, clear the land of existing structures, and then resell it to private developers.[3] The Housing Act of 1954 introduced the term "urban renewal" and gave new impetus to the federally subsidized effort by explicitly authorizing federal funds for the acquisition of property and the removal of buildings.[4]

My dual interests in urban renewal and archival research date back to the 1980s and my childhood in Winona, Minnesota. I recall an impressive collection of well-preserved nineteenth-century downtown buildings juxtaposed with two square blocks of 1970s-era apartment blocks, offices, and commercial buildings. These newer buildings represented Winona's built legacy of the federally funded urban renewal program. Even as a child, I was keenly interested in the buildings I saw around me in my hometown, and with my mother's encouragement and cooperation, I visited the local historical society archives on several occasions to learn about the buildings that were demolished to make way for the new. What I discovered was a collection of newspaper clippings, photographs, maps, and drawings that resonated with my own growing interests in architecture, drawing, and photography. Again with my mother's support and encouragement, I began drawing and photographing the historic buildings of downtown Winona.

Although these formative experiences with buildings and archival research clearly laid the groundwork for my education as an architect and my later career as a university professor of architecture, my interest in urban renewal lay dormant for many years. It was rekindled in 2013 when my university, North Dakota State, offered a research grant designed specifically to encourage and support research into the materials in the university archives. Remembering my time as a young man researching in the Winona County Historical Society archives, hunting for materials concerning Winona's demolished buildings, I wondered whether the North Dakota State University archives contained any material on Fargo's urban renewal projects. To my delight, online finding aids confirmed that the archives housed extensive collections of urban renewal materials, many of which derived from the personal collections of Earl Stewart, a former professor in my own department who had passed away some years before I became aware of the collection.[5] I wrote a successful proposal to the grant committee that centered on the construction of a digital model of downtown Fargo and digital mapping of archival materials. The Gunlogson Award also allowed me to hire a half-time graduate research assistant.[6]

The project related to my broad research interests concerning *architectural and urban epistemology*. In general, my research considers the ways in which knowledge about the built environment is produced, manipulated, structured, disseminated, consumed, and archived, in both historical and contemporary practices.[7] For this project I proposed to study the archive's collections of images, texts, maps, and models associated with Fargo's urban renewal program from 1955 to 1974 and, specifically, to use digital technologies to organize, cross-reference, and analyze selected materials. As a topical subject within the field of architectural and urban epistemology, urban renewal constitutes a rich field for inquiry: the contested ground at the heart of the program was historically subject to diverse and often contradictory forms of mapping and documentation resulting in a significant—though in Fargo's case largely untapped—corpus. The archival material concerning Fargo's urban renewal program consists of maps, photographs, meeting minutes, project files, personal correspondence, newspaper clippings, and similar materials. The majority of these materials remain unpublished and reside in the collections of North Dakota State's Institute for Regional Studies. Published materials concerning Fargo's urban renewal program are few, and with the exception of a 1966 thesis, no general overview of the program's history has been produced.[8] Some photographic material housed in the archive is publicly available through an online portal called Digital Horizons.[9] To date, the photographs on Digital Horizons represent only a small fraction of images in the institute's collection. The items on Digital Horizons are accompanied by professionally researched, robust textual descriptions, but they are not referenced to maps of the urban renewal area.

I became especially interested in how photography was used in the early stages of Fargo's urban renewal program, particularly how the camera was used to selectively frame and highlight existing conditions and patterns of use as well as to promote new possibilities for development resulting from the clearance of older buildings. The City of Fargo's application for federal funding to support initial surveys included photographs that the city's Urban Renewal Agency clearly selected to highlight substandard existing environments to promote their clearance to make way for the construction of new buildings. These photographs served the ends of the Urban Renewal Agency precisely because they could be carefully positioned and framed to emphasize the worst aspects of the existing conditions.

As I investigated these photographs further, I found the introduction of digital tools to be invaluable in specifying and clarifying the bias that I had initially observed. In particular, I worked to develop a process of placing sampled historical photographs into a digital model. By itself the process of digital modeling is a logical contemporary outcome of the long-established practice of accurately documenting the measurable, physical attributes of the built environment.[10] Digital modeling offers the opportunity to document a three-dimensional built reality to a high degree of precision, thus providing a means of recording physical attributes in perpetuity for the use of researchers and educators. Moreover, when digital modeling is supplemented by the ability to produce photorealistic renderings, researchers gain the ability to produce simulated photographic views from any vantage point within the modeled environment. This in turn makes it possible to depict past states of a built environment in a familiar manner, facilitating comparison with present-day conditions. When further augmented by animation and virtual-reality technologies (including wearable devices), this approach makes it possible for a viewer to explore a simulated environment in a visually convincing, full-surround manner. Clearly, the technology has vast potential for researchers, particularly preservationists, seeking to understand the visual impact of the built environment on perception and on culture.[11]

My research approaches the technologies of digital modeling and photographic sampling with a somewhat different goal in mind. Rather than attempting to construct visually convincing replicas of simulated environments, my research relies on digital technologies to deconstruct biases inherent in historical photographs. In this essay I describe and reflect on my approach as it developed over the course of my research into Fargo's urban renewal efforts.

Concealing

As my graduate assistant and I began our work in 2013, I was struck by how few photographs Fargo's Urban Renewal Agency used to substantiate its original claim for federal funds. In its original context, the city's request for funds was subject to federal guidelines, which required that the area targeted for redevelopment meet certain criteria for "blight." Moreover, the Urban Renewal Agency was obligated to demonstrate the existence of "blight" to the satisfaction of the federal Urban Renewal Administration.[12] As we continued our work, I became interested in trying to specify in some way precisely *how* the photographs operated selectively.

An initial solution was to geo-reference the photographs to a map of the project area—something that was, in fact, done as part of the city's original application for funds. I felt, however, that this did not go far enough in emphasizing the specific tactics used in the original application. By inserting scanned photographs into the digital model, my research assistant and I produced new images with the same geometry as the original photographs. More importantly, by generating views with only the photographed surfaces rendered, we began to see how much of the area was not photographed—in short, how much of the area was not visible to the people making decisions about how to spend public money. We also verified that the photographs tended to concentrate on the worst-maintained buildings and most deteriorated conditions in the targeted area.

The photographs we examined resulted from the initial application for urban renewal funding prepared by Earl Stewart, professor of architecture at North Dakota State University, who was hired in 1955 by the City of Fargo to formally request federal survey and planning funds. At that time Fargo was a city of nearly forty thousand people that had experienced steady growth since its initial settlement in 1871, at a location chosen by the Northern Pacific Railroad for its crossing of the Red River of the North.[13] Despite Fargo's steady population growth and its position as a regional center for transportation, manufacturing, and trade, by the 1950s areas in and around downtown Fargo had deteriorated in value and in physical condition.[14] This deterioration, associated with a visible lack of maintenance of private buildings, was due in part to the relocation of established businesses and residents into newly developed areas outside the city's historic core and in part to poorly maintained public infrastructure in and around downtown.[15] These deteriorated conditions were particularly evident in a district between Fargo's downtown core and the Red River. On behalf of the City of Fargo, Stewart requested $47,000 from the federal government to study the redevelopment of this district, which was ultimately designated the R-1 project area.[16] A roughly contemporaneous application was made for what became the R-2 project area south of downtown, but the federal government advised the Fargo agency to pursue one project at a time.[17]

Stewart's application for federal funds (approved by the federal government in 1956 at a reduced amount of $37,000) consisted of nearly one hundred pages of completed forms, prepared narrative, and maps.[18] In its favor, the application constituted the first large-scale organized effort toward documenting the existing conditions in the R-1 project area. Unfortunately for later historians, the application did not differentiate among buildings and landscapes with historical value and those that genuinely needed improved maintenance or outright removal: the entire subject area was uniformly targeted for clearance and redevelopment. Moreover, no recognition was given to the role these places played in the history of the city. In keeping with the times and consistent with the tone of then-contemporary narratives for similar inner-city projects elsewhere in the country, the application made extensive reference to "unsatisfactory" and "blighted" conditions without formally defining these terms or their specific referents. The Urban Renewal Agency prepared four maps for the application: a map indexing the five photographs selected to document existing conditions, a map depicting current uses of buildings in the district, a map showing areas regularly subject to flooding, and, finally, a map titled *Buildings Considered Substandard,* with individual buildings identified—although the agency included no explicit criteria as a basis for this determination.

Prior to the onset of the urban renewal program in Fargo, both the R-1 and R-2 project areas consisted of a mix of commercial, residential, and light-industrial structures typical of midsize American cities in the Great Plains and upper Midwest. The R-1 project area in particular was characterized as an "amalgamation of heterogenousity [*sic*]," i.e., a diverse collection of structures in varying degrees of repair. Given subsequent (i.e., postrenewal) developments in Fargo and, particularly, in light of today's incentives encouraging mixed-use development, it is especially ironic that the mixed use of downtown in 1956 was identified as a liability. In requesting federal funds for redevelopment, Stewart's narrative noted the lack of zoning controls and identified the then-current mix of structures, "including industrial buildings, warehouses, grocery stores, apartment buildings, houses, hotels, churches, restaurants and commercial buildings."[19]

The first photograph to appear in the application, taken at a location at the far north end of the R-1 project area, depicts a lumber storage yard in a clear state of disarray (Figure 1).[20] The photograph is dominated by disorganized stacks and piles of lumber and other building materials both old and new, relegating the permanent built structures in the area to the background (Figure 2). Although other areas similar to the lumber storage yard existed within the R-1 project area at the time of application, they were not typical, representing only a small portion of the overall land use, and were found in marginal locations. The photographer clearly constructed the image to foreground disorganization, poor maintenance conditions, and impermanent rubble while drawing attention away from the built structures in the area. Stated differently, the photographer made a deliberate choice to focus

Figure 1. Lumber storage yard, north end of R-1 Urban Renewal Area, Fargo, North Dakota, photograph circa 1955. Photograph from the collections of the NDSU Institute for Regional Studies and University Archives, Mss. 22, Box 1, Folder 4, document titled *Survey and Planning Application.*

Figure 2. Thematic categorization of photograph content, color coded to show the photograph's focus on impermanent rubble and debris (*gray shading*) as compared with permanent built structures (*black shading*). Image by Mike Christenson.

Figure 3. Flamer Hotel and the 1st Avenue Cafe, Fargo, North Dakota, photograph circa 1955. Photograph from the collections of the NDSU Institute for Regional Studies and University Archives, Mss. 22, Box 1, Folder 4, document titled *Survey and Planning Application.*

attention on a feature of the urban landscape that could reasonably be addressed through *maintenance* rather than one that required *demolition.* Yet the Urban Renewal Agency selected this photograph as a means of persuading reviewing officials of the necessity of taking action, presumably in the hope that a view of obviously ill-maintained conditions would provoke the desired outcome: the receipt of federal funds.

The second photograph in the application, taken by Fargo photographer Everett Brust, shows structures on the north side of First Avenue between Third and Fourth Streets, the current site of the Fargo Public Library (Figure 3).[21] The wood-framed commercial building in the photograph is the Flamer Hotel and 1st Avenue Cafe, which was notable for having survived Fargo's fire of 1893. To the east of the hotel stands a single-family home. The building visible at the right of the photograph, though evidently larger and more substantial than the Flamer Hotel building, is clearly not the focus of the photograph. Instead, Brust centered the older building in the photograph while excluding the newer, more substantial building (Figure 4), despite the fact that all three buildings in the photograph were earmarked for demolition. The Urban Renewal Agency's selection of this photograph from a larger collection was clearly done to draw federal officials' attention to the unfavorable characteristics of the R-1 area, effectively rendering the nearby well-maintained structures invisible to those officials.

These two photographs illustrate distinct though related approaches taken by the Urban Renewal Agency in the interest of promoting its agenda for renewal: first, the selection of photographs to highlight poorly maintained areas and, second, the framing of photographs to exclude relatively new structures free of "blight." The other three photographs in Stewart's application for survey and planning funds provide additional examples of these approaches.[22] Although the five photographs depict examples of the then-existing conditions within the R-1 project area, the photographs are notable for what is left out—namely, well-maintained, substantial, and useful properties. Due to the selection of photographs for the application, these properties remained literally invisible to the federal officials responsible for reviewing and approving the City of Fargo's application for funds. Had the federal officials exercised independent inquiry, they would have quickly discovered that the conditions documented in the application were neither typical nor representative, and it is possible that the City of Fargo's application would have been rejected.[23]

The Case of the Berry Building

A year after the City of Fargo's initial application for survey and planning funds, the Fargo Urban Renewal Agency applied for an expansion of the R-1 project area.[24] The project area was enlarged to include properties at the margins of the original application, including a property at the corner of First Avenue and Fourth Street occupied by a three-story commercial building known as the Berry Building. The Berry Building was not identified by name in the grant application documents but was instead noted as a "property involving comparatively high cost [of acquisition]."[25] The application described the unnamed building: "In relatively good condition . . . [it] is a three story reinforced concrete structure approximately 40' × 140' built in 1916. . . . This building must be demolished *because its location is unsatisfactory with regard to the redevelopment of the project area.*"[26]

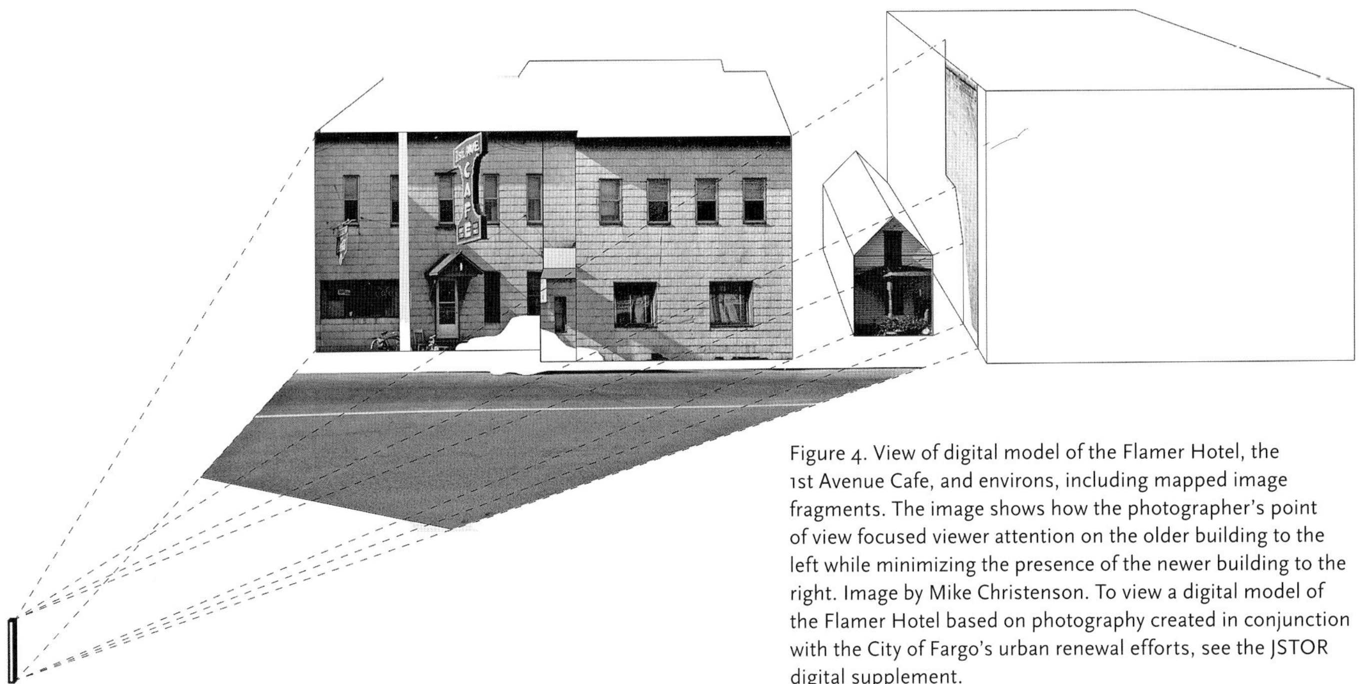

Figure 4. View of digital model of the Flamer Hotel, the 1st Avenue Cafe, and environs, including mapped image fragments. The image shows how the photographer's point of view focused viewer attention on the older building to the left while minimizing the presence of the newer building to the right. Image by Mike Christenson. To view a digital model of the Flamer Hotel based on photography created in conjunction with the City of Fargo's urban renewal efforts, see the JSTOR digital supplement.

Figure 5. Berry Building, rear and side, Fargo, North Dakota, photograph 1957. Photograph from the collections of the NDSU Institute for Regional Studies and University Archives, Mss. 22, Box 1, Folder 5, document titled *Application for Loan and Grant.*

The single photograph of the Berry Building in the application document is significant for its vantage point as well as its framing (Figure 5). The Berry Building was of a standard type in American cities: the building's street façade was designed with attention to architectural detail and reliance on relatively high-quality materials when compared with the sides and rear, which were constructed with plainer, less-expensive materials. The vantage point from which the Berry Building was photographed directs attention to the building's east and north sides, which were designed to be interior to the city block rather than the main (street) façade. Clearly, the photographer deliberately captured the building at an aesthetic disadvantage. The photograph emphasizes the unkempt surroundings of the building. In particular, the image depicts as much as possible of the unmaintained empty lot on the east side. In short, the photograph appears to have been deliberately positioned and its content carefully considered in order to bolster a case in favor of demolition.

After the city made the application for a federal loan, the Berry Building was photographed from the street façade to supplement a market appraisal (Figure 6).[27] Although the casual appearance of this photograph suggests that it was taken with a handheld camera (i.e., as distinct from tripod mounted), it is obvious that the Berry Building could have been photographed from an angle revealing more of its distinct architectural character for the federal application. Of course, such a photograph would have been inadequate evidence in support of a case for demolishing the building, as it would have depicted

Figure 6. Berry Building, façade, Fargo, North Dakota, photograph circa 1957. Photograph from the Institute for Regional Studies, NDSU, Fargo (Photo.2012.3.5).

a well-maintained, attractive building that was at the time only forty years old. The applicants clearly chose photographs that would justify a program of urban renewal, paralleling the practice of Farm Security Administration photographers during the Depression, who selected photographs specifically in order to justify continuing federal support for the agency's programs.[28]

Digital modeling shows this deliberate photographic construction (Figure 7). Significantly, the mapping of the photographs into a digital model indicates that the photograph used in the formal application (see Figure 5) was taken from a vantage point on private property, whereas the more flattering street façade could have been photographed from the public street. This suggests that the photographer deliberately sought out an unobvious vantage point to further the agenda of the forces advocating demolition.

The preservation of the Berry Building was not a contentious issue, given that the urban renewal efforts predated the national and, certainly, the local preservation movement. Although the question of preserving the Berry Building triggered a court challenge to the city's urban renewal program, photographs were not used as a means of emphasizing the building's value, as they likely would have been had the project taken place ten or fifteen years later, at a time when historic preservation had gained traction. Photographs served the ends of the forces advocating renewal because their content could be carefully managed to emphasize the worst aspects of the existing conditions. If the historic preservation movement had developed earlier in

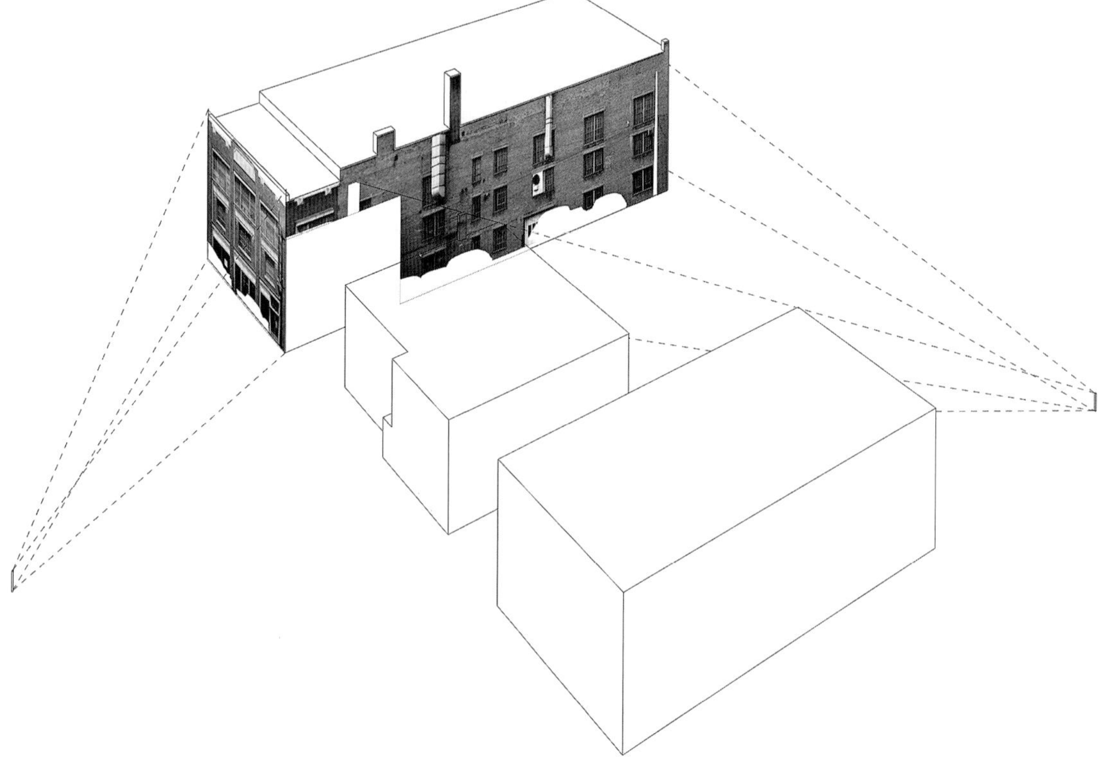

Figure 7. View of digital model of the Berry Building and environs, including mapped image fragments. The two points to either side of the Berry Building represent photographers' positions. Image by Mike Christenson. To view a digital model of the Berry Building based on photography created in conjunction with the City of Fargo's urban renewal efforts, see the JSTOR digital supplement.

Fargo, it is possible that photographs would have been strategically used by preservationists to aid their cause, as was typical of other, later attempts to raise awareness of and preserve historic buildings and districts.[29] This is not to say that Fargo's urban renewal projects proceeded without opposition, but rather that photographs were deployed in a decidedly one-sided manner in the process. Ultimately, the only significant form of organized public resistance to Fargo's urban renewal program appears to have been the Fargo Taxpayers Committee, which publicly resisted the Main Avenue (R-2) project on the basis of an anticipated increased tax burden.[30]

Promoting the New

As the projects progressed, the Fargo Urban Renewal Agency sought to organize and disseminate information to publicize and promote new development. Materials published in newspapers or as standalone brochures are typified by an advertisement placed in several national newspapers in 1960 (Figure 8).[31] The published advertisement includes a photograph of an architectural model of the R-1 project area, depicting the city hall (constructed in 1959), the proposed library, and the auditorium at the center of the image, with office buildings and a midrise hotel in the background. Headlined "Opportunities in Fargo North Dakota," the advertisement emphasized the notion of the city as a tabula rasa ready for new development. The text accompanying the photograph describes "87,000 square feet of cleared land," which referred to the parcels of land made vacant by the wholesale demolition of buildings and houses under the urban renewal program.

The photograph of the model was strategically composed so as to emphasize downtown Fargo as a place unencumbered by the past. A small tower visible at the top edge of the published image is one of Fargo's two train stations, and an existing

opportunities
in fargo
north dakota

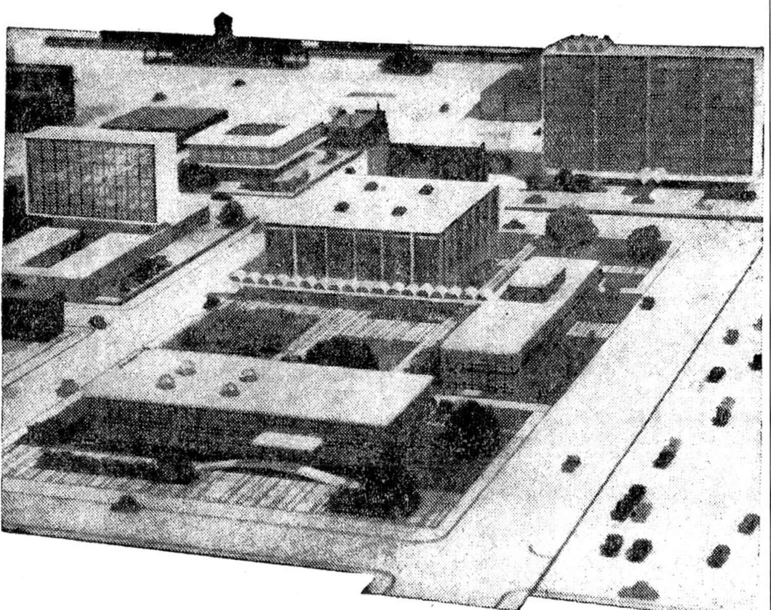

new development

87,000 SQUARE FEET OF CLEARED LAND
IN DOWNTOWN AREA AVAILABLE FOR NEW
COMMERCIAL DEVELOPMENT. WRITE OR
CALL:

EARL E. STEWART, AD 5-2761
URBAN RENEWAL AGENCY
FARGO, NORTH DAKOTA

BID OPENING OCTOBER 31, 1960

Figure 8. Advertisement for land sale in downtown Fargo, 1960. Image from the collections of the NDSU Institute for Regional Studies and University Archives, Mss. 22, Box 8, Folder 3.

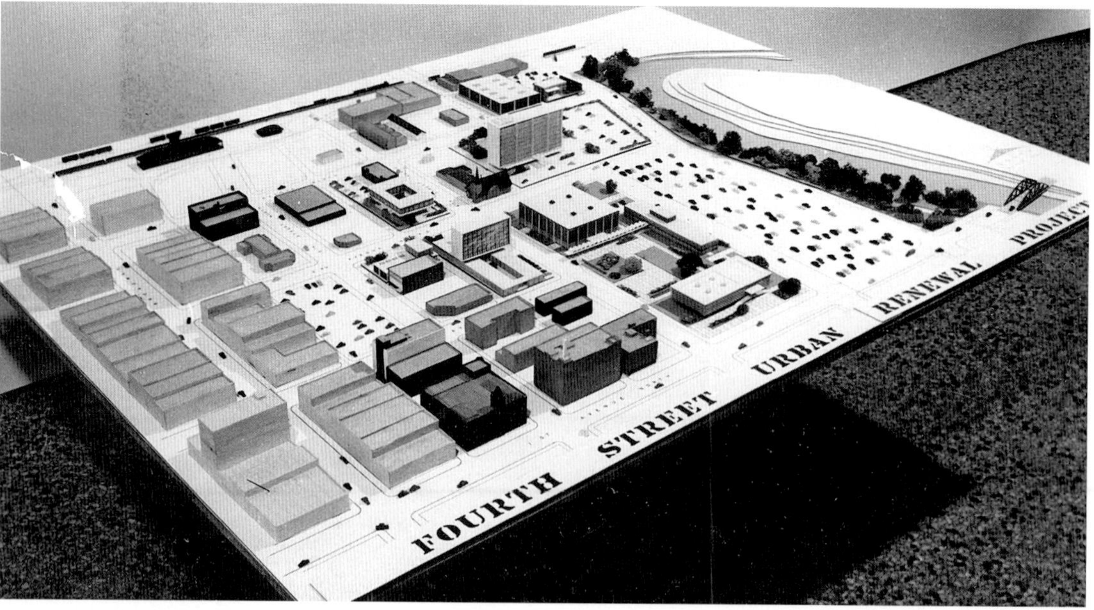

Figure 9. Model of the Fourth Street Urban Renewal Project, Fargo, North Dakota, circa 1960. Photograph from the Institute for Regional Studies, NDSU, Fargo (Photo.2012.12.01).

Lutheran church on Fourth Street is, upon careful inspection, visible near the center of the image. These two registers of historical context are unique within the image that is otherwise dominated by the proposed modern structures. Due to the photograph's vantage point and the high-contrast image, both the train station and the church appear to recede into the background. In particular, the characteristic church steeple is almost impossible to discern within the otherwise ubiquitous context of flat-roofed, dichromatic modern buildings.

While it is true that other photographs of this model could have been used in the advertisement, they would not have been as effective in depicting the modern context of downtown Fargo that the Urban Renewal Agency sought to project. The published image is successful in emphasizing the new at the expense of the old. For example, a general overall view of the model clearly shows existing historic structures along Broadway, downtown Fargo's main north–south thoroughfare (Figure 9). Although the model showed the entire urban renewal area, it did so in a wider, less controlled context than that shown in the image selected for advertising purposes. For this reason the Urban Renewal Agency did not select the image for publication; the advertisement was deliberately designed to promote a specific and highly constructed view of the city.

Consequences on the Urban Landscape

Ultimately, the City of Fargo's Urban Renewal Agency designated an area totaling over five square blocks adjacent to the Red River near the center of the city for redevelopment. The agency demolished the existing buildings in this area, as well as in a separate area along Main Avenue to the south of downtown (the R-2 project area), and subsequently prepared the land for new development.[32] In keeping with a plan formalized as early as 1952, the agency earmarked the R-1 area as the location for the city's unified public center. The City of Fargo subsequently constructed new buildings for a city hall, a library, and a public auditorium—together with a "convention hotel," extensive parking areas, and landscaped grounds across the cleared site. The clearance of buildings along Main Avenue resulted in the construction of new commercial and residential projects (including a residential high-rise tower named for Mayor Herschel Lashkowitz, himself an instrumental figure in Fargo's urban renewal efforts).

In an ironic twist, the public buildings constructed as part of the urban renewal program themselves fell victim to later efforts directed toward downtown renewal. The public library, constructed in 1968, was demolished and replaced thirty-nine years later with a new library building.[33] The city hall, designed by noted modernist architect Ralph Rapson, is slated for demolition and replacement in 2016 with a new, larger city hall building; the convention hotel sits empty and abandoned, awaiting demolition to facilitate the construction of a flood protection system.[34] Fargo's public auditorium survives, although it is unrecognizably transformed through additions and remodeling into the Fargo Civic Center.[35]

Conclusions

Within the context of the federally funded urban renewal program in Fargo, photography was employed as a powerful tool in the effort to promote redevelopment from the mid-1950s into the 1960s. A wider, more consistently executed photographic survey of the existing conditions—including the several buildings in good repair throughout the district—could have resulted in greater ambiguity concerning the suitability of wholesale removal and may have cast the receipt of federal funds into doubt.

That Fargo's Urban Renewal Agency used photography in the manner it did is not in itself surprising; after all, the agency had a vested interest in securing the funding, and to that end, it was clearly to the agency's advantage to depict the existing environments and structures in the least favorable light. Although fundamentally misleading with respect to the overall condition of the area slated for demolition, Fargo's application for federal funding was prepared in conformance with the federally established rules for such documents. With hindsight and with the aid of digital technology to trace photographs and to map them into a comprehensive digital model of the area, the selective nature of the photographs shows the extent to which the City of Fargo's applications for federal funds were misleading. Ultimately, I hope to extend this inquiry to a wider collection of images and maps, bringing contemporary modeling and imaging technologies to bear on archival materials in pursuit of unique and revealing insight into the ways that information is structured to promote specific ideas and agendas.

The images I have constructed from digital models (see Figures 4 and 7) are not intended to simulate views achievable through real experience—indeed, the physical vantage point required to produce photographs from these angles would require being aloft—but rather to view the "space of photography" from a vantage point permitting a simultaneous view of the photographer's position and subject matter.[36] Instead of attempting to visually re-create a possible past experience, my research seeks to expose the practices employed by individuals and groups with a vested interest in a particular outcome—in this case, the demolition of historic buildings and their replacement with new structures.

Although my use of digital technology—in particular, the use of digital modeling in combination with sampled photography—is not focused on the question of reconstructing historical views, it is nevertheless relevant to the practices of historic preservation. This is because preservation as a practice seeks to understand not only the physical attributes of the built environment but also the culturally and historically significant behaviors informing the questions of *what to preserve* and *what to discard*. In the case of Fargo and other cities subjected to the destruction of urban renewal, distance in time makes it possible for us to appreciate the value of what was destroyed, while digital technology provides us with unique insights into how the decision to demolish was made.

AUTHOR BIOGRAPHY

Mike Christenson, AIA, is a registered architect and an associate professor of architecture at North Dakota State University in Fargo. Christenson's research examines questions of architectural and urban epistemology: how knowledge about the built environment is produced, manipulated, structured, disseminated, consumed, and archived. Christenson's research is aimed at developing media-based strategies and tools suited for both analytic and design-generative purposes. Christenson has published and presented his research nationally and internationally and is an associate editor of the international journal *Architectural Science Review*. He serves on the board of directors of the Association for Computer-Aided Design in Architecture.

NOTES

Research described in this paper was partially funded by the Gunlogson Award, given by North Dakota State University (NDSU) in 2014, and by a subsequent 2014 award for a graduate research assistant from the NDSU Department of Architecture and Landscape Architecture. The author is indebted to the staff at the NDSU Archives, particularly Trista Raezer-Stursa and John Hallberg, for their continuing support and assistance. Alex Carlson and Troy Räisänen, graduate research assistants from NDSU's Department of Architecture and Landscape Architecture, assisted with data collection, archival work, and digital model construction. My colleague, Professor Steve Martens, assisted me in my pursuit of information concerning Gunnlauger Bjarni Gunlogson, the namesake of the fund that provided initial support for the project.

1. Housing Act of 1937, Pub. L. No. 75-412, 50 Stat. 888 (1937).

2. Housing Act of 1949, Pub L. No. 81-171, 63 Stat. 413 (1949).

3. Samuel Zipp, *Manhattan Projects: The Rise and Fall of Urban Renewal in Cold War New York* (Oxford: Oxford University Press, 2010).

4. Housing Act of 1954, Pub. L. 83-560, 68 Stat. 590 (1954).

5. The online finding aids are managed by the NDSU Library. I referred to *Finding Aid to the Fargo Urban Renewal Agency Fourth Street Project Records,* NDSU Libraries, 2009, http://library.ndsu.edu/repository/bitstream/handle/10365/187/Mss0022.pdf; and *Finding Aid to the Fargo Fourth Street Urban Renewal Photograph Collection,* NDSU Libraries, 2011, http://library.ndsu.edu/repository/bitstream/handle/10365/13830/Photo2012.pdf.

6. The Gunlogson Award is named for G. B. Gunlogson. G. B. (short for Gunnlauger Bjarni) Gunlogson, born and raised on a farmstead in rural North Dakota, was a tireless advocate of rural preservation of heritage and natural environments. His contributions to agricultural and mechanical invention are significant in the region's history. His remarkable legacy, values, and ethics live on in endowed programs, including North Dakota State University's Gunlogson Endowment, which is intended to enhance NDSU's land-grant mission though projects that preserve North Dakota's cultural history. See the *National Register of Historic Places Registration Form for the Gunlogson Farmstead Historic Site,* completed by Steve C. Martens, 2007, unpublished.

7. For a fuller discussion, see Mike Christenson, *Beginning Design Technology* (New York: Routledge, 2016).

8. The best general overview of the R-1 project is Gerald Dwight Anderson's "The R-1 Project: A History of Urban Renewal in Fargo, North Dakota" (master's thesis, North Dakota State University, 1966). John R. Borchert, Earl E. Stewart, and Sherman Hasbrouck, *Urban Renewal: Needs and Opportunities in the Upper Midwest,* Urban Report No. 5 (Minneapolis, Minn.: Upper Midwest Economic Study, 1963), focuses primarily on Fargo and provides a good summary of the program. Nicholas Bauroth, "The Reluctant Rise of an Urban Regime: The Exercise of Power in Fargo, North Dakota," *Journal of Urban History* 37, no. 4 (2011): 519–40, and Nicholas Bauroth, "The Possibility of a Housing Authority: Elite Negotiations and the Establishment of an Urban Renewal Relocation Plan in Fargo, North Dakota," *Journal of Planning History* 13, no. 4 (2014): 341–56, provide detailed analysis of specific aspects of the program.

9. The website for Digital Horizons is http://digitalhorizonsonline.org. Of the photographs discussed in detail in this essay, two of them are currently available online.

10. See John A. Burns, *Recording Historic Structures* (Washington, D.C.: American Institute of Architects Press, 1989), 20–21.

11. The relationship between historic preservation and photography has long been both mutually constitutive and problematic, and the advent of digital technology has not simplified matters. See, for example, two special issues of *Future Anterior* devoted to the topic of "Photography and Preservation," *Future Anterior* 10, no. 3 (Winter 2013), and *Future Anterior* 11, no. 1 (Summer 2014), particularly Sarah Rojon, "Postindustrial Imagery and Digital Networks: Toward New Modes of Urban Preservation?" *Future Anterior* 11, no. 1 (Summer 2014): 85–98.

12. For a detailed account of the processes composing the federal urban renewal program, see Malcolm J. Montague, "Urban Renewal: An Outline for the Practical Lawyer 'A Bombshell in a Nutshell,'" *Willamette Law Journal* 2 (1963): 359–83.

13. See Carroll Engelhardt, *Gateway to the Northern Plains: Railroads and the Birth of Fargo and Moor-*

head (Minneapolis: University of Minnesota Press, 2007); see also Arthur Henry Moehlman, "The Red River of the North," *Geographical Review* 25, no. 1 (January 1935): 87.

14. For an account of Fargo's historical development as a regional center, see John R. Borchert, *America's Northern Heartland: An Economic and Historical Geography of the Upper Midwest* (Minneapolis: University of Minnesota Press, 1987), esp. 69–75.

15. See Borchert et al., *Urban Renewal,* 12; and Bauroth, "The Reluctant Rise of an Urban Regime," 523–24.

16. *Survey and Planning Application,* Collections of the NDSU Institute for Regional Studies and University Archives, Mss. 22, Box 1, Folder 4, 1956.

17. Anderson, "The R-1 Project," 35.

18. However, not all of this material was prepared specifically for the application. Several of the pages in Stewart's application were taken directly from the City of Fargo's then-current master plan: I. S. Shattuck, *Fargo Master Plan: Report to the City Planning Commission, City of Fargo, North Dakota* (Fargo, N.D.: Pierce, 1952).

19. *Survey and Planning Application,* 3–4.

20. The five photographs selected for inclusion in the *Survey and Planning Application* were part of a larger collection of photographs, most of which were taken by Fargo photographer Everett E. Brust under commission from the Fargo Urban Renewal Agency. Prints of several of Brust's photographs are in the Fourth Street Urban Renewal Photograph Collection of the NDSU Institute for Regional Studies and University Archives; a selection of Brust's photographs have been digitally scanned and are available online at Digital Horizons.

21. In addition to appearing in the *Survey and Planning Application,* a copy of this photograph is filed separately in the Institute for Regional Studies' collections, with the title "Flamer Hotel and 1st Avenue Cafe, Fargo, N. D."

22. The third photograph, taken roughly at the location of the current Fargo City Hall, combines the two approaches in that it centers the photograph on a dilapidated structure, and it is carefully framed to exclude immediately adjacent structures in much better condition. The fourth photograph shows an auto salvage operation at the southern end of the project area, another location that though obviously poorly maintained was far from being typical of conditions within the overall project area. The fifth and final photograph shows the Grand Hotel, an apartment building located on a site currently occupied by city park land and specifically identified in the application as "considered substandard." *Survey and Planning Application,* section R-105, 13.

23. The failure of local efforts to systematically and fairly document existing conditions for purposes of federal review is certainly not unique to Fargo. See, for example, Francesca Russello Ammon, "Commemoration amid Criticism: The Mixed Legacy of Urban Renewal in Southwest Washington, D.C.," *Journal of Planning History* 8, no. 3 (August 2009): 175–220. Ammon writes: "As in many clearance projects, select photographs of particularly dilapidated sites helped cement a picture of the neighborhood that ignored the presence of other, unpictured, sound, and well-maintained structures" (213).

24. *Loan and Grant Application,* part 1, Collections of the NDSU Institute for Regional Studies and University Archives, Mss. 22, Box 1, Folder 5, 1957.

25. *Loan and Grant Application,* part 1.

26. *Loan and Grant Application,* part 1 (emphasis added).

27. "Market Value Appraisal for the Urban Renewal Agency of the City of Fargo, North Dakota, July 24, 1959, 313–15—1st Avenue North," Mss. 22, Box 5, Folder 3, 1959.

28. See James Curtis, *Mind's Eye, Mind's Truth: FSA Photography Reconsidered* (Philadelphia: Temple University Press, 1989).

29. See, for example, Richard Cahan, *They All Fall Down: Richard Nickel's Struggle to Save America's Architecture* (Washington, D.C.: Preservation Press, National Trust for Historic Preservation, 1994); or *With Heritage So Rich: A Report of a Special Committee on Historic Preservation* (New York: Random House, 1966)—a seminal and influential document in the development of the historic preservation movement, one that relies extensively on photography and that was published in the year of passage of the National Historic Preservation Act.

30. Bauroth, "The Reluctant Rise of an Urban Regime," 519.

31. In addition to the local *Fargo Forum,* the Urban Renewal Agency advertised in the Bismarck (N.D.), Milwaukee, Chicago, Des Moines, and Minneapolis

daily newspapers; national publications, including the *Wall Street Journal, Commercial West, Chain Store Age,* and *Business Week*; and nine North Dakota newspapers and three daily Minnesota papers. See Anderson, "The R-1 Project," 118.

32. A third area at Golden Ridge, an inner-ring suburban area to the northwest of downtown Fargo, was identified in 1955 as a "slum" subject for renewal. Shortly thereafter, in 1957, a devastating tornado struck Golden Ridge, destroying homes throughout the neighborhood and killing ten people. The urban renewal program was seen as an opportunity to leverage federal funds to rebuild homes in the area. A fourth area identified for renewal, the Morton-Doty subdivision in south Fargo, was redeveloped with private funds.

33. The 1968 library building was designed by the Fargo architectural firm of Seifert & Staszko Associates. The firm's records, including materials concerning the library's architectural design, are in the Institute for Regional Studies' collections. The 1968 building was demolished in 2007 and replaced by the present structure, designed by the Minneapolis architectural firm Meyer, Scherer & Rockcastle. See "Fargo Public Library," NDSU Archives, http://library.ndsu.edu/fargo-history/?q=content/fargo-public-library; and *Finding Aid to the Seifert & Staszko Associates Architectural Records,* NDSU Libraries, 2009, http://library.ndsu.edu/repository/bitstream/handle/10365/6729/SeifertandStazsko.pdf.

34. The Town House Motor Hotel was constructed in 1961–62 and is slated for demolition in 2016. For a brief review of the hotel's history, see "Town House Motor Hotel," NDSU Archives, http://library.ndsu.edu/fargo-history/?q=content/town-house-motor-hotel. Photographs of the hotel exist in the Institute for Regional Studies' collections and online at Digital Horizons, http://digitalhorizonsonline.org/cdm/ref/collection/uw/id/8053.

35. The Institute for Regional Studies houses several photographs of the Fargo Municipal Auditorium in its files and online at Digital Horizons. See, for example, "City Hall and Civic Memorial Auditorium, Fargo, N.D.," Digital Horizons, http://digitalhorizonsonline.org/cdm/singleitem/collection/uw/id/8072/rec/1.

36. I define and discuss the "space of photography" concept in "On the Architectural Structure of Photographic Space," *Architectural Science Review* 54, no. 2 (2011): 93–100.

Reviews

Cary Carson and Carl R. Lounsbury, editors
The Chesapeake House: Architectural Investigation by Colonial Williamsburg

Chapel Hill: The University of North Carolina Press in association with the Colonial Williamsburg Foundation, 2013.

xiii + 471 pages, 350 black-and-white and color illustrations.

ISBN: 978-0-8078-3577-7, $63.00 HB

ISBN: 978-0-8078-3811-2, $29.99 EB

Review by Kathryn E. Wilson

Examining the nature of architecture and landscape in one East Coast region from colonial settlement to the early nineteenth century, *The Chesapeake House,* edited by Cary Carson and Carl R. Lounsbury, is an accessible and beautifully designed volume that presents the work of an interdisciplinary team of historians, archeologists, conservators, and curators working for the Colonial Williamsburg Foundation over the past two decades. Moving well beyond the original site of Williamsburg to survey other extant buildings across Maryland and eastern Virginia, their work yields insights into the development of a distinct regional architecture and culture over time, grounded in the deep analysis of a wide variety of buildings and landscapes.

The book is divided into four sections—"Ends & Means," "Design & Use," "Materials," and "Finishes"—followed by a conclusion. The first two provide a larger sociohistorical context for the study of architecture in this period and lay out a research agenda that seeks to advance the study of the early American built environment, outlining underexplored aspects of the design process and highlighting social issues embodied in material forms that have too often been overlooked. The chief argument, Carson writes in his introduction to the collection, is that architecture gives "physical form to the way people treat other people who share their space" and that fieldwork, which "lays bare" a building's social uses, is "indivisible from the interpretation of architecture as social history" (12–13).

"Ends & Means" includes an overview by Lorena Walsh of the larger social, ethnic, and economic history of the region in terms of tobacco agriculture and slave labor and an excellent essay by Edward Chappell on fieldwork. Good fieldwork, according to Chappell, is based on the close observation of building features, recorded in annotated measured drawings, with the aim of "recognizing changes, sorting out dates, and discovering variability that reveals human choice and ideology" (32). Also of note is the discussion of the innovative (to this folklorist) microanalysis of materials that is allowed by new technologies, such as dendrochronology, to accurately date architectural remnants and map change over time with greater precision than previously possible. Spatial and chronological contexts matter, Chappell points out, highlighting by way of example how decorative elements varied among floors or rooms of a house, with differences in finish communicating status or directing movement through domestic space.

Much of the evidence marshaled implicitly points to the role that living history at Williamsburg has played in driving new analysis. One example is the restoration of the courthouse on Market Square. To create a fully functioning eighteenth-century space and reenact larger social power relations between various players, physical evidence was mined to reconstruct the daily procedures of the chamber in which a variety of people worked, stood trial, or watched the proceedings. Elsewhere, hierarchies were discovered in the spatial arrangement and decoration of domestic interiors, shaping how individuals were brought together or kept apart and how specific rooms were outfitted to fulfill both private and public functions. Here, one perceives the influence of performative approaches to architecture, especially in attention given to the processual nature of space. Entrances and exits indicate how different kinds of people moved in and out. The quality of locks and hinges signified who would come and go. Molding, trim, and paint color indicated which rooms were higher status or served more public functions.

These ideas are echoed in the section "Design & Use," which examines the processes that shaped housing design and rebuilding across different periods, with a specific focus on the plantation form. In an essay on the design process, Lounsbury outlines the emergence of a regional style and the persistence of local conditions, social customs, and conventional building techniques amid the introduction of classical principles and British high-style design in the eighteenth century. The chapters "Plantation Housing" and "Town House and Country House" by Carson and Mark Wenger, respectively, which provide an effective synthesis of a generation of cultural landscape and vernacular architecture studies conducted since the 1970s, link the form of houses to a variety of historical processes and transformations: the transfer and circulation of architectural ideas from the old to the new world, economic and agricultural diversification, and perhaps most significantly, the region's dependence on chattel slavery and the social relations it produced.

The two later sections of the book, "Materials" and "Finishes," offer an encyclopedic compendium of information about traditional

especially studies on the relationship of power and space. Needless to say, the book takes on a very disturbing topic, and Stratigakos handles it masterfully. Despite the difficult emotions *Hitler at Home* arouses, it is a significant contribution to the study of ordinary buildings with regard to things we know that need reinforcing. It shows the power of architecture to seduce millions of people. It shows the capacity of architecture for multiple interpretations. It connects domestic architecture to masculine power. And finally, it uncovers architecture's unmatched capacity to remember.

AUTHOR BIOGRAPHY

Annmarie Adams is William C. Macdonald Professor at the School of Architecture, McGill University. Her research explores gendered spaces, domestic architecture, health care architecture, and their discreet intersections.

James A. Jacobs

Detached America: Building Houses in Postwar Suburbia

Charlottesville: University of Virginia Press, 2015.
viii + 261 pages, 61 black-and-white illustrations.
ISBN: 978-081-393761-8, $45.00 HB
ISBN: 978-081-393762-5, $45.00 EB

Review by Barbara Miller Lane

Between 1945 and 1970, new housing types transformed the American city and suburbs. Millions and millions of "tract houses" constructed and designed by builders ringed the older urban cores. Nearly all were ranches, split-levels, or other new forms of two-story houses. Each was different from previous American houses in design and spatial arrangement. But because the new types have been thoroughly disliked for most of their history by cultural critics—and by architectural historians—we know astonishingly little about them. Only in the past few years have scholars turned sustained attention to the new houses and the neighborhoods of which they were a part.[1] James A. Jacobs is one of the first to focus specifically on the design of these houses and, so far, the only one to emphasize the plans of the houses almost exclusively.

How does one select what to study, given the gigantic number of houses? Architectural history, at least, has never confronted this problem. The social sciences, more accustomed to dealing with modern mass phenomena, suggest several methods. Sociology relies on random samples, surveys, and interviews, while history and anthropology favor the case study as a microcosm from which generalizations can be extrapolated. Jacobs has employed all of these approaches, and his results are compelling.

The "case study" at the core of this study is a builder, Ryan Homes. Ryan Homes started out as a small Pittsburgh firm right after World War II and was hugely successful, growing into one of the largest homebuilders in the country by the 1960s. Jacobs unearthed a sizable collection of Ryan Homes records at Carnegie Mellon University: a rare gold mine because neither builders nor local offices have kept records in most cases. Jacobs also surveyed and interviewed original owners in several of Ryan and other Pittsburgh-area subdivisions, despite the difficulty of discovering these now very elderly people. In addition, he visited some Ryan subdivisions constructed in the 1960s—and, more briefly, a Levitt and Sons' development from this era in Bowie, Maryland—in order to view the houses, to understand the plans, and to talk with their current owners.

In order to put these examples into perspective and to attempt some generalizations that are valid for the national scene, Jacobs also studied the plans of houses as presented in magazines aimed at builders: the National Association of Home Builders' (NAHB's) *Correlator, American Builder,* and *Practical Builder.* Further, he worked through many issues of popular women's magazines and what he calls the "shelter press": *House and Home, Better Homes & Gardens, House Beautiful, House and Garden,* and *American Home.* Additionally, he sampled the real estate advertisements of four major newspapers: the *Pittsburgh Press,* the *Washington Post,* the *Chicago Tribune,* and the *Los Angeles Times.* He also gained access to the archives of the NAHB, which most researchers have found hard to do.

This is an impressive and well-conceived research program. Jacobs has extracted from these sources a great many house plans, which he has hired a draftsman to reproduce. The result is a handsome book that is far more informative than most publications about suburban houses after World War II.

From these plans he develops a hypothesis about the evolution of tract house plans, which he sees as falling into three periods that roughly correspond to the decades of construction (1940s, 1950s, and 1960s and after). The 1940s, he writes, were the decade of the "minimum house" (the label derived from the Federal Housing Administration's 1946 *Principles of Planning Small Houses*), a house of about nine hundred to one thousand square feet, with an "all purpose living room," a kitchen, one bath, and two or three bedrooms. In the 1950s, he says, buyers sought more living space, especially in the kitchen, so this was the decade of the "living-kitchen." Both decades, according to Jacobs, were characterized by an affirmation of "togetherness" for the family and by a "revolution in lifestyle": away from the formality of the prewar period to a love of casual living in the postwar era. In the 1960s a desire among buyers ("maturing families") for greater "apartness" led to the creation of more differentiated spaces, most notably the family room, the separate dining room, and the master bedroom suite. The result is what Jacobs calls the "zoned house," in which private and quasi-public spaces were differentiated. The first decade produced the ranch house, with its single story and open plan. The second decade produced the split-level house, which lent itself to the beginnings of greater spatial differentiation. In the third decade and after, new versions of the split and the return of the two-story house completed the evolution of the zoned house. Each of these developments is illustrated by many plans and by a great deal of helpful information about the layout of spaces in various models.

These shifts were driven, Jacobs argues, by the changing preferences of buyers as shaped by social change, with the first decade characterized by the movement of the "affluent working class" to the suburbs and the next two decades by the formation of a "new middle class" (204). Jacobs writes that the possession of a house with highly differentiated spaces eventually became a "marker" of membership in this new middle class. Extrapolating these developments toward the future, he states that "they are the grandparents and parents of today's much-maligned 'McMansions'" (210–11). This is a bold and in many ways very satisfying set of explanations for the evolution of typical American houses. Many of these observations are supported by my own research.[2] Jacobs's attention to variations in class is especially important, since most historians of residential architecture have seen suburban buyers as uniformly middle class.

But I think that applying these generalizations to the millions of houses built throughout the nation after 1945 is overambitious. There are many contrary examples. Buyers in the 1940s were already seeking large kitchens. A great many builders throughout the period offered dining ells, and some offered separate dining rooms. Versions of the family room also began quite early in many places, as enlargements of the living-kitchen or as a leftover space in the lowest level of split-levels. Two-story houses preceded ranches and splits as builders' houses in some metropolitan areas (in Philadelphia, for example), rather than being the end product of the evolution. The national scene in general was far more varied than Jacobs suggests: different house types predominated in different areas.

The choice of Ryan Homes in the 1960s as the principal example of a builder also raises questions. Ryan Homes was one of the giants among American building firms. Given the numbers of houses being built in the postwar era, there may have been tens of thousands of builders, and they ranged from very small to moderately large. But the great giants—Ryan, Centex, Kaufman & Broad, Lennar, and Pulte—were different; they built relatively small developments in many different locations at once, and they accounted for an extremely small proportion of the vast output of builders during the period. Unlike most other builders in the 1940s, 1950s, and 1960s, the giants usually did not engage in land development or community planning.[3] Thus, by focusing on Ryan Homes, Jacobs cannot generalize about the building process: how land was found and subdivided; how houses were sited, designed, and built; or how streets evolved in tandem with the siting of houses. Yet this is vital information in understanding buyers' preferences: buyers often cared more about the lot, the site, the street view, and the probable shape of the planned community than they did about the details of the house plan.

The sources of Jacobs's plans are also problematic. We see many plans, but because most derive from "shelter" magazines or *House and Home*, we cannot be sure whether they are from houses that were actually built. How do we know that they are typical of a larger group and not just one-off designs? This is a serious problem for all types of media studies, not least for the history of builders' houses. Newspapers are generally somewhat more reliable for these purposes, and Jacobs's use of newspapers is commendable. But why look at just one month per year (September)? Several months in the spring and summer might be better. And why not additional newspapers? The *New York Times* (which is online) would have been an important addition, as would the *Dallas Morning News* (also online) and the Boston and Philadelphia papers (not yet online). The *New York Times* is particularly useful for the study of split-level houses, which proliferated at an early date in the areas of New Jersey, New York, and Connecticut around the New York metropolitan area.

I do not agree with the premise that house plans can be detached from house forms and studied independently. For example, window treatment varied enormously from builder to builder and among house types. Thus, the relationship of indoors and outdoors, the flow of light into the buildings, and the views toward the outside varied dramatically, too. Split-level and two-story houses offered far less relationship to "outdoor living" than ranch houses, and they displayed very different street façades, changing the look of the community.

I would describe the postwar evolution of house design and the housing market somewhat differently. I believe that there was one overwhelmingly significant generational change in the production and consumption of single-family dwellings in the thirty years after the war. The first generation of houses (circa 1945–60) were rather close to the minimal level in size and often displayed the undifferentiated plans of the minimal dwelling. A high proportion of these houses were "ranch houses." The buyers, in many if not most metropolitan areas, came from the newly affluent working class. My own research suggests that these buyers tended to stay in their original dwellings, and when they needed more space, they added to their existing houses. They were not just homebuyers but also community builders.[4]

The second generation of buyers (from around 1960 to 1975 or 1980), who are the primary focus of Jacobs's book, probably came from a different class background and were seeking their second or third homes, at a time when the supply of affordable housing was dramatically shrinking. The house types favored by this group were larger ranches (on the West Coast and elsewhere), larger split-levels of various designs, and two-story houses (in the Midwest and on the East Coast). Housing economists show that during 1960–79 housing costs rose sharply and "affordability" plummeted.[5] So these later purchasers must have brought to the table a good deal more capital than the buyers of the 1940s and 1950s, and they frequently "traded-up" their house purchases. Which of these groups would have been "the new middle class"? Perhaps both, but if so, we need to know more about each and about how they lived together.

Jacobs's book offers a persuasive and important argument, but one that sometimes overreaches its evidence. I hope it will inspire further case studies that give more prominence to typical builders and their work on the ground, in many different geographical areas, and to the buyers, their housing preferences and their socioeconomic status.

AUTHOR BIOGRAPHY

Barbara Miller Lane is Mellon Professor Emeritus in the Humanities and a research professor in the Growth and Structure of Cities Department at Bryn Mawr College. Her most recent book is *Houses for a New World: Builders and Buyers in American Suburbs, 1945–1965* (2015), which is also reviewed in this issue.

NOTES

1. See, for example, John Archer, *Architecture and Suburbia: From English Villa to American Dream House, 1690–2000* (Minneapolis: University of Minnesota Press, 2005); Sandy Isenstadt, *The Modern American House: Spaciousness and Middle-Class Identity* (New York: Cambridge University Press, 2006); Becky M. Nicolaides and Andrew Wiese, eds., *The Suburb Reader* (New York: Routledge, 2006); Anna Vemer Andrzejewski, "Building Privacy and Community: Surveillance in a Postwar American Suburban Development in Madison, Wisconsin," *Landscape Journal* 28, no. 1 (2009): 40–56; Dianne Harris, ed., *Second Suburb: Levittown, Pennsylvania* (Pittsburgh, Penn.: University of Pittsburgh Press, 2010); Elizabeth Collins Cromley, *The Food Axis: Cooking, Eating, and the Architecture of American Houses* (Charlottesville: University of Virginia Press, 2011); Thomas Hubka, *Houses without Names: Architectural Nomenclature and the Classification of America's Common Houses* (Knoxville: University of Tennessee Press, 2013); Dianne Harris, *Little White Houses: How the Postwar Home Constructed Race in America* (Milwaukee: University of Minnesota Press, 2013); Robert A. M. Stern, *Paradise Planned: The Garden Suburb and the Modern City* (New York: Monacelli Press, 2013); Barbara Miller Lane, *Houses for a New World: Builders and Buyers in American Suburbs, 1945–1965* (Princeton, N.J.: Princeton University Press: 2015); and John Archer et al., eds., *Making Suburbia: New Histories of Everyday America* (Minneapolis: University of Minnesota Press, 2015). Pathbreaking early studies include Gwendolyn Wright, *Building the Dream: A Social History of Housing in America* (New York: Pantheon Books, 1981); and Barbara M. Kelly, *Expanding the American Dream: Building and Rebuilding Levittown* (Albany: State University of New York, 1993).

2. See especially the discussions of the family room and the "eat-in" kitchen in Lane, *Houses for a New World,* 21, 67, 78–79, 84-85, 108, 152, 166, 181–82, 186, 189, 202–3, 215.

3. See especially Leo Grebler, *Large Scale Housing and Real Estate Firms: Analysis of a New Business Enterprise* (New York: Praeger, 1973); and Witold Rybczynski, *Last Harvest: How a Cornfield Became New Daleville: Real Estate Development in America from George Washington to the Builders of the Twenty-First Century, and Why We Live in Houses Anyway* (New York: Scribner, 2007).

4. See especially Lane, *Houses for a New World,* chaps. 5 and 6.

5. Barbara T. Alexander, "The U.S. Homebuilding Industry: A Half-Century of Building the American Dream," John T. Dunlop Lecture, The Joint Center for Housing Studies, Harvard University, October 12, 2000, typescript, www.jchs.harvard.edu.

Barbara Miller Lane
Houses for a New World: Builders and Buyers in American Suburbs, 1945–1965

Princeton, N.J.: Princeton University Press, 2015.
xi + 305 pages, 224 black-and-white illustrations.
ISBN: 978-069-116761-9, $49.95 HB

Review by Richard Longstreth

Houses for a New World makes a significant contribution to the growing corpus of scholarly literature focused on the post–World War II tract house and residential development on what was then the metropolitan periphery. This volume is not only the most detailed study to date but offers an abundance of fresh material and, most importantly, substantial new insights on the nature of a phenomenon that became an emblem of the American landscape and American life, one that still profoundly affects our routines and our outlooks. Barbara Miller Lane takes her subject in a largely positive light that is framed by voluminous research over a period of many years. Her perspective accords with that of a number of other historians who have investigated this realm in recent years. At the same time, she is mindful that the postwar suburb still has its critics who variously deride it as physically banal, culturally deprived, environmentally harmful, and racially divisive. Lane not only acknowledges such invectives but also explores why these places were so demonized by sociologists, planners, architects, and others when they were new, and she provides a sound basis for refuting at least some of the arguments that persist.

Lane breaks new ground in several ways. First, she closely examines several kinds of tract development that for the most part have never received such attention before. The importance of her case studies is that they begin to give a more accurate reading of the complexion of postwar residential development than we have had to date. Many previous writings have been grounded in generalities, drawing from federal provisions and policies, broad demographic and sociological studies, a sampling of trade journals and shelter magazines, and trends in popular culture, among other sources. Beginning in the 1990s, more detailed explorations have been made on the Levittowns in Nassau County, New York, and Bucks County, Pennsylvania; Lakewood in Los Angeles County, California; and Park Forest in Cook County, Illinois.[1] But the first three of these developments entailed more than 17,000 houses each, and the fourth, nearly 5,500, in addition to a number of apartment buildings. In their size, scope, and support facilities, as well as in the case of Park Forest, with its focused application of garden city planning principles, these places were likely more the exception than the rule. Several case studies have been made of middle-class African American postwar suburban enclaves, the demographic nature of which renders them unusual.[2] An urbanistic perspective is afforded in what was a pioneering examination of Los Angeles that shows how postwar housing tracts (two of which are also examined by Lane) were key to shaping that metropolis.[3] Together, this work gives a more complex and nuanced picture of the seminal role of postwar developments of single-family houses in defining the United States during the second half of the twentieth century; however, it is hardly a complete picture.

Lane builds upon this research by taking a first, essential step in crafting a more truly national understanding of the phenomenon based on exploring the places themselves. Collectively, these examples offer more of a cross-section of the scope and nature of postwar house tracts than has previously been available. To advance the process, she focuses on twelve developments in four metropolitan areas: Los Angeles, Philadelphia, Boston, and Chicago. The projects vary considerably in size (from 135 to 6,829 houses, with most falling between 1,200 and 2,500 dwellings), layout, and appearance. Likewise, the builders differed in background and in the methods by which they established and operated their respective businesses. Lane profiles not only these individuals, but also others with whom they contracted to realize their work. The local context often figured prominently in the nature of what was done. To develop her portrayal, Lane has interviewed many of those people involved or their descendants. She has also drawn from the recollections of a number of early inhabitants. Finally, she has examined the physical character of these places firsthand, analyzing subdivision layouts, house forms, and interior spatial arrangements. Are these places more representative of the norm in postwar suburban development? Did a norm ever exist? Some examples, no doubt, represent widespread practices, but others less so, as with the stage-set imagery embraced in two Orange County, California, developments or the "flattops" that comprised the initial portions of Rose Tree Woods outside Philadelphia. Even when places seem typical, they may not be in all their dimensions.[4]

Beyond the array of case-specific information, Lane probes basic underlying issues. Who designed these places? Her conclusion is that the builders were primarily responsible. They often employed architects or other designers to draw up plans and also contracted with engineer-planning firms to prepare the subdivision layouts, but it was the builders themselves who seem to have set the parameters for what they wanted. Their goal, of course, was to provide what prospective homeowners would buy. (Lane's research, let us hope, puts an end to the persistent claim in some circles that purchasers were simply beholden to whatever builders would foist upon them.) The text explores a variety of ways in which builders conducted reconnaissance to determine what would attract consumers. But what did *they* want? Lane presents evidence that counters some often-noted assumptions of how prospective homeowners' ideas were influenced by shelter or even popular magazines, television shows, or movies. Instead, she suggests how ideas about dwelling were shaped by previous experiences—derived not so much from middle-class houses of earlier decades but from small, often overcrowded houses and apartments occupied during the Depression and military base housing of various kinds, much of it makeshift, as well as shipboard quarters during World War II. This latter exploration is one of the book's most significant contributions, for it begins to fill in a gap in the inquiry that, remarkably, has almost never been addressed before and goes a long way to explaining why suburban houses so disparaged by critics were vigorously embraced by the millions of Americans who moved to them.

Lane's interviews with twelve early inhabitants of her case-study tracts, gathered in the appendix, are a bounteous source unto themselves, giving a new dimension to why such places were (and often still are) so meaningful to those who occupied them. These developments seemed very new in their location, arrangement, and appearance (inside and out), but more than physical distinctions, they were part of a new experience. Lane gives fresh evidence to reinforce the work of others that these places comprised communities of a different sort from their counterparts of earlier decades—new in their perceived (and often actual) separation from established parts of metropolitan areas; new in their ethnic and religious (though not racial) diversity; new in the absence of an entrenched social hierarchy—everyone was relatively young, married, and with (or soon to have) children. The early occupants themselves got to create the institutions and activities that formed community.

Historians of planning may be disappointed that more attention is not paid to the nature of subdivision layout, to creating infrastructure, or to providing amenities. Lane's approach, however, provides a valuable foundation from which such matters can be pursued in detail by others. She emphasizes that her commanding study is hardly a definitive one, but rather it is an exploratory venture intended to stimulate much in the way of further research. How much did the tradition of grid planning affect postwar residential tracts outside Southern California, for example? Even a casual perusal of the real estate sections of major metropolitan newspapers of the era reveals that the choices available to persons in the market for a new house of relatively modest dimensions were considerable, arguably greater than the spectrum of designs illustrated in this book. The market was never uniform in its preferences, but how great was the scope? If we consider, on the one hand, the semidetached houses that continued to be built well into the 1960s on the edges of Philadelphia and, on the other, the arrestingly modern houses designed by Charles Goodman in the Washington, D.C. area or built by Joseph Eichler in Northern and Southern California, the range is dramatic indeed. To what extent did localisms—in layout, materials, and appearances (inside and out)—really play in the design of tract houses? How common was the establishment of homeowners' associations to assist perpetuating stability and continuity in such developments? The list of fruitful topics for further exploration is a long one.

Houses for a New World, then, is not the ultimate examination of postwar house tracts. Indeed, it is nicely complemented by another volume released just slightly earlier in the year. James A. Jacobs's *Detached America* (also reviewed in this volume) breaks new ground in its detailed investigation of the tract house as domestic space and how market demands and spatial configurations evolved over the postwar period, and it, too, is informed by extensive fieldwork and interviews.[5] A rich topic is getting more of the top-flight scholarly attention it deserves.

AUTHOR BIOGRAPHY

Richard Longstreth is professor of American studies at George Washington University and is currently vice president of the Frank Lloyd Wright Building Conservancy. His latest book is *Looking beyond the Icons: Midcentury Architect, Landscape, and Urbanism* (2015), which is reviewed in *Buildings & Landscapes* 23, no. 1 (Spring 2016).

NOTES

1. In chronological order, they are Barbara M. Kelly, *Expanding the American Dream: Building and Rebuilding Levittown* (Albany: State University of New York Press, 1993); Allison Leslie Baker, "The Lakewood Story: Defending the Recreational Good Life in Postwar Southern California Suburbia, 1950–1999" (PhD diss., University of Pennsylvania, 1999); Gregory Randall, *America's Original GI Town: Park Forest, Illinois* (Baltimore, Md.: Johns Hopkins University Press, 2000); Allison Baker et al., *The Lakewood Story: History, Tradition, Values* (Lakewood, Calif.: City of Lakewood, 2004); and Dianne Harris, ed., *Second Suburb: Levittown, Pennsylvania* (Pittsburgh, Penn.: University of Pittsburgh Press, 2010). Lane is incorrect in ascribing William Levitt as the principal designer of houses for his firm (16). An abundance of period accounts ascribe that role to his younger brother, Alfred.

2. Most notably, Andrew Wiese, *Places of Their Own: African American Suburbanization in the Twentieth Century* (Chicago: University of Chicago Press, 2003). In another important study, Margaret Ruth Little, "Getting the American Dream for Themselves: Postwar Modern Subdivisions for African Americans in Raleigh, North Carolina," *Buildings & Landscapes* 19, no. 1 (Spring 2012): 73–86, the author suggests that black families preferred houses that looked more "modern" than those locally popular among white households, which favored Southern "colonial" imagery.

3. Greg Hise, *Magnetic Los Angeles: Planning the Twentieth-Century Metropolis* (Baltimore, Md.: Johns Hopkins University Press, 1997).

4. I sought to emphasize this point in a case study of a tract in metropolitan Washington, D.C. See "Building Houses, Creating Community: Joseph Geeraert and the Development of Twinbrook," in *Looking beyond the Icons: Midcentury Architecture, Landscape, and Urbanism* (Charlottesville: University of Virginia Press, 2015), 195–221.

5. James A. Jacobs, *Detached America: Building Houses in Postwar Suburbia* (Charlottesville: University of Virginia Press, 2015).

Robert B. Riley

The Camaro in the Pasture: Speculations on the Cultural Landscape of America

Charlottesville: University of Virginia Press, 2015.
xii + 170 pages.
ISBN: 978-081-393715-1, $39.50 HB
ISBN: 978–081-393716-8, $39.50 EB

Review by Elihu Rubin

"The countryside just doesn't look like countryside is supposed to anymore," Robert Riley writes in the essay that gives this collection its name. "The tractor-tire garden out front is now an eight-year-old Camaro with a 'for sale' sign on it" (92). This unexpected new reality—Riley's "machine in the garden"—prompts a broader inquiry into the contemporary rural landscape in transition.[1] It used to be that people who lived on the land also earned a living from it. This old rural landscape played a stable role as both a physical place and an image of preindustrial wholesomeness in the spatial imaginary of the modern city. Today, however, much of the American countryside has shed its traditional associations and become part of the metropole, home to "commuters, retirees, or desktop publishers earning a living from their den," who "regard the rural landscape not as a productive system or a way of life but as a locational amenity" (94).

The Camaro in the Pasture, which brings together twenty-six essays and short reflections—half of them published previously, the earliest from 1958—represents Riley's more than fifty-year engagement with U.S. cultural landscapes, rural and urban, as a writer, educator, and designer. He is professor emeritus of landscape architecture at the University of Illinois and for nearly twenty years served as the editor of *Landscape*, the journal of human geography created by John Brinckerhoff Jackson in 1951. Riley dedicates this volume to his mentor, "in memory of Brinck." He is among those most influenced by Jackson's gift for seeing and analyzing the American landscape, and this book is a tribute and contribution to that tradition.

Jackson is perhaps best remembered for crafting pithy and evocative portraits of new metropolitan rituals, like the Sunday drive as a 1950s family outing. His wry description of the danger, hassle, and sensorial paucity of such an experience in "The Abstract World of the Hot-Rodder" sent him into an affectionate reverie for the past: "I find myself recalling the days when the streetcar was the chief means of Sunday transportation out of the city."[2] Jackson viewed the streetcar excursion as a spiritual and deeply ecological experience. He was not paralyzed by nostalgia, however. His genius lay in recognizing how new forms of mobility generated novel cultural landscapes. Jackson's essay goes on to explore the abstract world of the hot-rodder as the paradigm for a more visceral and direct type of engagement with the physical landscape in which the excursionist wanted to be *part* of the environment and not just its observer.

Hot-rodding—building, adapting, and racing cars—anticipated the rise of skiing, surfing, gliding, mountain climbing, and other less communal and more kinetic sports where the individual is at the controls. (This list also included motorcycle riding, well known to be Jackson's travel mode of choice.) At the time, Jackson's appreciation was all the more radical because the hot-rodder got no respect in highbrow circles: "What we notice in particular about his activities is the rubbish-strewn landscape, the disregard for time-honored esthetic values, the reckless driving."[3] Jackson resisted the urge to prejudge, however. The drag strip and the motorcycle excursion, like the Sunday family drive, were for him authentic expressions of culture, and their practitioners would create "a new poetry and a new nature mysticism," a prediction that just barely postdated an early example of such work: Jack Kerouac's *On the Road*.[4]

Though steeped in this tradition, Riley balances Jackson's imperative to observe with a competing one shaped by his role as designer and critic: to improve. J. B. Jackson was not averse to critique. In his essay "The Stranger's Path," for instance, he warned against the clearance of visitor-driven vice districts in the central city as part of urban renewal, pointing out the social functions of the tenderloin.[5] On the whole, however, Jackson's chief intent was to expand appreciation for the formation and meaning of ordinary landscapes. Riley's speculations, by contrast, are driven in part by the desire to extract lessons for his coprofessionals: trained landscape architects. His most trenchant essays are targeted to the field's educators and students. Consider three written in the mid-1960s. In one, "The Urban Cosmeticians," he laments the perseverance of conventional City Beautiful aesthetics in urban design. In another, "Understanding the Strip," he suggests remedies such as strengthening the intensity of its street crossings. In a third, he asks designers to abandon "The Search for Certainty" and to take a more tolerant view toward diversity and difference in the landscape.

Despite his appreciation for the topic, Riley worries that there is little concrete for the landscape designer to draw from an examination of common, everyday environments. In one essay he suggests that "vernacular" may become just another fad for designers: just as shabby becomes chic, so does elite design appropriate the ordinary as a style. Elsewhere, Riley notes the rise of the concept of "palimpsest" to describe how sites are built up, adapted, and rebuilt over time. A palimpsest alludes to authorship, erasure, and rewriting; it suggests that settings are more layered and more contested than an observer might immediately apprehend. Although potentially a useful metaphor, Riley's concern is its misappropriation by designers: "There's a big difference between viewing the site as a palimpsest for design inspiration and assuming that it will be read as such by those who use it." A contrived palimpsest can turn into a "litter bin," he warns, or an "assemblage approaching terminal nostalgia" (120). Ever alert to intellectual posturing and empty rhetoric, Riley would like to see more substantial design research in the studio and exhorts students to spend more time in the field and less time spouting what he calls "pseudotheory" (115). Elsewhere, in an invaluable essay speaking directly to educators of landscape architects, Riley reflects on the role that history plays in design education and outlines three versions of a landscape history course, reminding us that "the history we teach must depend upon who we want to be" (37).

Interspersed with longer essays are shorter reflections that read a bit like the offhand blog posts of a witty curmudgeon. In one, Riley takes aim at the McMansion—or "Nouveau Baronial," as he dubs the style. "The mailbox is enclosed in a big brick pier, ostentatiously expensive, looking secure enough to resist a nuclear attack" (68). In another he asks what happened to the garden as a metaphor and a literal place for sex, citing the Song of Solomon, Arabian Nights, and the Villa d'Este as imagined in Anthony Hecht's poetry. Riley ridicules our current iteration of this erotic tradition: "Drinking a mojito in a Home Depot hot tub?" (43). These interjections, while amusing, often stray from Jackson's appreciative tone to point out the poverty of contemporary landscape experiences compared with their precedents.

Many of the essays draw on Riley's fascination with the connections between memory and place. He recognizes that many of our most powerful landscape experiences are forged as children, when we form indelible perceptions of our physical surroundings. Do our remembered childhood landscapes shape our ability to understand, to appreciate, and, ultimately, to design more satisfying environments? "Can we design for the smell of freshly mown grass, frying chicken, or spring-moist soil, or for the sounds of crickets and spraying hoses, or for twilight, or the feel of the air on the first day of autumn?" (59). For readers of a journal like *Buildings & Landscapes,* it may be enough to reflect on the psychological and emotional impacts of early memories on our environmental perceptions, a process that may help us understand why some places appeal while others alienate. But can designers imitate the innate appeal of childhood landscapes? Probably not. The best we can do is to generate designs that do not actively prohibit the formation of memorable experiences like these.

In one of his earliest essays, written in 1958, Riley calls for more criticism of landscape architecture. Today, he might be pleased to have witnessed the ascendancy of that field in design discourses and its claims on urbanism. And though Riley does not respond directly to recent trends like the so-called landscape urbanism—perhaps trying to quell academic faddism—his voice represents a key link in the heritage of landscape thinking and writing. Readers from that field will appreciate his searching efforts to reconcile design practice with the traditions of observation and analysis so persuasively advanced by Jackson.

AUTHOR BIOGRAPHY

Elihu Rubin is associate professor of architecture, urbanism, and American studies at Yale. He is author of *Insuring the City: The Prudential Center and the Postwar Urban Landscape* (2012), which received the Lewis Mumford Prize for Best Book from the Society of American City and Regional Planning History and the Kenneth Jackson Award for Best Book on a North American topic from the Urban History Association.

NOTES

1. Robert Riley's title cannot help but recall Leo Marx, *The Machine in the Garden: Technology and the Pastoral Ideal in America* (New York: Oxford University Press, 1964).

2. J. B. Jackson, "The Abstract World of the Hot-Rodder," *Landscape: Magazine of Human Geography* 7, no. 2 (Winter 1957–58): 22.

3. Jackson, "The Abstract World of the Hot-Rodder," 25.

4. Jackson, "The Abstract World of the Hot-Rodder," 27; Jack Kerouac, *On the Road* (New York: Viking Press, 1957).

5. J. B. Jackson, "The Strangers' Path," *Landscape: Magazine of Human Geography* 7, no. 1 (Autumn 1957): 11–16.

Stephen Fan, curator
SubUrbanisms: Casino Urbanization, Chinatowns, and the Contested American Landscape

Kerri Culhane, curator
Chinese Style: Rediscovering the Architecture of Poy Gum Lee, 1923–1968

Exhibitions at the Museum of Chinese in America, New York, September 24, 2015 through March 27, 2016.

Review by June Williamson

With *SubUrbanisms* and *Chinese Style,* the Museum of Chinese in America has staked a broadened claim for the role of Asian immigrants—Chinese Americans in particular—in the production of metropolitan cultural landscapes beyond traditional Chinatowns. The museum, founded in 1980 and housed in lower Manhattan since 2009 in a greatly expanded space designed by Maya Lin, is an ideal location to examine the material in these concurrent exhibitions.

The larger of the two shows, *SubUrbanisms,* invites the visitor to travel from crowded Mott and Canal Streets in Manhattan to the west bank of the Thames River in eastern Connecticut, where sits the Mohegan Sun, a megacasino resort. Dozens of buses travel to the casino from Chinatown—and from every other Chinatown in the Northeast—daily; many cater to gamblers from Asian communities, as evidenced by radiating red threads in one of a series of provocative diagrams and mappings that provide spatial and temporal context in the exhibition, curated by architect Stephen Fan with graphic design by Shane Keaney.

Originating in 2014 as *SubUrbanisms: Casino Company Town/China Town* at the Lyman Allyn Art Museum in New London, Connecticut (winner of VAF's 2015 Buchanan Award), the show is accompanied by a graphics-packed catalog with contributions from Abigail Van Slyck, Chloe Taft, Ellen Pader, and Aron Chang.[1] The exhibition (like the book) is organized around four primary themes: "Casino Sub-urbanization," "Learning from Los Chinos," "Single/Multi Family Hybrid Housing," and "Sub-Urban Urbanism." It features large photographs of places and people, infographic charts and maps, full-scale mock-ups of domestic spaces, documentation of houses in plan and model, and hypothetical architecture and urban design proposals by Fan. Robert Venturi, Denise Scott Brown, and Steven Izenour's symbolic readings of Las Vegas and Levittown are obvious touchstones to the design research into casino landscapes and postwar ranch houses.[2] The "kind of looking" provided here, however, is markedly different, as Van Slyck notes in the catalog.[3] As the subtitle of *Learning from Las Vegas* reminds us, Venturi and Scott Brown sought to highlight and mine the "forgotten symbolism of architectural form" in ordinary commercial and domestic buildings. Fan, by contrast, redirects our gaze to subtle signs of hidden daily practices and cultural preferences that reframe, trouble, and subvert the symbols on the surface, likening the built environment to a "prism" through which to understand larger dynamic forces.[4]

The Mohegan Sun casino, complete with a thirty-four-story hotel tower, was built on a Superfund site formerly used by a manufacturer of casings for submarine nuclear reactors. The exhibition (like the catalog) situates this suburban megacasino in various narratives. One is the history of company towns, including nearby Norwich, once a center of textile production by Irish and French Canadian immigrant workers. Another is the growth and dispersion of Asian immigrants in the United States, who comprise a hefty proportion of both casino patrons and workers (Fan estimates 20 to 30 percent and 10 to 25 percent, respectively, at Mohegan Sun). A third is the recent explosive growth of casino development—on Native American reservations, on postindustrial sites, and along state and national borders. A Native American–owned redevelopment, the Mohegan Sun is not subject to local permitting and public approvals processes. Large color photographic prints, one reproduced on the catalog cover, highlight how the shimmering glass tower seems to rise out of the tree canopy, like a singularity. Obscured in the glossy images are the local, regional, and indeed global footprints of the thousands of workers necessary to sustain the mirage.

"Learning from Los Chinos" picks up their story. Fan maps the constellation of businesses that are Asian owned and/or cater to Asian customers around Mohegan Sun, including his parents' Chinese restaurant in Norwich, and the high number of Asian-owned houses in neighboring subdivisions in suburban Montville. By pairing photographs, culled from thirty research visits to ten houses over two years, with remarks, often racist, by non-Chinese neighbors expressing anxiety about the new arrivals, the exhibition presents the story of a "suburban uncanny," wherein things seem, to some, to be "just not right." In a pointed example of insensitive and derogatory language, white neighbors dubbed the unsanctioned path through the woods that Asian workers have carved from their ranch houses to the casino as the "Ho Chi Minh Trail."

In a note on representation in the exhibition's brochure, Fan explains the appropriation of tactics from dada and surrealism and commercial advertising. A framed patch of artificial grass paired with a "keep off the grass" sign is an example of the former. An example of the latter is the pairing of identical photos, each with a different word superimposed in bold white text, such as a rustic gate fronting an untidy lawn labeled both "refuse" and "reuse," echoing the Hong Kong Shanghai Bank's Different Values ad campaign, prominent in New York's airports and subway tunnels a few years ago (Figure 1). These tactics are part of a strategy to elevate the material for the museum context and to urge viewers to reexamine their preconceptions about suburban disorder. Some uses of these tactics, including the framed patch of grass, come off as precious, while others are affecting, such as the laundry line strung diagonally across one of the rooms, from which hangs underwear, newspapers, and other personal effects, reproducing one of the common hidden daily practices observed in the house visits. *SubUrbanisms* documents a new twist on an old story of residents squeezing use-value out of their property, from taking in boarders to pay the mortgage to front lawn vegetable gardens to hooks for drying self-caught fish.

Figure 1. Stephen Fan, "Refuse/Reuse," from *SubUrbanisms,* 2014. Courtesy of Stephen Fan.

These observations are amplified with architectural documentation of new living patterns. Chinese casino workers have transformed single-family houses into shared homes of various types, from multigenerational family dwellings to de facto dormitories for single workers. Meticulously drafted plans and models show the dwellings "as inhabited," to use the term of Renee Chow, from whose work Fan appropriately borrows both language and methods of documentation and analysis.[5] Fan finds in the raised ranches of Montville additional sleeping areas carved out of living rooms, basements, and garages; new privacy thresholds and storage niches; and entries modified to accord with *fung shui* principles. Exhibition panels illustrating traditional and contemporary housing in China—*tulou* round housing, *tiang jing* "sky well" houses, high-rise apartment blocks, and suburban *bie shu* "villas"—reinforce the notion that Chinese immigrants are accustomed to high-density living. They also beg questions about perceptions of crowding and how suburban Americans might adapt to living with less space, whether by choice or necessity.

A final section of the exhibition presents hypothetical proposals designed by Fan for retrofitting three types of sites to produce higher dwelling densities and a greater mix of uses. Navigating a shift in role from ethnographic observer to visionary architect is challenging. The retrofit designs—for a mat-urbanism base supporting microunit residential towers in downtown Norwich, for apartments wrapped around Mohegan Sun's employee parking garage, for in-filling the space between ranch houses in culs-de-sac—are well executed and delineated. But they seem detached, even a bit naïve, when viewed against the analytical lens employed elsewhere in the exhibit. Are we to understand all the research as background, culminating in these hypothetical proposals, thereby reproducing "research as design" methods from VSBA (Venturi, Scott Brown and Associates, Inc.) and contemporary firms like OMA (Office for Metropolitan Architecture) and BIG (Bjarke Ingels Group)? Or are these designs meant to represent just a few of the many possible design iterations that might fruitfully emerge from the project of retrofitting suburbia for changing demographics, dramatically altered economies, and environmental imperatives? Assuming the latter, I found the schemes optimistic and fresh.

A second, smaller exhibition, *Chinese Style,* curated by architectural historian and preservationist Kerri Culhane and more modest in scope and ambition, returns us to an earlier generation of immigrants, unearthing the professional archives of architect Poy Gum Lee (1900–1968). It traces his path from a merchant family childhood on Mott Street and Beaux-Arts architectural training to a thriving practice in Shanghai and Nanjing to post–World War II repatriation back to New York and a second career. As Culhane writes in the exhibition's brochure, "A son of Chinatown, Lee brought western modern architecture and technology to China, and re-imported them to Chinatown, inflected with the ideals of the Chinese Republic" (15). Lee's route was the inverse of a stereotypical immigrant experience, although one that was apparently not all that rare among Chinese in the early twentieth century and that is becoming increasingly common in this century as hyphenated Americans, the progeny of various global diasporas, decide to become "returnees" as opportunities arise.

Culhane tells a story of stylistic evolution and hybridization in Lee's prodigious output. His career in China coincided with the professionalization of architects under the Chinese Republic, and his American credentials and connections and his talent helped him land key commissions there in the service of modernization. Culhane describes how a hybrid modern architecture emerged in China, with details like the *dougong,* a traditional timber bracket, transformed into a cast-concrete stylistic element.

After he returned to New York, Lee cultivated private clients in the Chinatown business community, for whom he designed civic buildings, restaurants, and monuments. He also labored for the New York City Housing Authority (NYCHA) from 1951 to 1962. Supervising the fifteen-acre China Village Title I Urban Renewal Plan (unbuilt), he proposed integrating Chinese-style elements in a towers-in-a-park scheme. The project and its patrons, however, were ridiculed by Robert Moses and Lee's NYCHA superiors. In an example of professional prejudices of the time, the exhibition includes a mocking cartoon sketch of one of the complex's towers, with curved roofs and hanging lanterns, labeled "Chow Mein Houses." In this way and others, the exhibit deftly problematizes a simplistic reading of the "Chinese style" in these projects as tourist-pleasing Orientalist kitsch. The hanging scroll-type display in the center of the room of delicate pencil-on-trace drawings of Lee's late projects reinforces this theme, while nicely resonating with the installation of hanging newspapers and clothing in *SubUrbanisms.* In content and form, there are rich provocations in both shows.

AUTHOR BIOGRAPHY

June Williamson is associate professor of architecture at the City College of New York. She is author of *Designing Suburban Futures: New Models from Build a Better Burb* (2013) and, with Ellen Dunham-Jones, *Retrofitting Suburbia: Urban Design Solutions for Redesigning Suburbs* (2009, updated edition 2011).

NOTES

1. Stephen Fan, ed., *SubUrbanisms: Casino Urbanization, Chinatowns, and the Contested American Landscape* (New London, Conn.: Lyman Allyn Art Museum, 2014).

2. Robert Venturi, Denise Scott Brown, and Steven Izenour, *Learning from Las Vegas: The Forgotten Symbolism of Architectural Form,* rev. ed. (Cambridge, Mass.: MIT Press, 1977).

3. Abigail Van Slyck, foreword to Fan, *SubUrbanisms,* 13.

4. Stephen Fan, "Introduction: Sub-Urban Casino Company Towns / China Towns," in Fan, *SubUrbanisms,* 45.

5. Renee Y. Chow, *Suburban Space: The Fabric of Dwelling* (Berkeley: University of California Press, 2002); and "Ossified Dwelling: Or Why Contemporary Suburban Housing Can't Change," *Places* 17, no. 2 (Summer 2005): 52–55.

Nicolas A. Brown and Sarah E. Kanouse, editors

Re-Collecting Black Hawk: Landscape, Memory, and Power in the American Midwest

Pittsburgh, Penn.: University of Pittsburgh Press, 2015.
xi + 296 pages, 167 black-and-white illustrations.
ISBN: 978-082-294437-9, $39.95 HB
ISBN: 978-082-298039-1, $39.95 EB

Review by Justin M. Carroll

When I receive books in the mail, I tear open the packaging, check the cover, read the back jacket, and flip through the pages. I followed my usual practice upon the arrival of *Re-Collecting Black Hawk: Landscapes, Memory, and Power in the American Midwest,* a stunning and provocative image-and-text collection edited by Nicolas A. Brown, a professor of geography and American Indian and Native studies, and Sarah E. Kanouse, an artist. Rifling through, I accidentally landed on a black-and-white photograph of a street sign from Freeport, Illinois. Set against a dull gray sky, the sign demarcated the intersection of West Empire Street and South Blackhawk Avenue. I stared at it for a moment before closing the book and setting it on my desk. I did not know it then, but the image proved to be a perfect encapsulation of the volume as a whole: this book is about the intersection of American empire and the appropriated language, imagery, and memories of Chief Blackhawk and Blackhawk's War—and the myriad ways in which both the man and the war haunt and contour the settler imagination inscribed in the built environment of the American Midwest.

Makataimeshekiakiak, or Black Hawk (1767–1838), was a Sauk war leader. Born in the Illinois Country, he contested the expansion of the United States, fought with the British Empire during the War of 1812, and, in 1828, was forced to move west across the Mississippi River. Four years later, he and 1,500 Sauk men, women, and children crossed back into Illinois before they were attacked by state militias and the U.S. Army. The Sauk suffered nearly six hundred casualties over the course of four months. Imprisoned for a year, U.S. authorities then paraded Makataimeshekiakiak through major cities of the East Coast, where, rather ironically, whites lionized him as protector of his land and people. The mythos of Black Hawk as the noble savage was born.

In *Re-Collecting Black Hawk,* Brown and Kanouse draw attention to, and complicate, appropriations of Makataimeshekiakiak's memory through an innovative pairing of photographs and texts, some embodying the Black Hawk fetish and some questioning it. At the core of the book are 170 wonderfully conceived, original, black-and-white photographs of historical markers, sports teams, consumer products, subdivisions, road signs, advertisements, and other white-settler exploits of the name, visage, and history of Black Hawk. Brown and Kanouse pair these images with two sets of post–World War II texts. The first are drawn from governmental reports, white and indigenous histories, recipes, press releases, newspapers, and letters to the editors from local newspapers. The second are writings from and interviews with tribal officials, activists, and scholars. These encounters between text and image speak to "the various and conflicting ways the history of that war [Black Hawk's] and the memory of that person [Black Hawk] function in the present," inviting readers to draw new connections between a colonial past, the colonizing present, and new found disjunctures that offer openings for reinterpretation of a familiar landscape (5). Ultimately, the goal of the book, as the authors put it, is to force us to confront "the importance not only of remembering and forgetting—present tense practices—in shaping both history and the landscape but also recognizing the power geometries within which these contemporary mobilizations of the past are situated" (5).

One of the many vital themes of the book is that in enshrining Black Hawk across the landscape, midwesterners—the cultural (if not literal) ancestors of those who dispossessed local indigenous communities—erase the histories they aim to commemorate. As the authors suggest, "the widespread practice of using Black Hawk's mystique to name parks, decorate car washes, or anoint a new subdivision" has the unanticipated effect of decontextualizing, detemporalizing, and dehumanizing a real historical actor (7). Consequently, these efforts transform Black Hawk into little more than an icon: "a flat image printed on a sign or invoked through Roman letters" (7). Appropriated imagery and names became "floating signifiers or empty signs" of settler colonialism that in celebrating triumphant narratives of the past contribute to the silencing of indigenous voices in the present. The preponderance of these "empty signs that circulate in the landscape," the authors argue, "diminish our capacity to imagine alternative[s]" (8).

Luckily, the processes that underwrote settler colonialism proved incomplete. The indigenous peoples of the Midwest, as elsewhere in the Americas, did not assimilate nor vanish entirely. Instead, they practiced "survivance," as articulated by Ojibwe scholar Gerald Vizenor: an active continuing presence that allows indigenous peoples to contest and shape the places in which they live.[1] Brown and Kanouse's pairings of image and text reveal this dynamic. Even when texts do not comment directly on the photographs they accompany, they "refute [the photographs'] ideological certainty" (16). The variety of voices included similarly "forestalls the transmission of a single message" and destabilizes claims to any single "authentic or historically accurate picture" (13). Instead, the authors test new and more nuanced narratives by grounding their photographs in the contemporary issues of Indian country today: sovereignty, ecology, health, language recovery, poverty, and violence. And they remind us that "Indian Country" is "not just 'over there' on the rez but also in our own backyards" (14).

Considering the photographs separately from the texts, I was struck with an incredible sense of oppressive banality. Although taken from across the Midwest, the same themes and imagery appear repeatedly: virtually identical park signs, statues, recycling cans, and even housing developments. Whether in Illinois, Wisconsin, or Iowa, the appropriations of Black Hawk and Black Hawk's War seem interchangeable. The similarities across such a broad swatch of landscape speak, of course, to the generic character of much of the contemporary American built environment. But they also suggest the completeness of the American colonial project. Black Hawk was here, now he is gone, and while you can travel around in search of his legacy, you will find him only as we see fit. And yet Brown and Kanouse's image–text pairings also highlight the dearth of the settler colonial imagination today. Having overinvested our built environment with this once potent symbol of westward expansion and white-settler dominance, we now seem unable to incorporate new narratives.

While depressing, the project also often struck me as humorous, and discovering these moments made the book a pleasure to read. For example, a 2007 press release from the Illinois Historic Preservation Agency announced a new exhibit entitled *The Transformation of Black Hawk: Frontier Terrorist to Advertising Icon, Sainthood and Beyond.* Those who held tickets to a special wine and cheese gala were promised "a premier bottle of Black Hawk or Elizabeth [Illinois] wine from Mossbach Ridge Winery" (171). As if that were not absurd enough, below the text Brown and Kanouse placed a photograph from Elizabeth showing a sign for an interpretive center with a museum store replete with a portrait of Black Hawk for sale. I am struck by the intersection of historical storytelling and profit making. Elsewhere, a photograph of a park sign featuring a stereotypical image of an Indian chief's head reads: "Black Hawk Park: Take Nothing but Pictures, Leave Nothing but Footprints." Below the image a quotation from historian Daniel K. Richter's *Facing East from Indian Country* reads: "As White Americans wrote their nation's past, their greatest erasure of all was of memories of Indians who neither uncompromisingly resisted like the King Philip of their imagination nor wholeheartedly assimilated like the Pocahontas of their fantasies."[2] Take nothing but pictures, leave nothing but footprints, indeed.

Ultimately, though, the book's tone is not one of despair or irony but of optimism. And herein lies the true value of *Re-Collecting Black Hawk: Landscape, Memory, and Power.* Brown and Kanouse offer a portrait of past and present landscapes that contain the seeds, if the reader digs, of a different future. *Re-Collecting Black Hawk* "arise[s] from the dense, fraught, and layered territory of history, memory, and cohabitation that is our colonial inheritance, implicating the reader in the labor of weaving together these fragments and conceptual disjunctions and leaving it up to us—readers, writers, image makers, Natives, and non-Natives—to make something like justice of it" (10).

AUTHOR BIOGRAPHY

Justin M. Carroll is assistant professor of history at Indiana University East and studies the British fur trade in the Great Lakes. He is currently working on a book about the indigenous histories of nineteenth-century Chicago.

NOTES

1. Gerald Vizenor, *Manifest Manners: Narratives on Postindian Survivance* (Lincoln: University of Nebraska Press, 1999), vii.

2. Daniel Richter, *Facing East from Indian Country: A Native History of Early America* (Cambridge, Mass.: Harvard University Press, 2003), 252.

Wolfgang Tillmans, curator
Book for Architects

Exhibition at the Metropolitan Museum of Art, New York, January 26 through November 15, 2015.

Review by Gabrielle Bendiner-Viani

Enter a darkened room dominated by a large structure with its back to you. Climb a set of stacked benches to see a corner brightly lit by a changing pair of projected images, one on each wall. You see some familiar high-design architectural marvels as well as many ordinary anonymous places. Sometimes there are whole buildings, more often fragments: doorknobs, signs, satellite dishes. Everything is photographed like a snapshot rather than through the perfecting lens of the professional. Most of the sites depicted show their age, their wearing down, and their building up through use. As 450 photos flash by in a forty-one-minute video loop—approximately four pairs of pictures every two minutes—this installation creates its own geography. While an introductory text on the gallery wall states that "there is no soundtrack for this exhibition," the whispers of the gallerygoers humanize the space.

Wolfgang Tillmans, who came to prominence in the mid-1990s with his riveting portraits of European club kids, has created this *Book for Architects.* Conceived for the Fourteenth International Architecture Exhibition (commonly called the Architecture Biennale) in Venice in 2014, the project was reinstalled at the Metropolitan Museum of Art in New York in early 2015, where it ran for ten months. Tillmans culled the series from his archive of photographs made over a ten-year period in thirty-seven countries. We see aerial views shot from skyscrapers and airplanes showing the patterns of mass housing: tracts of suburbs and the x's of high-rises. Streetscapes contrast with everyday objects: sidewalk bollards and the profile of a PlayStation 4 videogame console. There are portions of gleaming office towers, including a sidelong look at Frank Gehry's IAC building in New York. Just as often, we see generic conference rooms, elevators, and hotel corridors. The tactility of the spaces appears frequently, as in a pairing of four stuccoed interior walls alongside the flat surfaces of a staircase. Close-ups show a mess of infrastructure, awkward attachments, modifications, exposed ducts, and insulation. Elsewhere, we see other kinds of things that we are also not meant to notice: people queuing for toilets and, for that matter, toilets themselves of all kinds. Other more voyeuristic images show homeless encampments and refugee tents. We also have promised environments, in the form of advertisements for buildings under construction. Sometimes, people are important: a woman in her kitchen is next to a view of an unfinished building; in other images the frame cuts them off at the legs.

In its title, *Book for Architects* confounds. Examples like the IAC building aside, Tillmans's installation does not feature structures most architects would include in a portfolio—and when it does, the images are not ones they would favor. Many of the places are formulaic in design; many are not professionally designed at all. Even the well-known buildings are more familiar than awe inspiring (the New Yorker in me smiles when I see the Flatiron Building appear). Instead, Tillmans has created a primer on the importance of buildings that are not architected, perhaps, rather provocatively, to remind professional designers that these are the vast majority we experience or to school them on the challenges of planning for the rigors of use. Indeed, the most poignant element of the project is its documentation of the myriad ways people fix, jury-rig, and modify the built environment to suit their needs, suggesting an inspiring agency as well as indicating ways that people are at the mercy of the spaces built for them.

This exhibition is surely not only for architects, however, since that would be a very small audience, even at the Venice Bienniale. Who else could it be for? It might be for all of us: an admonition to care more about the everyday and to think more critically about the designer's viewpoint, which too frequently refuses to consider a building beyond its moment of unveiling. Like vernacular architecture and cultural landscape studies, Tillmans's perspective calls attention to the ordinary physical spaces we experience and makes them worthy of contemplation. And certainly, we have room for contemplation; rarely does an art piece present you the furniture from which to consider it. Here, we have a whole stand of wide wooden bleachers that invite you to view while simultaneously making you part of the show.

Is experiencing this piece a contemplative practice? Or is it one too similar to the flashes of visual material to which we are accustomed while surfing the Web? You can sit with these photographs, but unfortunately, they do not sit long with you. There are a few beautiful images (if often of ugly things)—light falling on a wall makes the surface luminous—yet it seems that very few of the photographs can stand on their own. Similarly, one could ask whether the built in benches afford attention or distraction. While I was in the exhibition, one couple exemplified this duality. He sat at the top of the bleachers, three levels up, watching the corner of a changing screen. She lay across the rest of the bench, her head in his lap, eyes firmly closed in the darkened room.

If this is a space that can be for either contemplation or its opposite, what might Tillmans be trying to say? The dual screen, never resting, brings us contrast after contrast. To the project's credit, these are rarely cheap pairings of stark differences or comedic similarities. Rather, they are formal; we recognize shared form between a mess of cables and a perfect arch or between a high design and a structure modified by its occupant. These juxtapositions enable us to see each image anew once its partner has been absorbed. Often, the sequences show a life cycle of structures: built, unbuilt, falling down. Frequently in this cycle we see shimmed, patched, and broken materials, in pairings that often elevate and honor vernacular buildings. While this project could have veered dangerously toward typology, it instead is full of what Tillmans calls "echoes" and in this way is sensitive to the messy lives of buildings.

Even though Tillmans states these are photographs made with a "kind eye," they are distressingly flattening. The great size at which the pictures are projected in conjunction with the unwavering digital brightness imbues the project with authority rather than opening up a dialogue with the viewer. The photographs themselves, as well as the form of their presentation, keep you at arm's length, hinting at the emotional distance—or even, one suspects, ironic detachment—of the maker from that which he depicts. While one might hope for the material to make a significant contribution to critical thinking on how people use and remake space—adding to discourses of urban anthropology, environmental psychology, and critical landscape studies—the photographs here do not read as ones made through stillness, or looking closely. Unsurprisingly, among the few images that I felt betrayed real warmth and that have stayed with me, are the ones of Tillmans's parents' house. In one interview he explained that these are "what I grew up with: like the red colour of the bathroom tiles I looked at for twenty years!"[1]

Much of rest of the installation, by contrast, leaves one with a feeling of passing through, even though Tillmans has said he edited out many photographs of airports and hotels. The series feels like photographs made on the way to something else, perhaps on the way to making a global art career, which brings to mind the critical work of art historian Miwon Kwon, who described the placelessness of international art stars like Tillmans as being "out of place all too often."[2]

Tillmans has suggested that the installation represents "the randomness, beauty and imperfection that characterizes [*sic*] built reality, both past and present."[3] Yet this collapsing of time through a focus on form combined with the (emotional) distance of the photographer from the spaces recorded leaves little room for context. The contrasts that let us see these images anew also leave us with a flattened globalized landscape, with each location defined by the universal rather than specificities of culture, site, history, and development. Kwon writes, as if as a caution to future work like Tillmans's, that truly engaging means "addressing the uneven conditions of adjacencies and distances between one thing, one person, one place, one thought, one fragment next to another, rather than invoking equivalences via one thing after another . . . so that the sequence of sites that we inhabit in our life's traversal does not become genericized into an undifferentiated serialization, one place after another."[4] Unfortunately, Tillmans's series of pairs and contrasts is, at its end, one place after another, in an unending present, making New York, London, Moscow, and Seoul equivalent and rarely asking why they might not be.

Where are we at the end of our time with this loop? While the "book" has taken us on a journey, its destinations will not stay with us as our bodies move out of the museum into our own everyday architecture. This lack of context through contrast and the lack of connection through contemplation are missed opportunities for real reflection on the critical importance of vernacular, lived space for architects and everyone else.

AUTHOR BIOGRAPHY

Gabrielle Bendiner-Viani is a photographer, urbanist, and principal of Buscada (www.buscada.com), a critical studio focused on place and civic dialogue. She is professor of urban studies and public art at the New School and has exhibited at institutions including MIT, Tate Britain, the Center for Architecture, and the Sheila Johnson Design Center.

NOTES

1. Rob Wilson, "A Warm Eye: Wolfgang Tillmans on his *Book for Architects*," *Uncube Magazine*, June 27, 2014, www.uncubemagazine.com.

2. Miwon Kwon, *One Place after Another* (Cambridge, Mass.: MIT Press, 2004), 156.

3. From exhibition wall text, quoted in Melinda Santillan, "Wolfgang Tillmans: *Book for Architects*," 01\|\|*Magazine*, July 8, 2014, www.zero1magazine.com.

4. Kwon, *One Place after Another*, 166.

List of Editors: *Buildings & Landscapes*

Perspectives in Vernacular Architecture 1 (1982), 2 (1986)
EDITOR: Camille Wells

Perspectives in Vernacular Architecture 3 (1989), 4 (1991)
EDITORS: Thomas Carter and Bernard L. Herman

Gender, Class, and Shelter: Perspectives in Vernacular Architecture 5 (1995)
Shaping Communities: Perspectives in Vernacular Architecture 6 (1997)
EDITORS: Elizabeth Collins Cromley and Carter L. Hudgins

Exploring Everyday Landscapes: Perspectives in Vernacular Architecture 7 (1997)
People, Power, Places: Perspectives in Vernacular Architecture 8 (2000)
EDITORS: Annmarie Adams and Sally McMurry

Constructing Image, Identity, and Place: Perspectives in Vernacular Architecture 9 (2003)
Building Environments: Perspectives in Vernacular Architecture 10 (2005)
EDITORS: Alison K. Hoagland and Kenneth A. Breisch

Perspectives in Vernacular Architecture: The Journal of the Vernacular Architecture Forum 11 (2004), 12 (2005), 13.1 (2006)
EDITORS: Jan Jennings and Pamela Simpson

Perspectives in Vernacular Architecture: The Journal of the Vernacular Architecture Forum 13.2 (2006/2007), Special 25th Anniversary Issue
EDITORS: Warren Hofstra and Camille Wells

Buildings & Landscapes: Journal of the Vernacular Architecture Forum 14 (Fall 2007), 15 (Fall 2008), 16.1 (Spring 2009), 16.2 (Fall 2009)
EDITORS: Howard Davis and Louis P. Nelson
BOOK REVIEW EDITOR: Marilyn Castro

Buildings & Landscapes: Journal of the Vernacular Architecture Forum 17.1 (Spring 2010), 17.2 (Fall 2010), 18.1 (Spring 2011), 18.2 (Fall 2011), 19.1 (Spring 2012), 19.2 (Fall 2012)
EDITORS: Marta Gutman and Louis P. Nelson
REVIEW EDITOR: Andrew K. Sandoval-Strausz

Buildings & Landscapes: Journal of the Vernacular Architecture Forum 20.1 (Spring 2013), 20.2 (Fall 2013), 21.1 (Spring 2014), 21.2 (Fall 2014), 22.1 (Spring 2015), 22.2 (Fall 2015)
EDITORS: Cynthia G. Falk and Marta Gutman
REVIEW EDITOR: Andrew K. Sandoval-Strausz

Buildings & Landscapes: Journal of the Vernacular Architecture Forum 23.1 (Spring 2016), 23.2 (Fall 2016)
EDITORS: Anna Vemer Andrzejewski and Cynthia G. Falk
REVIEW EDITOR: Matthew Lasner

Join the Vernacular Architecture Forum

Please enroll me as a member of the Vernacular Architecture Forum. I understand that membership entitles me to the next two issues of the biannual journal *Buildings & Landscapes: Journal of the Vernacular Architecture Forum* and electronic receipt of the quarterly *Vernacular Architecture Newsletter (VAN)*, and that my subscription will begin with the next issue of the newsletter after the receipt of my dues. Membership also includes registration discounts for the VAF annual conference and other sponsored events as well as access to the VAF member forums.

Membership Categories

☐ Active, $60* ☐ Multiyear Active, _____ x $60*

☐ Household, $80* (includes one copy of publications per household)

☐ Student, $30* (Name of School: ____)

☐ Institution, $90* ☐ Contributing, $90**

☐ Patron, $165** ☐ Lifetime, $2,000** (Payable in four $500 installments over a four-year period)

Membership Outside North America

☐ Add $5 to above categories, other than Lifetime, for postage

Enrollment Information

____

NAME(S)

____

ADDRESS

____

CITY STATE/PROVINCE ZIP

____

COUNTRY

____

EMAIL (IF YOU WISH TO JOIN OUR MEMBERS E-MAIL LIST) TELEPHONE

Go to http://www.vernaculararchitectureforum.org/join for further information, mailing address, and online payment options.

*Active, Household, Institution, and Student Members: Please consider an additional gift in support of VAF programs.

$ __________ Student and Professional Support Fund (including grants, fellowships, and awards)

$ __________ Publications Fund (including *Buildings & Landscapes*, *VAN*, and special publications)

$ __________ VAF Endowment Fund

**Contributing, Patron, and Lifetime Members: All receipts above the basic $60 active membership category will be applied toward the giving category or categories of your choice (please check one or more):

☐ Student and Professional Support Fund

☐ Publications Fund

☐ VAF Endowment Fund